■   ■   ■

ASIA-PACIFIC: CULTURE,

POLITICS, AND SOCIETY

SERIES EDITORS: REY CHOW, H.D.

HARTOONUNIAN, & MASAO MIYOSHI

GENDER AND NATIONAL

LITERATURE HEIAN TEXTS

IN THE CONSTRUCTIONS OF

JAPANESE MODERNITY

■ ■ ■ TOMIKO YODA ■ ■ ■

Duke University Press   Durham & London 2004

© 2004 Duke University Press ■ All rights reserved

Printed in the United States of America on acid-

free paper ⊛ ■ Designed by R. Giménez ■ Typeset

in Adobe Minion by Tseng Information Systems

Library of Congress Cataloging-in-Publication

Data appear on the last printed page of this book.

TO MY PARENTS,

Emi and Shōtarō Yoda

CONTENTS

ACKNOWLEDGMENTS

Academic research often seems like a solitary endeavor. As I recall the help I received from so many people in the course of completing this book, however, I am compelled to think otherwise. The book now appears less a product of the time I spent alone at libraries or sitting in front of a computer monitor than an outgrowth of interactions and conversations I had with teachers, friends, colleagues, and students. The shortcomings of this book demonstrate my limitations, but they would have been far more extensive and grave if not for the input I received from others too numerous to be fully acknowledged here.

The research for this book began during my graduate studies at Stanford University. My gratitude first goes to Tom Hare, my adviser, for his superb guidance, intellectual passion, and friendship, which have sustained me through my graduate years and beyond, and to Susan Matisoff for instructions and advice that have proved invaluable. I would also like to express my appreciation to many other teachers and friends I met at Stanford, who contributed greatly to my intellectual growth and are present in many fond memories of my time in Palo Alto, including Amy Borovoy, Thierry Delmarcelle, Marion Lee,

Felicia McCarren, Diane Middlebrook, Jutta Sperling, Haun Saussy, and Makoto Ueda. A graduate fellowship at the Stanford Humanities Center provided me with an interdisciplinary research environment where I began developing some of the questions I explore in this book. I am also much obliged to Edwin Cranston and Haruko Iwasaki, my teachers of premodern Japanese literature before I began my studies at Stanford.

I am most fortunate to have found an excellent cohort of colleagues in my home department at Duke University. I want to thank both past and present colleagues in the Department of Asian and African Languages and Literature, especially Leo Ching, miriam cooke, Hitomi Endō, Bruce Lawrence, Jing Wang, and Eric Zakim, for their support and wonderful camaraderie. Outside the department, Anne Allison has been a valued colleague and a caring friend. I have drawn much sustenance from her generous spirit and intellectual energy.

Teaching at Duke has afforded me numerous opportunities to exchange ideas and work with colleagues in diverse fields, which have affected this book in both direct and indirect ways. Robyn Wiegman has injected a tremendous new energy into the Women's Studies Program at Duke, spearheading many exciting activities around it. The faculty research seminar Gender and Sexuality Studies, which she conducted with Elena Glasberg, helped me rethink some of the major debates in contemporary feminist theory; many thanks to the organizers and all the participants for great discussions. I have gained much from my affiliation with the Asian-Pacific Studies Institute at Duke. I would like to thank all the colleagues with whom I have worked at the institute and in its research clusters, including Nan Lin, Ralph Litzenger, Kris Troost, and Kären Wigen. The Marxism and Society Group has been a marvelous forum for exploring a wide range of social and theoretical issues. I want to thank its participants, particularly Michael Hardt, Fred Jameson, Charlie Piot, and Ken Surin. I have also benefited from many other formal and informal exchanges with friends and colleagues at Duke and in the Triangle Area. I thank Stan Abe, Cathy Davidson, Arif Dirlik, Judith Farquhar, Ranji Khanna, Diane Nelson, Kathy Rudy, Barbara Herrnstein Smith, and Brian Cantwell Smith for friendship and intellectual stimulation. Jan Radway and Ken Wissoker gave me indispensable advice on how to navigate the increasingly treacherous terrain of academic publishing.

Works by contemporary scholars of Heian studies in Japan have been extremely important to my research, and during my repeated research trips to Japan I received much help from many of these researchers in person. During my earliest extended research in Japan, Hinata Kazumasa was a generous host and mentor. A research group on Heian literature, Monogatari kenkyūkai, offered me an ideal opportunity to get to know and learn from both younger and more established scholars in the field. Among the members of the group, I want to particularly thank Takahashi Tōru, Fujii Sadakazu, Mitamura Masako, Mitani Kuniaki, Takagi Makoto, and Andō Tōru. I have been immensely rewarded by my conversations with Kawazoe Fusae, not only on Heian literature but on topics that include feminist scholarship in Japan today.

I would like to acknowledge many people who have read or listened to parts of the manuscript at various stages of its development and offered me feedback and encouragement, including Tani Barlow, Gus Heldt, Mack Horton, Terry Kawashima, and Joshua Mostow. I would like to thank Michael Bourdaghs for kindly sharing the editor's and author's introductions to his English translation of Kamei Hideo's *Transformations of Sensibility* before its publication. Norma Field provided incisive comments on my research on numerous occasions and offered much appreciated support and encouragement.

Some of the final revisions of the manuscript were made while I was teaching at Cornell University during the fall of 2002. I thank all the members of the Department of Asian Studies and the Japan Studies faculty at Cornell, particularly Brett de Bary, Edward Gunn, Victor Koschmann, and Naoki Sakai, for providing a most intellectually invigorating environment. My manuscript received extremely helpful responses and provocative questions in a graduate seminar I team-taught at Cornell. It was a true luxury to discuss my work in a series of meetings with highly informed and sophisticated readers. I deeply thank the faculty members and students who participated in the seminar, especially Brett de Bary for her generous engagement with my project and for helping me to see it in a broader perspective, and Naoki Sakai for offering wonderful critical insights into many of the issues I treat.

I am greatly indebted to Harry Harootunian not only for giving me penetrating comments on multiple drafts of the manuscript but for his vast knowledge, critical acumen, and great generosity, which have helped and inspired me over years. Through his writing and in person, he has constantly reminded me not to take for granted the assumptions embedded in existing disciplinary frameworks. Tom LaMarre also read virtually every draft of this manuscript, and his astute critiques were indispensable to the development of the book. His research on Heian poetics and modern Heian literary studies have greatly influenced my own thinking.

At Duke University Press I could not have asked for a more supportive and skilled editor than Reynolds Smith. Without his strong advocacy, the publication of this book would not have been possible. I also thank Sharon Torian, Justin Faerber, and my copyeditor, Janet Opdyke.

Research for this book was supported with an Arts and Sciences Research Council grant from Duke University; an Association for Asian Studies, Northeast Asia Council, Japan studies grant; a Duke University, Asian-Pacific Studies Institute, Travel Fund award; and a Harvard-Yenching Library travel grant. The National Endowment for Humanities Fellowship and a junior sabbatical leave from Duke University allowed me to take some time away from teaching and other regular duties to concentrate on writing. The publication of this book was supported by generous funding from the office of the Dean of the Faculty of Arts and Sciences at Duke University.

An earlier version of chapter 3 appeared as "Reading Literary History against the National Frame, or Gender and the Emergence of Heian Kana Writing," *positions* 8:2 (2000); an earlier version of chapter 4 appeared as "Fractured Dialogues: Mono no Aware and Poetic Communications in *The Tale of Genji*," *Harvard Journal of Asiatic Studies* 59:2 (December 1999).

■   ■   ■

Güven Güzeldere has been my most trusted interlocutor not only in convictions we share but in matters on which we do not agree. As I complete this book, I realize how much he has affected its content and the ways in which it developed. I thank him for his constant encouragement and prodding—always there when I needed him most—and for cheering up those long evenings when we burned the midnight oil together.

Finally, these acknowledgments would not be complete without mention of my family. My sister, Junko Yoda, and my brother-in-law, Michael Soucy, generously invited me to stay with them while I conducted some of my early research in Tokyo and helped make those stays not only productive but most enjoyable. My parents, Emi and Shōtarō Yoda, have supported me unflinchingly in all the paths and detours I have taken. This book is dedicated to them with gratitude and love.

NOTE TO THE READER

In this volume, I cite terms and passages in the original Japanese (rendered in romanization or Japanese script) when I consider them particularly helpful to the reader or pertinent to my discussion. The romanization of modern Japanese words follows the Hepburn system. In romanizing texts and words from pre-Meji periods, however, I replicate the kana transcription of standard *kogo* (classical Japanese) dictionaries or the modern annotated texts I used.

Throughout this book, East Asian names are cited with family names first (exceptions are the names of scholars who are based outside of Asia or have published in English). In reference to pre-Meiji Japanese figures, I follow the Japanese convention of referring to them in shorthand by their given names.

All the translations from Japanese texts are mine unless otherwise noted.

The following abbreviations were used for serials and collected works.

HYS: *Haga Yaichi senshū*, ed. Haga Yaichi senshū henshū iinkai. Kokugakuin, 1982–92. 7 vols.

MBZ: *Meiji Bungaku Zenshū*. Chikuma shobō, 1965–85, 100 vols.

MNZ: *Motoori Norinaga zenshū*, ed. Ōno Susumu. Chikuma shobō, 1968–77. 23 vols.

NKBT: *Nihon koten bungaku taikei*. Iwanami shoten, 1957–68. 102 vols.

NKBZ: *Nihon koten bungaku zenshū*. Shōgakkan, 1970–79. 51 vols.

NKT: *Nihon kagaku taikei*, ed. Sasaki Nobutsuna. Kazama shobō, 1956–65. 10 vols.

NST: *Nihon shisō taikei*. Iwanami shoten, 1970–82. 67 vols.

INTRODUCTION

How are we to stage productive dialogues between the study of Heian literature and contemporary feminist and gender studies? This was one of the principal questions with which I began the research that culminated in this book. This initial question has remained with me through the many years it has taken to complete this project. Yet my views on how to approach Heian texts from a feminist perspective and how to rethink feminism through the study of Heian texts have changed substantially over time. Initially, I was drawn to the wealth and sophistication of women's writing in the Heian period—narrative fiction, poetry, and memoirs that evoke complex insights into matters such as romance, literary discourses, familial relations, and sexuality. They seemed to promise rich material that could be studied from a perspective informed by contemporary feminist and gender theories. Through the examination of these texts, I hoped to participate in the ongoing debates over the diverse construction of gender and sexual identity, social organization of gender, and different forms in which the politics of gender may be articulated across the historical and cultural spectrums. In the early 1990s, when I began to research Heian texts, little attention was being paid in the field to the recent developments in feminist and gender studies.

Furthermore, I believed that Heian literature could serve as a site from which to address some of the thorniest problems involved in establishing a feminist perspective in the field of Japan studies, namely, how could feminist scholarship intervene in the conventional discourses on the national ethos that *already* emphasized feminine qualities in, and to some extent women's contribution to, Japanese culture? It has been one of the enduring clichés in modern Japanese culturalism to assert the uniqueness of the Japanese national identity (i.e., its difference vis-à-vis the West) through its identification with the "feminine." As Rey Chow comments on the similar difficulties faced by feminist criticism in China studies, significant roles assigned to "women" and "feminine" in the mainstream national self-construction have complicated the task of carving out a distinct position from which to launch feminist inquiries in the Japanese context.[1]

On the modern Japanese cultural horizon, Heian literature, firmly placed at the center of the national literary canon, has been one of the most concentrated points of intersection among national culture, literary tradition, and women/femininity. Analyzing the feminization of Japanese culture through Heian literary texts and modern studies on them therefore has broad ramifications for feminist scholarship on Japan. In particular, it prompts us to question the essentialized notions of gender and national culture that the received understanding of Heian literature has encouraged — the assumption that categories such as *women* or *Japanese culture* have transhistorical and homogeneous referents. Such discussion of Heian literature can help locate cleavages between "women" and "Japan" that can serve as spaces for feminist critique.

The National Subject and the Disciplinary Critique

A feminist study of Heian literature therefore calls for engagement with the existing discourses on Heian literature. In the contemporary field of Heian literary studies, this means critical examination of both traditional and revisionist currents in the field. With regard to traditional scholarship, a major point of contention is the essentialized notions of women and the feminine embedded in the kind of scholarship that refers to *ōchō joryū bungaku* (female literature of the Heian court) as the object of its analysis. This term not only particularizes women's literary production but implies slippage from the female attributes of the author to the femininity of her writing. Indeed, a substantial portion of this scholarly genre consists of biocritical readings in which the reification of the authorial presence licenses the unexamined presuppositions about her female experience and feminine sensibilities projected onto Heian texts.

More recent developments in textual, formal, and narratological studies of Heian literature, which began in the early 1970s, present a different set of problems for feminist criticism. There we have to address the apparent dearth of interest in gender issues. The trend was catalyzed as a reaction against many of the central tendencies of traditional scholarship, for instance, the notion of authorship, the positivism of philological study, and the realist assumptions regarding the relationship between a text and its context. In the process of the "textual turn" of the discipline, issues such as female authorship or women's experience in the society became secondary to the investigation of the text's formal structure and the textual construction of narratorial voice. Some even questioned the relevance of the concept of "gender" as an analytical tool for examining Heian texts, arguing that in Heian Japanese there is no equivalence of linguistic gender such as we find in European languages. There was a general skepticism within the revisionist trend as to whether feminist criticism can bring anything to the field that has not been already covered by more traditional scholarship, which has avidly discussed Heian literature in relation to "women" and "femininity." In other words, revisionist critics have not pursued the possibility that textual discourses themselves (without having to posit the identity of author) may implicate the gender of the narrator or of the audience or that the discursive effect of the text may rely on its relation to the sociocultural organization of gender. Furthermore, the disciplinary critique by these revisionist scholars largely bypassed the issue of sexist assumptions in the field. It was as if they considered the problem of sexism in Heian literary scholarship resolved itself simply by eliminating the realist authorial presence from the critical perspective.

In order for the feminist study of Heian literature to intervene in this disciplinary condition, it needs to demonstrate both compatibility with and dissent from the revisionist intellectual projects and their critique of traditional scholarship. It must challenge the reified understanding of terms such as *feminine* and *women's literature* in the disciplinary orthodoxy while questioning the very process through which revisionism had largely displaced gender issues from the field of inquiry. In order to develop such a two-pronged strategy in a coherent manner, we need to examine the relation of continuity as well as the break between traditional and revisionist currents in the field. Only then can we understand how a feminist approach is capable of offering new perspectives into the disciplinary critique by identifying points of complementarity between mainstream postwar scholarship and the critique of it. It was issues such as these that led me to pay increasing attention to the history of Heian literary scholarship and to trace it back to the beginning of the modern discipline of literary studies in Japan.

Through research into the history of modern scholarship on Heian literature, I realized that the gender ideology of the discipline is much more complex than I had assumed. Even the link between Heian literature, femininity, and national culture was far from simple, articulated through different and at times conflicting points of view. Since the modern discipline of literary studies was established in Japan in the late nineteenth century, the scholarly discourses on Heian literature have been revised and transformed, variously responding to the disciplinary debates as well as the broader historical conditions surrounding them. At the same time, attention to the disciplinary history brought into sharper focus certain sets of common conceptual frameworks underwriting diverse understandings of Heian literature in modernity. In particular, it became increasingly clear that the discipline's gender construction had to be examined in relation to modern understandings of sociality, history, and subjectivity, which presupposed the nation-state as a principal point of reference.

In the modern humanistic tradition, literary art is considered to be a significant site of collective as well as individual subject formation. It is understood to enable some of the most genuine expressions of human interiority as well as one's relation to the external world. It allegedly articulates universal conditions of humanity, raising essential questions about human existence by representing highly individuated experiences and emotions. Literature is also believed to be a medium in which language — the most basic and ordinary means of communication shared by a human community — may achieve the singularity and profundity of an aesthetic object. The ways in which literature is thought to bring together the particular and general or ordinary and sublime help us to understand how it has served as one of the most potent bases for constructing collective, or more specifically national, identity. Particularly since the late eighteenth century, literature has often been viewed as expressing the elusive essence of national identity — the kernel of national character that is more than just a composite of shared language, tradition, ethnicity, territoriality, and so on. For the advocates of national literary studies, literature has been upheld as both the hallmark of human civilization in general *and* the expression of a discreet national culture. Any nation worthy of civilizational status, in other words, must possess a unique literary tradition. Thus, modern discourses on literature have typically invoked, explicitly or implicitly, the presence of a national subject, organizing diverse forms of literary discourse (produced in different times and places and associated with various strata of society) in relation to the unifying principle of nation.

As many have argued, "literature" is not a neutral descriptive category but a construction that emerged under specific historical conditions of possibility. Central to this process in Japan as elsewhere was the formation of the academic discipline of national literary studies occurring alongside the establishment of a modern university system.[2] In Japan, the discipline known as *kokubungaku* (national literature studies) emerged in the late nineteenth century to design the national literary canon and literary history, disseminating a specific set of definitions of what literature is and how it should be studied. The period when kokubungaku, and thus the creation of literature itself, took shape was the historical juncture in which Japan was consolidated as a modern nation-state and began its foray into imperial ventures. As we will see, the academic discourses on literature were closely linked to the political and social transformations in this era, which is known for its nationalistic fervor. Some of the initial impulses for the development of kokubangaku germinated in the late nineteenth century when many among the ruling elites in Japan began sounding the alarm over excessive Westernization during the first phase of nation building, calling for a national identity firmly based on the country's unique national character and tradition. Mainstream kokubungaku developed under a mandate to become the guardian of the classical literary canon and the promoter of national identity based on that heritage. It was not until after World War II, and some say not until the 1970s, that many of even the "modern classics" of late-nineteenth and early-twentieth-century literature were fully canonized as proper objects of study by the discipline. This does not mean, of course, that academic discourses on literature were completely disassociated from contemporary literary practices at the time kokubungaku emerged. In fact, the ways in which kokubungaku scholars viewed the literature of the past was closely aligned with emerging trends in Meiji literature (e.g., the elevation of the prose narrative in the generic hierarchy under the vogue of the modern novel). It may be said that in late-nineteenth-century Japan the modern academic study of literature developed not around but parallel to literary practice, which was undergoing a process of profound and complex transformation, responding to changes in social, economic, political, and cultural conditions in the country while rapidly absorbing the influences of European literature and literary theories. The modern academic discipline of literary studies was also engaged in the process of *modernization* but through its construction of the literary discourses of the past. Kokubungaku studied traditional literary discourses through the modern conception of literature and its alleged indispensability to the concept of nationhood.

In recent years, there has been a growing body of scholarship on the invention of national tradition in the fields of history and literary/cultural studies.[3] My book draws on these studies while focusing on the less scrutinized issue of how gender has figured in this process. I examine, through the genealogy of modern discourses on Heian literature, the process through which the discipline *gendered* literature: the analysis of literature through the gender of the author and the audience, the use of gendered metaphors and terms to describe particular literary aesthetics and styles, or the association of a genre of literature or a period in literary history with femininity or masculinity. Through the modern construction of Heian literature—which may be one of the most salient cases of feminized literary tradition in Japan—I also consider the more general significance and function of gendering literature and literary history in the context of literary modernization and nationalization.

Gender and National Literature argues that modernizing discourses on literature in Japan used gender difference as a foundational asymmetry—a vitally interconnected and hierarchically differentiated binary. Through the manipulation of this gendered structure, furthermore, literature was constituted as the expression of a unified and autonomous national subject. By "national subject," I mean not simply the alleged organic wholeness of a particular national community, but an essence that underwrites the national identity, integrating its diverse constituents, or the overarching continuity of the national history, underlying its incessant permutation. The national subject unfolds in time and yet is also primordial to this process, guaranteeing in advance the unity among its specific moments. History in this schema is understood as a process through which the unique interiority of the nation expresses itself, advancing toward its full realization.

Of course, the relationship between the modern individual subject and the collective national subject is not merely additive (meaning that the amalgamation of the former produces the latter) but structural. Autonomous and singular, an individual subject in modernity is the entity that gives meaning and coherence to the linear and segmentalized sense of time. It is transcendent in its ability to unify diverse and at times conflicting properties as its own. In other words, the liberal humanistic subject and the modern national subject both perform such transcendent and synthetic functions that guarantee individual/collective identity. Moreover, their historical effects have been indissociably intertwined: the ideology and institutions of the nation-state have operated as powerful apparatuses for constituting its population as modern subjects, and liberal humanism has served as a great mobilizer in social and political movements that have helped establish the global nation-state system. My discussion of modern individual and national subjects is built on this relation of mutuality. Approaching the problematics of the subject at both these levels is also methodologically significant for my study. While the *modern subject* draws our attention to the psychological, experiential, and philosophical significance invested in the modern conception of subjectivity, the *national subject* helps us to focus on specific links between these conceptualizations of subject and concrete historical processes and material conditions particular to modernity, including the nation-state system.

In this study I argue that specifically feminine literary aesthetics or feminine moments in literary history were typically constituted as the negativities to be overcome or sublated (both repressed and conserved) when literary discourses of the past were reconstituted in the framework of the modern national subject. The sublation of the feminine, furthermore, guaranteed the emergence of a fuller and more transcendent realization of literature as the expression of a national subject. We need to note that this process involved not simply negating the feminine but recognizing and elevating it within the context of national unity. Here we begin to see the common logic operating in the modern discipline's varied assessments of feminized Heian literature. I argue that the gender ideology of the modern discipline must be understood through the process in which the feminine is recognized, canceled, and then contained within the national framework articulated in masculine terms. The present study explores this structurally masculinist organization of literature and the modern national subject through discourses on Heian literature in Japanese modernity.

The Problem of the Discursive Subject

So far I have discussed how this study examines the intersection among modern subject, nation-state, and gender ideology in the construction of Heian literature. A question not yet addressed is whether such a perspective is relevant for the critique of more contemporary scholarship in the field. What I have referred to as the textual turn in Heian literary scholarship since the 1970s has already challenged the modern construction of literature and the modernizing impulse of conventional kokubungaku, highly skeptical of many of the basic assumptions held by the discipline. The scholars who led this movement came of age in the mid- to late 1960s, a generation that questioned the commitment to the historical process of modernization that a broad spectrum of postwar Japanese intellectuals had shared.

The call to study Japanese texts from the distant past through the critique of modernity in general and the modernizing operation of kokubungaku in particular, however, was not a project pioneered by the post-1970s revisionists. As early as the 1920s, the *minzokugaku-*

sha (folklorist) Orikuchi Shinobu had launched a persistent antimodernist challenge to the academic establishment of kokubungaku.[4] He argued that the historicism, rationalism, and scientific pretensions of the modern discipline obscured the true meaning of national literature. Deeply sympathetic to eighteenth-century nativism, he sought to recover from textual records the archaic, preliterate literature of the folk. National literature was to be redefined via the imaginative grasp of the originary state of literature that seamlessly mixed the religious, literary, and collective agrarian practices of the native community. Although Orikuchi was considered to be outside the professional circle of kokubungaku, he exerted considerable influence on the study of premodern Japanese literature. Particularly in the postwar period, kokubungaku scholars who denounced the discipline's complicity in the nationalist propaganda of the wartime state saw in Orikuchi's work inspiration for redefining the nation and the national on the basis of the genuine community of the folk—to be distinguished from the rational unity of the state.

While post-1970s revisionist scholars expressed affinity with the folkloric project, they also developed theoretical and methodological approaches that clearly set them apart from Orikuchi and his followers. Central to this distinction was the displacement of the explanatory force of the origin (as well as evolutionary teleology) in the textualist methodology. In other words, textualists, unlike Orikuchi, refused to subordinate Heian literary texts not only to the modern concepts of literature but to the traces of preliterate and oral origin in archaic songs and ritual performances. Mitani Kuniaki, a representative scholar of the textual study of Heian literature, identifies his refusal to explicate a text in relation to its origin as a phenomenological approach. He claims that rather than exercising the inductive logic that explains the effect (literary text) in terms of the cause (origin), he prefers the phenomenological stance that focuses strictly on the effect (text).[5] We may note here that the bracketing of the causal relation foregrounds the text itself as the field of investigation.

What is at stake in Mitani's avoidance of the causal explanation and the epistemological privileging of the origin is the problem of representation. If earlier scholarship construed literature as that which represents some form of preexisting positivity (whether it be the intention of an individual author, collective body, or some more impersonal social or historical milieu), the textual approach examines literary texts as *effecting* or rendering intelligible that which it appears to merely represent. If this is the case, the issue is not *what* the text represents but *how* it represents. What is being put aside, therefore, is not only the question of origin but of ontology in general. This is why the issue of language or signification—linguistic, rhetorical, stylistic mechanisms and diverse relationality located on the textual surface—became the primary concern of textual literary analysis. This methodological orientation and aim clearly situate the textual critique of modernity/kokubungaku in Heian studies within more global developments in contemporary literary criticism.

The fact that the critique of modernity in post-1970s Heian literary scholarship has revolved around the issue of representation and signification helps explain why its theoretical inspiration is derived less from Orikuchi than from the work of the antimodern linguist Tokieda Motoki. Tokieda's "language process theory" (presented in a book published in 1941) approached language as a dynamic process rather than a fixed system enacted by a subject speaking in a concrete communicative context. He developed his theory in reaction to what he perceived to be the dominant current in contemporary linguistics, which reduced language to an inert mechanism that conveys meaning. He sought instead to understand language through performative and subjective functions that he felt were being ignored. Language process theory insisted on defining *language* as a radically pragmatic and contextual operation in which subjective and objective were inextricably linked in a communicative situation. Thus, it rejected as a fallacy the kind of analytical perspective that objectified the linguistic process as a static entity.

This antiobjectifying stance also underwrote Tokieda's opposition to the universalizing claim of modern linguistics as a study of language in general, as if it had unproblematic access to the understanding of language in its totality. Instead he argued that an essential and genuinely theoretical understanding of language can be developed only through the study of a particular linguistic practice—in his case Japanese. In other words, he opposed the universalizing understanding of language to the extent that he defined *language* as a process that always operates from the specific positionality of a discursive subject and thus cannot be dissociated from the particular language it deploys.

He searched, therefore, for a way to theorize this subjective function working through the language without petrifying it into an objective facet of a linguistic system. He argued, furthermore, that thinking through Japanese grammar and rhetorical forms offered a unique opportunity to illuminate the discursive and performative rather than the referential and static nature of language.

It is important to note that Tokieda's insistence on speaking from the specificity of Japanese rejected not only the hasty references to language in its universality but the particularistic stance of naive linguistic nationalism. "Japanese" for Tokieda was not to be identified with a reified national subject that can be taken for granted—identified, for instance, with the unity of the state, ethnicity, or territoriality. Instead it is a concrete yet open-ended problematic, an understanding of which is pursued by his discipline, *kokugogaku* (national language studies). Similarly, the subject of linguistic performance, *shutai*, was not a conventional modern subject—a unitary entity that objectifies the world and also itself from a detached interior consciousness. Instead, he spoke of a subject as always situated in a concrete discursive context and understood through the discursive act—through its agency of creating meaning for itself and others. This subject is to be grasped through its dynamic function and not as an isolated and objectifiable entity that nominal first-person reference "I" seem to represent.

In the above passages, I have sketched out the manner in which the theorization of discursive subjectivity, the critique of modernity, and the antiuniversalizing (and anti-Eurocentric) perspective came together in Tokieda's thought. This interconnection sheds light on the links among various facets of post-1970s revisionist scholarship in Heian literary studies—its attention to the contextual nature of Japanese language; its critique of modern, realist formulations of subjectivity and representation; and how it questioned the modernization of Japanese literature through the examination of Heian texts. In particular, thinking through Tokieda's theory helps us to see that while textualists insist on the specificity of Japanese language (largely through the invocation of Tokieda's theory) they are not nationalist in the sense of modern kokubungaku or folkloric neonativists.

Just as important, however, the examination of Tokieda's theory helps us to understand how in some crucial respects contemporary

Heian literary studies that have adopted Tokieda's theory of language and subjectivity fall short of fully displacing the national subject and the universalizing/totalizing stance of the modern discipline. At first glance, the discursive subject posited through the relationality and performative operation of discourse/text appears to effectively subvert the conventional notion of the modern subject. Tokieda's effort to define the discursive subject from a nonobjectifying stance disrupts the contradictory unity through which the modern subject is identified: on one hand, a free, self-constituting power of subjectification; and on the other hand its status as a singular entity in the world (which cannot be established unless it is put into a relation with other subjects or situated in an objective spatial and temporal context). In other words, the concept of a modern subject typically conflates the first-person sense of subject (as the ultimate reference point through which the world and the self are known and made meaningful) and the self objectified from the third-person perspective. Tokieda's strategy was to resolve this antinomy by eliminating the second half of the untenable conjunction. As I argue, however, this approach targets the fallacy of objectifying stance without simultaneously attending to the problem on both sides of this formulation. In other words, even if the subject is understood purely performatively, without positing its preexisting ontological status or hypostatized sense of inner life, Tokieda's theory preserves the integrity, if not the unity, of the subject. By retaining the subject (or subjective process) as an unalienated and noncontradictory ground of language, Tokieda falls short of radically contesting the objectifying, totalizing frame of modernity as well— unable to recognize the need to develop an alternative approach not only to the subjective but to the objective. My objection to Tokieda's theory and its use in Heian literary scholarship ultimately rests on its displacement of, rather than critical engagement with, the problem of history and the sociality of discourse. In other words, by retaining the undivided subject (and the coherence of language based on it), he foreclosed the problematics of history.

Thus, while he critiqued the dichotomy of universal versus particular conceptualizations of language that reinforced the axiomatic status of modernity/the West, and while he dissociated Japanese from the existing national unity embodied in the state, Tokieda's theory nonetheless neglected to provide an alternative account of the historicity

12   Gender and National Literature

of discourse. I contend that this is why his theory could be assimilated into the logic of the imperial subject, which is defined not statically through objectified attributes but through its ever-expanding dynamics. The politically and socially reactionary possibilities of Tokieda's theory pose serious questions about the relatively uncritical deployment of it in contemporary literary scholarship. Furthermore, it brings to light a question that applies equally to the textual approach to Heian literature and Tokieda's theory. How do we develop a study of textual/linguistic forms and processes that opens up inquiries about the sociality and historicity of the text, and by so doing consistently resist the national/imperial identity? In other words, the formalist and textualist critiques of the modern historicist and realist conceptualization of literature must be directly engaged with an alternative understanding of discourse/text as a social and material practice that refracts an ideological closure. It is at this theoretical juncture that my study suggests turning to feminist criticism as a possible form of intervention in the study of Heian texts—an approach that can stimulate the theoretical integration of linguistic and social, textual and historical.

Feminism and Heian Studies

As mentioned at the beginning of this introduction, this study has been shaped in part by the question of how to inject feminist perspectives into Heian literary scholarship and also how to rethink feminist theory through the study of Heian texts. *Gender and National Literature* responds to this question by linking feminism and Heian texts via critical examination of the modern national construction of literature and the notion of subjectivity constituted therein. The recognition that the association of Heian literature with femininity coalesced in the process of modernizing and nationalizing literature has profound implications for designing a feminist approach to Heian texts. It suggests that the critique of the gender ideology of the modern discipline cannot simply focus on reclaiming Heian women's writing from gender stereotypes and misogynistic assumptions or on excavating their contribution to the history of Japanese literature. In kokubungaku discourses, we do find misogynistic denigration of Heian literature for its feminine qualities and condescending attitudes toward Heian female writers that deserve to be questioned. At the same time, however, we need to locate the masculinist construction of literature and literary history underlying the valorization of the association between Heian literature and femininity and the veneration bestowed on these feminized texts in the Japanese literary canon. Thus, I draw attention to the sexism deeply ingrained in categories such as "literature" and "literary history" despite their appearance of gender neutrality. These terms have been taken for granted as those through which literary discourses and their histories are construed—the stable ground on which qualifications such as "*female* literature" or "*Heian* literary history" are overlaid. I argue that without interrogating the gendered inflections of these categories, which are foundational to kokubungaku, we can only critique the discipline's sexism at the level of its discrete content, failing to address the more pervasive ways in which masculinist premises permeate its methodologies. What I am invoking here is the critical function that historicization plays in the methodology of this study. By historicizing, I mean not only the historical contextualization of the object we study but a self-reflexive investigation into the historicity of the conceptual frameworks through which we make objects intelligible. To this extent, historicization always concerns the present, the subject, and the relationship between ourselves and what we posit as our object of study.

The historically inflected understanding of the modern construction of Heian literature suggests the inadequacy of challenging the gender ideology of modern literary scholarship simply through a critique of its sexism or even its gender essentialism. Such a charge may denaturalize the attitudes about gender identity assumed by the discipline while not necessarily historicizing them. We may easily find in cultural and historical locations other than our own what may appear to be a relatively invariant understanding of the distinctions between men and women or feminine and masculine or justification for the inferior status of women in society by invoking some form of suprahistorical principle. The critical question for feminist criticism as I see it, however, is how assumptions concerning gender difference (whether this division is understood to be fixed or fluid) have been constituted historically, through their links to diverse sets of institutions and ideas, forming complex forces that authorize hierarchical, discriminatory, and exploitative social structures and practices. To analyze the historicity of gender construction from a feminist standpoint is to understand it in such relationality and thereby to account for its function and persistence in ways that contribute to feminist political and critical agendas. In this study, therefore, I seek to analyze the logic that runs through diverse assessments of Heian literature (and its feminine attributes) in relation to gender ideology and other regulatory structures of modernity that have shaped kokubungaku.

Such a historicization of gender ideology in kokubungaku, in turn, is integral to historicizing Heian texts themselves, reading them *against* the modernizing/nationalizing perspective of the discipline. This is so, in part, because the gender-constructionist perspective does not automatically translate into historicization, for the specificity of gender formation in the Heian period can be acknowledged in a rather ahistorical manner. One may endorse the possibility that categories such as "woman," and "man" had very different significance for Heian aristocratic culture than they do in our own society. Such a recognition, however, has limited critical impacts unless it is accompanied by the awareness that what *we* mean by these terms is far from transparent. In order to explore the distinct organization of gender in Heian society, we need to continually explore our understanding of how we conceptualize gender and how these ideas are produced and reproduced in a complex relationship with varieties of social practices and institutions. Such a self-reflexive critique provides an indispensable theoretical reference point from which we can begin to investigate the difference between gender construction in the Heian context and that of modern society.

Sensitivity to the historicity of the modern conception of gender, however, does not mean abandoning the use of terms such as *gender* and *women*. In this study, I use these terms with the recognition that their meanings are vitally linked to the specific context of their circulation and deployment. I do not wish to argue that *gender* has a proper referent in the Heian world or that *woman* has transhistorical significance. At the same time, these terms function as signifiers precisely to the extent that their values are heterogeneous rather than monolithic. Their meaning cannot be fully fixed even by the most dominant definition of them in a given historical context—open to the possibilities of recontextualization and resignification. The argument that a term such as *gender* should not be used in discussing Heian society because the concept did not exist at the time implies that there are terms (native to the textual context) that prevent us from committing a fallacy of historical anachronism. Yet any term, even those found in the Heian lexicon, can be deployed to project thoroughly modern assumptions onto Heian texts. What is at issue is not the use or disuse of a specific category in itself but the ways in which it is used and contextualized. In this study, therefore, I refer to *gender* in the discussion of Heian texts. At the same time, I also consider how terms such as *men* and *women* are defined in relation to each other and also to other categories in Heian texts in ways that diverge from meanings assigned to them in modernity. In other words, I use them heuristically, simultaneously drawing attention to and mapping their historically constituted usage in modernity while deploying this schema to explore alternative means of contextualizing them in relation to Heian texts. Furthermore, I consider the implications that such an exercise may have for feminism as well as for Heian literary studies. Weaving the discussion back into contemporary debates, I locate the purpose of recontextualizing highly fraught gender categories not in the demonstration of their fluidity or polysemy per se. Rather, I hope to show that questioning them via Heian texts can help us find new ways to contest the persistence of modernist frameworks and their effects, not only in Heian literary studies but in feminist studies as well.

The Relevance of Premodern Studies

I want to take a moment to briefly restate some of the methodological issues already touched on in this introduction in order to situate my study in the current state of scholarship on premodern history and culture in humanistic disciplines. The methodological organization of this book attempts to respond to some of the challenges facing the research and teaching of literary texts from the distant past. Once we historicize the concept of literature as a construct and expose the modern "invention" of literary tradition, what do we do with these texts and how do we formulate the intellectual rationale for continuing to study and teach them? A study of *modern* literature can be reflexive of the very process through which literary production in modernity has been constituted and reconstituted by the formation of the category "literature." It can avoid reifying literature by recognizing the ways in which literary texts themselves actively reproduce and often subvert the codes and conventions through which they are understood in the modern world. With texts from the distant past, however, the relevance of studying them after the demise of modernizing concepts such as "national canon" seems highly problematic.

Compared to, say, modern Japanese literature, "Heian Literature" invokes a more radically disjunctive formation — records of literary texts and the long history of their transmission from vastly different moments of history that come to us mediated by modern concepts and institutions. Teasing apart the layers of this contradictory and fragmentary configuration, I believe, calls not only for the study of the literature's modern interpretations but for a renewed engagement with the Heian texts themselves. In other words, the understanding of the modern discipline itself cannot be conducted in isolation from the practice of rereading the textual sources. Thus, I use the disciplinary critique as a catalyst for experimenting with a feminist counterreading of Heian texts. I historicize the modern interpretive frameworks not simply by means of contextualization — showing how they are informed by modern ideas and institutions — but by counterpoising them against a reengagement with Heian texts. The dissonance thus discovered between Heian texts and the discourses on them can help us probe the distinct sets of assumptions with which these texts appear to be working.

This manner of examining textual sources through the historicization of modern construction and vice versa may seem digressive and ponderous. It may appear, furthermore, to impose heavy constraints on our ability to claim knowledge about these texts. Indeed, readers will find that I do not offer a comprehensive analysis of issues such as the economy of gender and the gendered subject in the Heian context. What I do suggest about the gender organization of culture and society that Heian texts invoke barely scratches the surface of this vast and complex topic. I nevertheless believe that this circuitous and circumspect methodology opens up the possibility of reaffirming the pertinence of studying texts from a radically different time for a broad range of contemporary intellectual inquiries — to inherit this past part and parcel with the reading tradition that has sedimented around it. In taking such an approach to Heian texts, my study aims not for the veracity of the interpretations I offer but for its coherence and innovation with respect to proposed critical agendas. It should be added, however, that the critical frame against which I have tried to gauge the efficacy of my interpretation has continually been transformed through the process of analysis. I described earlier how my project of bringing Heian literary studies and feminist theory into a fruitful dialogue underwent a series of changes while I worked on this project. Thus, what Heian texts have provided my study is not a body of information to be simply appropriated and familiarized or, inversely, held up as an exotic Other (which often predictably conforms to our expectations and desires for alterity). Rather, they have offered, above all, stimuli for developing a frame from which to rethink our historically situated knowledge and imagination, to explore our horizon of interpretation that is opaque to us. I hope this study conveys some of the rewards that grappling with such a challenge provides and its relevance to our understanding of the present.

An Overview

The book is roughly divided into three parts, each addressing different moments in the history of modern scholarship on Heian literature: (1) the emergence of national literature studies in the late-nineteenth to early-twentieth centuries; (2) postwar developments in the discipline; and (3) the post-1970s theoretical and methodological shift in the field, which continues to shape the discipline. A rough chronological ordering of these three parts, however, is not meant to create an impression that this book is a survey of modern scholarship on Heian literature. While the present study is concerned with *historicizing* some of the major claims made and assumptions held in modern discourses on Heian literature, it is by no means an exhaustive examination of the disciplinary history. I refer to these three moments, in varying degrees of detail, for specific critical purposes. They work together to suggest that, despite the transformations of the discipline and its historical environment, some of the central interpretive models that emerged in Meiji kokubungaku have not been brought under full scrutiny. In particular, I am concerned with the persistence of the modern paradigm of national subject and the attendant conceptualization of gender. At the same time, I try to recognize the fault lines and contradictions within the discipline, paying attention to the debates in the field, which often revolve around the different ways in which past scholarship is claimed and disclaimed. Thus, I hope to complicate overly neat and chronological constructions of the disciplinary history, pointing out multiple ways in which kokubungaku has constituted itself and its own past.

The first two chapters trace the historical permutation of the association between Heian literature and femininity, from eighteenth-century poetics to the modern discipline of national literature studies. Chapter 1 locates an important precedent of the modern feminization of Heian literature in the eighteenth-century nativist discussion of poetry. While the focus of my study is on the modern (i.e., post–Meiji Restoration) construction of Heian literature, the analyses of eighteenth-century poetics serve a number of purposes for this project. First of all, it sheds light on the historical circumstances under which the femininity of Heian literary discourse gained currency and became a topic of debate. In other words, I try to distinguish between the general perception that Heian court culture was effete, which we find articulated in a variety of sources from different time periods, and more specific discourses on the femininity of Heian literary aesthetics that appeared in the eighteenth century. Second, the reference to the eighteenth century, which in Japanese historiography is sometimes referred to as the "early modern," helps me to complicate the term *modernity*.

Eighteenth-century poetics began articulating literary discourses and aesthetics in gendered terms as it sought to formulate new standards of poetic value based on authentic and immanent human experience rather than normative doctrines. Analyzing this facet of eighteenth-century poetics, I identify important prefigurations of the modern, interrelated construction of gender, literature, and social formation. Thus, rather than reducing the modern construction of literature to "Westernization," I call attention to historically concrete problematics that connect the eighteenth-century debates on poetry with modern discourses on literature. At the same time, I underscore a profound break between Tokugawa nativism and post-Restoration national literature studies. In part, through the examination of this rupture, chapter 2 sheds light on the specificity of the kokubungaku construction of literature, which subordinated a diversity of literary forms and history under the unity of a national subject. The chapter then discusses the effects that this transformation had on the assessment of Heian literature and its association with femininity.

The first two chapters interrogate some of the dominant assumptions in the discipline of kokubungaku by pointing out their contingencies vis-à-vis the modern structure of knowledge organized around national ideology. In the third and fourth chapters, I use the critique of modern scholarship as a basis for rereading Heian texts. The discussions in the two chapters move back and forth between critiques of modern discourses on Heian literature and close analyses of Heian texts. In terms of disciplinary history, they address the construction of the national subject, gender, and literature since the end of World War II, situating them in the postwar historical context. I consider both the continuity and discontinuity between the paradigms established by Meiji kokubungaku and those that emerged in the postwar discipline. Some of the perspectives discussed are still part of mainstream kokubungaku scholarship today, especially in what I referred to earlier as the more traditional as opposed to the textualist current in the field.

Chapter 3 focuses on one of the most powerful means by which the modern discipline has constituted the links among the nation, women, and literature in their understanding of Heian cultural history. It problematizes the standard representation of women's roles in the origin and development of kana, the native script, and the literature written in kana during the Heian period. I argue that received knowledge about the history of kana writing and literature takes advantage of the paucity of existing historical materials in order to posit a number of unexamined assumptions about women and their literary practices at the Heian court, turning them into a guarantor of purity and the autonomy of the national language. By drawing on some recent scholarship that redefines the contrast between kana and *mana* (a term conventionally understood to mean Chinese characters) primarily as a calligraphic rather than an orthographic or linguistic distinction, I question the widely accepted notion that women, due to their exclusion from the masculine linguistic domain of Chinese, functioned as the receptacle of native speech and helped develop kana writing and literature during the Heian period.

Chapter 4 examines the highly influential understanding of *The*

Tale of Genji developed by the eighteenth-century nativist Motoori Norinaga and the early postwar scholarship that sought to liberate the *Genji* from this perspective. By comparing the two approaches to the text, I examine their distinct assumptions about literary genres, the social function of poetry, and the nature of genuine sociality constituted through poetic communications. While chapter 2 discusses the affinity (as well as the discord) between eighteenth-century nativism and modern national literature studies, this chapter suggests that the reconstruction of the postwar discipline involved a challenge against the nativist legacies mediated by kokubungaku. The chapter then presents my own reading of the ways in which the *Genji* constitutes poetry and romantic relations against the two competing perspectives. Postwar critics sought to contest the view attributed to Norinaga that Heian kana narratives simply evoke the romantic world of aesthetic/affective harmony centered on poetic communion. Instead, they insisted on a more political and contentious understanding of the texts and their history. I argue, however, that their humanistic and masculinist notion of political agency precluded them from recognizing the tension and negotiation that revolved around the gender difference inscribed in the texts' poetic dialogues between lovers. This oversight in the modernist interpretation highlights the theoretical challenges involved in locating "political" or "critical" perspectives in Heian literary discourses.

The last two chapters propose new directions in the disciplinary critique and the study of Heian texts to be explored in view of post-1970s developments in the field. Chapter 5 analyzes the textual approach that has become a dominant methodology in the field in relation to the theory of Japanese language developed by Tokieda Motoki. As I have already summarized this discussion, I will not repeat it here. Instead, I would like to comment on the relations between the moments in the disciplinary history treated in chapters 2 and 5—the launch of the modernization project of kokubungaku and a clear critique of modernization voiced from within the field since the 1970s. Intellectual projects that I identify in these two historical conjunctures may appear to many to imply the modern versus postmodern divide. I do not explicitly make this association, in part because I wish to avoid the impression of linear ordering and the sense of a clean break that this pair of notions, "modern/postmodern," often inspires. Instead, my discussions focus on traces of the modern (national) subject that haunt the contemporary textual approach, despite its concerted effort to critique the modernist formation of language and subjectivity. Furthermore, I make this argument by analyzing the influence of Tokieda Motoki's work (published around the beginning of the Pacific War) on the textualist study of Heian literature. Setting Tokieda's work against the historical context, I try to suggest not so much the the possibility of history simply repeating itself (the antimodernism of the 1940s resurfacing as the postmodernism of the 1970s) but the ways in which the critique of modernity has been an integral facet of Japanese modernity and modernization. The fact that the modernity of Tokieda's antimodernism remains largely unacknowledged in the post-1970s appropriation of his theory in Heian literary studies, also reveals some of the limitations of the latter's attempt at overcoming kokubungaku methodologies.

The sixth chapter in many ways puts into practice some of the critiques I develop in chapter 5 through an examination of the intersection between the study of narrative forms and gender construction in Heian texts. Focusing on *Kagerō nikki*, the text often held up as the epitome of so-called Heian female diary literature, the chapter interrogates the common perception that the text is narrated in the narcissistic and self-absorbed voice of the female author. I suggest that Kagerō nikki is *not* written in the first-person voice (as conventionally defined), challenging the use of modern narratological concepts of voice and perspective in the study of Heian texts. Through this analysis of textual form, I question the realist and autobiographical reading of the text together with the assumptions concerning the authorial gender that has been projected onto it. At the same time, I argue that the narrative economy of the text also refracts the subjectification of the narratorial discourse in the manner proposed by the advocates of Tokieda's theory. Rather than identifying the subject supposedly implicated by the narration, I draw attention to the text's construction of a socially situated self that speaks through and against existing expectations about women and female destiny. In my analysis, the issue of gender is reintroduced to the study of Kagerō not as a property of the subject (i.e., understood as the unity of heroine and the narrator/author). Rather, I examine how gender serves as a significant social inflection of the textual discourse and its constitution of self.

Finally, in the epilogue I consider how such an approach to Heian narrative form and the question of gender that it raises may intervene in the ongoing debates on subjectivity and agency in contemporary feminist theory. I suggest that the study of Heian texts can help us question whether the postmodern critique of gendered subject is the ultimate horizon for rethinking feminist subject and agency today.

CHAPTER ONE

The Feminization of Heian and
Eighteenth-Century Poetics

Given the widely accepted image of the Heian court as populated with effete aristocrats and the reputation of the Heian period as the golden age of women's writing, the association between Heian literature and femininity seems all but inevitable. Historically, however, the identification of mid-Heian literature with feminine qualities was a notion that gained currency through the discussion of poetics during the eighteenth century.[1] While the perception of Heian aristocratic society and culture that developed during preceding centuries no doubt informed it, the feminization of Heian literature in the eighteenth century must be understood in relation to debates over the nature of poetry and its function within the society of the time. A closer look at the principal sources from the period suggests that the identification of Heian literature in feminine terms was variously construed and contested. This chapter examines the complex sets of designs that were involved in ascribing femininity to Heian literature and identifies common concerns informing divergent perspectives. Through this analysis, I begin exploring the broader problem of how the gendering of literary history and aesthetics has functioned in the modern construction of literature.

I argue that the feminization of Heian literature and the use of gender metaphors to discuss literary discourses germinated in response to the problems specific to eighteenth-century poetics: the need to establish a new definition of poetry and its standard of evaluation in opposition to accepted paradigms. This development in poetics, furthermore, was inextricably connected to the destabilization of the existing social and intellectual formations increasingly apparent by the early to mid–eighteenth century—including the dysfunction of the political and economic structures of Bakufu (the Tokugawa Shogunate), the challenge against the neo-Confucian intellectual order, and impacts of expanding urban space and its population. Harootunian and others have identified in the eighteenth-century debates on poetics a profound anxiety that the contemporary world had lost the immanent, spontaneous, and transparent form of human sociality and communication. The critical question, then, was how to reconstitute a unity and order of poetic modes and values in light of this condition. The problem, furthermore, was directly linked to the more general project of locating the integrity among the diverse and seemingly fragmented human experiences in which the essence of poetry was to be found. The association between poetry and social harmony is an idea found in some of the earliest forms of poetics in Japan (as well as in the Chinese poetics that often served as the model). In the eighteenth century, however, the coherence and authenticity of poetic sociality was posited *against* the perceived sense of growing social and linguistic opacity.[2] It is in this context that we find the use of gender categories in the discussion of poetics. In particular, the "feminine" was constituted as a key signifier of negativity—that is, the inferior pole of an interconnected yet asymmetrical binary—in relation to which new visions of sociality, poetic theory, and poetic practice were constituted.

Eighteenth-century poetics offered highly sophisticated responses to the problem of how to identify coherence in the anomie of human experience and how poetry construed as the purest and most authentic deployment of language may figure in such a process. This explains why it continued to inspire Japanese intellectuals, who later sought the means to grapple with the deeply unsettling impact of modernity. This prefiguration of modern discourses on literature by eighteenth-century poetics offers an important perspective on how the feminization of the Heian and the use of gender metaphors in discussing literary values and types in general took shape in modern (i.e., post-Restoration) studies of literature.

Kamo no Mabuchi and the
Feminization of Heian Poetry

The picture of elegant Heian aristocrats inhabiting an exquisitely refined court society—immersed in the pleasures of art and literature and shunning prosaic concerns such as economic affairs, military training, and even official matters of the state bureaucracy—has circulated widely through the popular reception of mid-Heian texts such as *The Tale of Genji*. Takahashi Masaaki traces back the roots of these conventional images not to the Heian period itself but to the nostalgic construction of it by the courtiers of later centuries who idealized the mid-Heian period as the apogee of aristocratic culture, taking the world depicted in the *Genji* at face value.[3] By the mid–fifteenth century, the economic and political power of the courtiers had undergone a marked decline and the capital they resided in had been badly damaged by repeated battles. Under such circumstances, courtiers sought to preserve their prestige, in part, by becoming purveyors of traditional arts, including poetic composition and criticism. During the Tokugawa period, the links between the courtiers and the arts were institutionalized by a Bakufu policy that removed the imperial family and courtiers from political arenas while offering them patronage for their roles as guardians of traditional learning and artistic practices. The historical transformation of the status and role of courtiers in Japanese history reinforced the perception of an effeminate and precious Heian aristocracy.

The association between Heian literature and femininity that is often taken for granted today, however, has more specific sources in eighteenth-century poetics, particularly in the work of Kamo no Mabuchi (1697–1769).[4] In "Nihimanabi" (ca. 1765), he writes:

> Since the Yamato region [where the capital was located during the Nara period] was a land of valiant men, in ancient times even women followed the masculine mode of composing poetry. Thus,

the poems of the *Man'yōshū* are composed in the masculine style. Because the Yamashiro region [where the Heian capital was located] was a land of women, even men followed the feminine mode, so the poems of *Kokinwakashū* are mostly composed in a graceful feminine style (*tawoyameburi*). Furthermore, when *Kokinwakashū* evaluated the styles of the six poets (poetic sages), it favored a tranquil and clear style of poetry, criticizing the strong and firm style as rustic. This is because they considered the poetic style of its particular time and place as the standard, without taking into consideration archaic poems.[5]

Mabuchi equates the rise of feminine style with the degeneration of poetry, attributing this downturn to the decline of direct imperial rule (the domination of the court by powerful aristocratic families), as well as to the popularity of Chinese literature and culture in the early Heian period.

Mabuchi posited the femininity of Heian society and its poetry in contrast to the masculinity of ancient poems, particularly those collected in an anthology of the Nara period, *Man'yōshū*.[6] For Mabuchi, *Man'yōshū* epitomized the essence of waka — the unadorned and straightforward expression of feelings unsullied by artificial embellishments or intellectual manipulations.[7] Mabuchi argued that this authentic articulation of emotion was adulterated and finally lost through the influence of Chinese language and thoughts in Japan. In order to purge such corruption, one had to develop a correct understanding of the words of the ancients through their poems and through this understanding gain access to the minds of the ancients.[8] In contrast to *Man'yōshū*, the Heian poetic anthology *Kokinwakashū* (compiled in the tenth century and destined to become the most canonical text of waka in subsequent centuries) does not help us to emulate the archaic mind according to Mabuchi. This is because the poetry in the later collection had already been affected by artificiality and Chinese influences. Labeling Heian poetry as feminine and weak, therefore, helped shore up the alleged strength and emotional authenticity of the earlier poems found in *Man'yōshū*.

Mabuchi's view of Heian poetry and the use of gender metaphors must be understood in relation to the ferment over new forms of waka poetics that arose in the eighteenth century around what we commonly refer to as *kokugaku* ("nativism" or more literally "native learn-ing," as opposed to the scholarship on Chinese sources), loosely linked schools of learning concerned with a wide variety of subjects, includ-ing language, religion, and poetics studied through classical textual sources. Kokugaku challenged the two dominant currents of poetics in existence: on one hand, the reduction of poetry to (moral) didacti-cism and political utility assumed in the Confucian tradition; and on the other the conservatism, rigidity, and institutional insularity of the orthodox study of waka controlled by poetic schools with aristocratic lineages.

By the early Tokugawa period, courtiers' poetics had calcified into staid conservatism, adhering closely to the sanctioned diction, theme, and rhetorical forms established largely by Heian imperial antholo-gies of waka. Fidelity to this canonical style of poetry was enforced by numerous arcane rules and regulations transmitted from masters to students. These teachings constituted jealously protected esoteric doctrines that conferred power and prestige to the houses of waka that claimed them. A relatively straightforward (i.e., not too tech-nically complex) and standardized style was valorized by the main-stream courtier's poetics as the orthodoxy; and the miniscule varia-tions within sanctioned forms and themes were cast as the sublime art of poetic composition, shrouded in pseudospiritual and mystical profundity.[9]

The first major challenge to the established waka criticism by ko-kugaku circle took shape over the controversy provoked by Kada Ari-maro's poetic treatise *Kokka hachiron* (1742).[10] In the text's central and the most controversial section, Arimaro offered an unequivocal rebut-tal against the view that poetry has any beneficial effect on the gov-erning of the state or has any utilitarian value in general. Instead he argued that it has no other function than to generate aesthetic enjoy-ment—when it achieves formal beauty and the depth of meaning, it impresses the audience and gives pleasure to the one who composed it.[11] This view clearly dissented from the Confucian tradition of poet-ics as well as from the belief in the spiritual force of poetry proclaimed by the courtiers' poetics.

Despite the apparent devaluation of poetry into a source of amuse-ment—defining it as an artifice to be judged primarily by its formal beauty and the pleasure it offers — *Kokka hachiron* helped stimulate exploration into the intrinsic criteria of poetic evaluation. Mabuchi's view that poetry simply expresses true human feelings may be seen as both a further engagement with the questions raised by *Kokka hachiron* and a rejoinder to the specific response it offered.[12] While the notion that poetry merely amuses and pleases the poet/audience tends to detach it from human affect, Mabuchi argued that poetry in essence is a pure expression of concrete human feelings.

The definition of *poetry* as an expression of the human heart is of course one of the most orthodox doctrines of waka poetics that can be traced back to the "Kana Preface" of *Kokinwakashū*. Mabuchi, however, radicalized its implication, divorcing it from formal technique and the normative aesthetic paradigm of courtly elegance. Thus *Man'yōshū* poetry, which is identified with the pristine and straightforward style, is held up as the supreme exemplar of waka. Mabuchi's idealization of *Man'yōshū* and his insistence on its virile aesthetics, therefore, was underwritten by his specific understanding of poetry and the relations among human affect, the process of composing poetry, and the basis for evaluating poetic merits.

Mabuchi's archaism should be distinguished from conservatism in that his call to return to the poetry of the ancients was based on his specific theoretical grasp of a poetic essence that defied waka orthodoxy. In this connection, we also need to note that Mabuchi's poetics, which privileged *Man'yōshū*, was supported by the philological methodology for studying Japanese classical texts introduced by the priest Keichū (considered to be one of the founders of kokugaku). It was through philological study that *Man'yōshū*, which had been marginal to mainstream waka poetics, was made more accessible, providing a foundation for the heterodox view proposed by Mabuchi and others. The philological and empirical study of ancient texts gave Mabuchi the authority to speak about the originary form of waka from a perspective unencumbered by insular esoteric doctrines.

As for the question of instrumental and didactic values of poetry, Mabuchi did suggest the interrelations between politics and poetics. He wrote that, although poetry does not seem to have obvious utility, it could help maintain the political order by calming and soothing the minds of the people.[13] Clearly, however, this was not the focus of his poetics. More important, his notion that in ancient times poetry sprung forth naturally from one's sensitivity and that the state was governed *spontaneously* (*onozukara*), without any contrivance and coercion, suggests that the relation between politics and poetics is noncausal or noninstrumental.[14]

Kageki's Critique of Gendered Periodization

Nearly half a century after Mabuchi's pronouncement of Man'yocentrism and his characterization of the Nara period and *Man'yōshū* as masculine and the Heian and *Kokinwakashū* as feminine a systematic critique of his views was launched by an influential poet and critic, Kagawa Kageki (1768–1843).[15] In "Nihimanabi iken" (ca. 1811), Kageki rejected Mabuchi's association of gender with geographic locations (the Yamato region identified with the Nara period versus the Yamashiro region identified with the Heian period) and historical eras (Heian versus Nara). He argued that if the Yamato region and the poems composed in it were masculine then poems from that region should have remained so throughout different historical periods.[16] This would contradict Mabuchi's claim that the Heian period as a whole capitulated to the effeminate style of poetry.

More important, he questioned the rationale for associating the forceful style of poetry with masculinity and the gentle style of poetry with femininity.[17] Kageki accepted the general contrast between Man'yō poetry's forcefulness and simplicity as opposed to Kokin poetry's gentle gracefulness. He argued, however, that this distinction would be better described as one between the naive rustic style and the elegant sophistication of the capital style — consonant with the transformation of the environments in which the poems collected in the anthologies were produced (the Heian culture is often identified with the establishment of the first full-scale imperial capital in Japan, Heiankyō, which was modeled after the capital of the T'ang dynasty in China).

In other words, although he admitted that different eras of waka history may be identified with certain overarching characteristics, he deemed masculine versus feminine to be inappropriate categories for describing these poetic styles. For one, Kageki pointed out, the pair insinuates misleading associations between the poetic styles and genders of poets (as if poems in *Kokinwakashū* were composed primarily by female poets). For another, referring to an entire period of poetic history as masculine would undermine the possibility that even in such an era poems composed by women may be relatively more feminine than those composed by men. Thus, it unduly underplays the variations that exist among poems of the same period. Ultimately, Kageki charged Mabuchi with manipulating the gender metaphor in order to give a positive cast to the simple and unadorned poetic style he identifies in *Man'yōshū*. The difference between qualities such as ornate versus stark acquires hierarchical nuances by being illustrated by masculine-feminine contrast. The conventional sociocultural privilege of masculinity over femininity, in other words, is superimposed on the relationship between *Man'yōshū* and *Kokinwakashū* by identifying the strong and simple with masculinity.[18]

Kageki's objection to Mabuchi's use of the gendered metaphor developed into a broader challenge to the latter's Manyōcentrism. Kageki rejected the hierarchical grasp of waka history, placing one era (that of *Man'yōshū*) ahead of the other (that of *Kokinwakashū*). Instead, he believed that the differences among distinct periods of poetic composition demonstrate the ever-changing cosmic rhythm expressed in poetry. Diverse styles of poetry in different historical times manifest the essentially poetic property of the world that is continually in flux. Although individual poets have their distinct modes of composition, they must be affected by the overall spirit of the particular era in which they live. Thus, rather than trying to mimic the poetic style of the past one should compose poetry consonant with one's time.

While clearly repudiating Mabuchi's archaism, Kageki was among the late Tokugawa critics whose theory extended some of the implications of Mabuchi's proposal: defining poetry as the genuine expression of concrete human emotions as such. This is precisely why he objected to Mabuchi's emulation of the ancient poetic style. From Kageki's perspective, this was itself a contrivance that contradicts the definition of poetry as a natural expression of human feelings. While Mabuchi identified the virtue in the simplicity of *Man'yōshū*, which was undervalued in traditional poetics, Kageki advocated the poetic authenticity of what was dismissed as vulgar — the use of ordinary words and themes consonant with the experience of contemporary everyday life. At least in theory, then, waka for Kageki was to be free from the formal/stylistic regulations imposed by Man'yō purism that Mabuchi preached (as well as by the orthodoxy of courtier poetics).

In practice, however, Kageki was not necessarily the most iconoclastic or experimental poet of his time, and even in theory he defended the virtues of the classical formal beauty of waka in *Kokinwakashū*.[19] As mentioned earlier, he argued that the ever-changing cosmic rhythm naturally shapes the waka of each period into a form appropriate to its time. If one simply composed poems according to one's emotions, the poem would take a particular *shirabe* (tone) because of this cosmic force.[20] The concept of shirabe, then, served as a conceptual conduit through which the concern for formal aesthetics returns to Kageki's poetics. Though cast as the natural effect of a cosmic principle, the notion of shirabe establishes an expectation of a formal standard that shapes poetry of each epoch. Kageki's backpeddling from the more radical possibility of the views he advocated suggests the difficulty of reconciling emotional authenticity and immediacy as the essence of poetic inspiration and the normative forms and conventions of waka. I examine in the following section the ingenious and complex ways in which Motoori Norinaga faced this challenge and the roles that gendered metaphor and Heian literature played in his thought.

Motoori Norinaga and the
Negativity of the Feminine

Although Motoori Norinaga was not directly engaged in the critique of Mabuchi's work, his approach to poetry and his use of the gender metaphor must be distinguished from those of Mabuchi as well as Kageki.[21] The specific ways in which he deployed the figure of "femininity" in his poetics had profound influences on subsequent discussions of not only Heian literature but literary aesthetics in general. Norinaga concurred with Mabuchi in defining the foundation of waka in terms of *ninjō* (human emotion). Yet, in a stark contrast to Mabuchi, Norinaga argued that *makoto no kokoro* (true human emotion) is *memeshi* (effete) and fragile.[22] No matter how wise and rational a person may seem to be, if one searches deeply within his heart, one will find qualities that are foolish and feminine inside him, no different from what is found in the minds of women and children.[23] He writes that Chinese texts may extol the heroism of a warrior who faces his death bravely. But if we see through his true heart as it really is, we will most likely find longing for his parents, a wish to see his wife and children again, and some regrets about having to sacrifice his life.[24] Masculine strength and composure are thus identified with the observation of artificial principles (promoted by Buddhism and Confucianism) that disavow personal feelings. They are charged with falsity, which obscures the true nature of the human heart and in turn the essence of poetry.

Like Mabuchi, Norinaga believed that poets in his contemporary society had lost the ability to compose poems that arise directly from one's heart and that the ideal mode of poetic composition had to be retrieved from the past through the study of ancient and classical waka.[25] Yet for Norinaga the most privileged past in the history of waka was not so much that of the Man'yō poets but the milieu of Heian court society. He states that from antiquity to the present *Kokinwakashū* represents the fullest and most complete development of poetry and the anthology offers the most paradigmatic style of waka to be emulated.[26] Furthermore, the importance of the Heian for Norinaga is attested by the fact that some of the most extensive elaborations of his poetics are found in his discussion of the eleventh-century narrative, *The Tale of Genji*, which he deemed indispensable for the study of waka.

Norinaga saw in the tale — which revolves around amorous affairs of characters who appeared effete, sentimental, and weak from his contemporaries' viewpoint — the most exemplary exploration of fleeting, ever-changing, and yet irrepressible human emotions.[27] He famously argued that the text's theme can be distilled to a single point, the recognition of *mono no aware*, the capacity to feel and be moved by the things and events in the world. Norinaga saw in Heian literature, and in the *Genji* in particular, a grace that arises from deep sensitivities toward human emotions and their failings. Thus, when he promoted the aesthetics of *miyabi* (elegance), he was referring not so much to the courtly sense of beauty canonized by traditional waka poetics. Rather, he was pointing to the shared aesthetic culture based on the sensitivity and forgiving attitude toward all forms of feelings that he identified in the *Genji*.

While Norinaga insinuated the association between Heian literature and femininity, he inverted the true-false dichotomy and the hierarchical relation that Mabuchi invoked through gender metaphor. Rather than using femininity as the mark of artificiality and degeneration, Norinaga deployed it as the signifier of uncensored, true feelings. Meanwhile, the masculine was no longer associated with the pristine native spirit expressed in poems from the ancient period. Rather, it stood for the artificiality exemplified by the foreign (Chinese) doctrines and the contemporary official order that had adopted them as its own.[28]

If, as Kageki argued, Mabuchi used the social and cultural prestige of the masculine to elevate the status of *Man'yōshū*, Norinaga used the inferior status of the feminine to exorcise what he perceived to be the hypocrisy and insincerity of the moralizing and didactic approach to poetry. He insisted on considering the affective source of poetry not on the basis of what *ought* to be but of what *is*, however transgressive it may be for the dominant ethical codes of the society. By associating poetry with the negativity of the feminine, he identified the emotional power of poetry in its very marginality to the sanctioned, clearly defined, prescriptive values. Norinaga's discussion of affect keeps turning to the shadowy realms of the human heart: the desire that crests against the prohibition, temptations that arise despite one's better judgment, and the ambivalence and vulnerability that haunt even sage priests and fearless warriors. By describing human emotion as abject and effete, Norinaga not only affirms its peripheral status but highlights its potency and ubiquity, which survive attempts to disavow it.

Norinaga's emphasis on the negativity of emotions through the use of the feminine metaphor underscores his understanding of affect on the basis of *how* one feels rather than *what* one feels. He insists that we need to look beyond the myriad contents of our emotional lives, which may be frivolous or degenerate, and discern their indubitable power to move us. He argues that *The Tale of Genji* does not necessarily promote illicit romances but uses them as devices through which the powerful emotions of its characters are invoked; he likens this to the beautiful and pure lotus flower that blossoms in muddy water.[29] By defining *emotion* in terms of its experiential forces, Norinaga not only divorces it from the criteria of morality and social utility but releases it from normative definitions in general. Human feelings, for Norinaga, escape the control of regulatory principles and rigid articulation — ever changing, multilayered, and often conflicted.[30] Herein lies

The Feminization of Heian   35

an important difference between Norinaga, on one hand, and Kageki as well as Mabuchi on the other. For Mabuchi and Kageki, authentic emotions have more or less specific contents—for the former, the simple and pristine feelings of the ancients and for the latter, sensibilities specific to the spirit of one's time. So they call on the poets to identify with these true emotions and express them in an appropriate manner (e.g., through the ancient or contemporary style of poetry). There are strong expressivistic tendencies in their poetics; the form is theoretically subordinated to the content.

Although Norinaga, like Mabuchi and Kageki, professes that poetry is the expression of human feelings, he does not presuppose direct and simplistic relations between the poet's emotion (understood at the level of content) and poetic discourses. He suggests that we cannot infer the formal characteristics of poetry (anticipate what poems should look and sound like) from its affective source if emotion as such cannot be grasped as a substantive entity. For Norinaga, therefore, poetry is *not* a spontaneous and artless expression of a particular feeling. This also means that the question of how to approach poetic form cannot be resolved through archaism—merging with the mind of the ancients and re-creating an unproblematic and natural unity between the heart and the word that existed in a purer state of human existence. At times, he explicitly cautions against idealizing the spontaneity of ancient poems, pointing out that there is no such thing as completely artless poetry, for even in ancient times poets embellished their words and desired to compose fine poems.[31] The issue of design and the effort to produce superior poems become even more significant in contemporary society, which has lost the innocence and purity of the distant past.

Thus, Norinaga refrains from denying the value of poetic regulations and conventions. When one composes a poem that seems true to one's feelings, using whatever words that come to mind, it is indeed authentic, regardless of unseemly diction or vulgar style. Ultimately, however, the lack of formal refinement would come back to haunt the poet, preventing him or her from reaping the full satisfaction of composing poems. This is because in general one is driven to express one's feeling in poetry not simply to satisfy oneself but to move others.[32] Here the need to adhere to the shared standards and formal regulations of poetry arises. The satisfaction of conveying one's feelings through poetry will not be achieved if one sees the audience unmoved by formally coarse and inferior poems.[33] This is why Norinaga insists that poetry must be composed with an attention to form, selecting appealing styles and words.[34] What mediates authentic feelings and formal regulations of poetry in Norinaga's theory, then, is its function as a social medium. The milieu of the Heian court and the literature produced therein is exemplary for Norinaga not because the society was so simple and unified that people "naturally" empathized with each other. Rather, he believed that poetry in that context performed its proper function of overriding the differences between people and generated the sociality of affective communication.

Gender and the Prefiguration of Modern in Eighteenth-Century Poetics

Harry Harootunian has analyzed kokugaku's cognitive strategy in terms of its principle of contiguity, contrasting it to Tokugawa neo-Confucianism, which apprehended the world in a series of resemblances.[35] According to Harootunian, this metonymic strategy of kokugaku allowed observers to make qualitative distinctions that previously, under the regime of the paradigmatic model of knowledge, had been difficult to make. And the establishment of such an evaluative model, in turn, enabled one to constitute a theoretical system that accommodates a greater degree of diversity and differences. Harootunian's perspective draws our attention to the fact that kokugaku was part of a broader movement in the eighteenth-century intellectual world that arose in response to the growing awareness that the existing epistemological frameworks were failing to respond to the social diversity and mobility emerging in Tokugawa society (e.g., the rigidly hierarchical and monolithic neo-Confucian worldview or the traditionalism and ritualism sustained through the insular and esoteric system of master to disciple transmission of knowledge). The seventeenth and eighteenth centuries saw rapid growth of the monetary economy and urban centers such as Edo, with the attendant expansion of the economic, cultural, and sociopolitical dynamism of townspeople. The Bakufu's political and economic organizations were eroding, and among the rural peasantry as well as the urban population there was a mounting sense of discontent against the regime. The development immediately consequential to the transformation of poetics was the spread of print technology, the growth of literacy among a larger segment of the population, and the proliferation of new forms of literary production and circulation, especially in the milieu of townspeople. These developments were among the conditions under which the challenges against the orthodoxy of poetic theory and practices, and the exploration of new approaches to poetry and its function within the society took place.

In this context, debates on waka poetics revolving around figures such as Mabuchi and Norinaga sought to establish a way to discuss waka that both breaks from the rigid adherence to received norms (whether it be based on waka orthodoxy or neo-Confucian diadacticism), and avoids slippage into pure subjectivism. Meanwhile, the introduction of sophisticated philological methodology helped raise poetic texts to an unprecedented level of empirical scrutiny, stimulating new perspectives on the history of waka. The antinormative and empirical thrust of kokugaku poetics foregrounds its decidedly "modern" properties. Its seemingly romantic, antirational, and antiquarian tendencies have, in fact, highly rational bases.[36] The fresh current of eighteenth-century poetics displayed the impetus for developing a general theory of poetry that accounts for historical differences and variations of waka style. Moreover, it sought to locate poetic authenticity in the experience available through concrete everyday practices. That is to say, they articulated the sense of truth confirmed not by a static authority but primarily through one's tangible experiences and interactions in the world. Mabuchi and Norinaga reached into the distant past in search of poetic authenticity not so much to deny or dismiss the experience in the present but to counteract the falsity that had, in their views, obscured truth in the contemporary world.

For Norinaga as well as Mabuchi, waka was not a mere contrivance divorced from true feelings, as Kada Arimaro suggested. Its privilege lay in its ability to convey genuine feelings like no other form of human discourse. The question, however, was that if we posit the poetic essence in concrete affective life, with all its variation, fluidity, opacity, and disorder, how can we also insist on a formal standard and system of values that hold the identity of poetry together? For Norinaga, the emotive essence of poetry and its aesthetic/conventional form come together in poetry understood as a social medium — defined by its function of staging empathetic communion. Thus, powerful feelings in a poet effect beautifully crafted poetry that moves the audience. Through such reflection into the relation between the affective essence of poetry and its formal aesthetics, waka was understood to be a constituent of genuine sociality. In other words, poetry mediates concrete human experience in the world, overcoming the difference between one individual and another not through an extrinsic principle imposed from above but by bringing forth something general and commutable that exists at the very heart of what appears divisive. This poetic function was deemed more significant than ever given the growing sense of opacity in human relations and linguistic communication in the present.

Norinaga's complex and at times elusive theory weaves subjective experience with shared social conventions, articulating a conception of social unity that defies static normativity. The influence that Norinaga's thesis had on subsequent Japanese intellectual history may be understood, in part, by the prescience with which his poetics anticipated the conceptualization of literature in a modern sense: the "concrete universal" that brings together individuality and collectivity, particularity and generality, or unity and difference. And the feminine, as the signifier of half-formed, shadowy, abject, and undisciplined forces of affect and desire, emerged at the center of Norinaga's understanding of social cohesion. In its very negativity, the effeminate heart of man guarantees the genuine communality in the fissures of positive regulatory structure stipulated by the public order.

The features of eighteenth-century poetics we have examined can help us to better understand how the gender metaphor was activated in the debates on poetry at the time. Feminine versus masculine represented a binary and asymmetrical set of values that were also vitally interconnected. It facilitated the articulation of a poetic universe envisaged as a diversity that forms hierarchical coherence, a unity wrought from different forces at work. Moreover, in Norinaga's poetics gender as the signifier of the difference within a whole helped to affirm the existence of authenticity in the midst of falsity, fragmentation, and corruption. His idealization of the past notwithstanding, he did not urge his contemporaries to travel back in time and *become* ancients.[37] There was no need to seek the truth outside one's present environment because it already existed as the negativity (that which is despised and disavowed) immanent in the present. This is why the abject feminine, defined by its status as the alterity to the masculine, figured as one of the most powerful signifiers of truth in Norinaga's thought.

The gender metaphor also helped to link poetry to human experience on the broadest spectrum, from the most particular, mundane aspects of everyday life to the broader principle of sociality. In the context of discussing Heian literature, the application of the gender metaphor provided a more generalized concept with which to analyze its aesthetics compared to the traditional sense of courtly beauty. In other words, while the notion of miyabi, for instance, invoked a specific set of orthodox poetic doctrines and canonical practices, the feminine was a much more plastic notion, one that could invite a wide range of associations and connotations that reached far beyond the scope of conventional poetics.

It was precisely due to the complex functions played by the gender metaphor that a significant degree of disagreement over the coupling of Heian literature and femininity ensued from the moment the notion crystallized in eighteenth-century waka poetics. We have seen how, for instance, Mabuchi and Norinaga made use of the asymmetrical binary of gender in a contrasting manner—the former manipulated the superiority of the masculine while the latter used the inferiority of the feminine to overturn received assumptions about poetry and human nature. We will bear in mind the theoretical complexity and multiple historical inflections that affected the feminization of Heian literature in the eighteenth century as we move to the next chapter, where we shift our attention to the rise of modern literary scholarship in Japan. The present chapter serves as a backdrop against which we study how the feminine-Heian nexus and gender metaphor became rearticulated vis-à-vis the "nation form"—the dominant frame of sociocultural identity in post-Restoration Japanese discourses on literature.

CHAPTER TWO

Gender and the Nationalization

of Literature

The emergence of the modern discipline of kokubungaku in the late nineteenth century is inextricably related to the formation of Japan as a nation-state. This chapter analyzes how gender and national identities intersected in kokubungaku's construction of Japanese literary history and the status of Heian literature therein. The first section considers the formation of Meiji kokubungaku and its appropriation and rejection of kokugaku legacies. I highlight the manner in which kokubungaku reformulated some of the elements of kokugaku as it built its disciplinary coherence around the concept of nation or national subject expressed through literary history. This process had profound consequences for the modern understanding of Heian literature.

The rest of the chapter analyzes the works of two principal figures of Meiji kokubungaku: Haga Yaichi and Fujioka Sakutarō, who produced some of the first sophisticated studies of Japanese literary history. In particular, I address the ways in which Heian literature and its alleged feminine properties played important roles in their attempts to forge the unity of national literary history, constructing the literary and the national in relation to each other. The distinct perspectives presented by the two scholars on how to articulate the unity of Japan's national literature highlight the complexity and contradictions that haunted the project. The difference in their strategies accounts for their divergent approaches to Heian literature and the roles they assigned to women and femininity in Japanese literary history as a whole. By juxtaposing the two distinct models for nationalizing literature, the chapter attempts to locate in Meiji kokubungaku not only an overt display of sexism but a more paradoxical process—how its deployment of modern conceptions of nation and national history precipitated the celebration as well as the devaluation of feminized Heian literature. Through this discussion, I hope to explore the modernity of gender ideology mobilized in kokubungaku discussions of literary history, women's literary production, and literary aesthetics.

The Birth of Kokubungaku

The history of Meiji kokubungaku is closely linked to the establishment of a modern university system by the Japanese state, modeled largely after European universities. Tokyo University was founded in 1877, with the scholars of *yōgaku* (Western learning) seizing the leadership and eclipsing the factions of Chinese and Japanese studies scholars that initially engaged in a fierce competition over institutional control. The development of the imperial university was an important facet of the state's program of transforming Japan into a powerful and prosperous modern nation.[1] The university represented the pinnacle of the national education system, a conduit for importing the latest technology and information from abroad. As an institution for training elites, particularly the top bureaucrats and academics, it helped the state influence an important segment of the ruling class and extend its control over the production and dissemination of knowledge. The institutional history of kokubungaku can be traced through the permutations of academic organization at Tokyo (Imperial) University that led to the birth of the department bearing this very name. The process unfolded through the increasing specialization of academic fields, mirroring the disciplinary divisions found in European universities.

In the 1880s, a wave of support for the study of Japanese classical literature arose in academia. It was fueled by a burgeoning nationalistic current that called for curtailing the excessive level of modernization and Westernization which had supposedly occurred during the first decades of the Meiji period.[2] This newly aroused interest in Japanese literature was institutionalized at the Imperial University through the establishment of the *wabungakuka* (Department of Japanese Letters) in 1885, splitting up the *wakan bungaku ka* (Department of Sino-Japanese Letters). At this point, however, wabungakuka covered materials that would later be siphoned off into fields such as history, law, and politics. In 1889, wabungakuka was renamed kokubungakuka and subdivided into *kokugo* (national language) and *kokubun* (national literature). It was not until 1901, however, that the modern form of kokubungaku, as the discipline of national *literature*, solidified.

By the 1890s a new generation of kokubungaku scholars, familiar with European literary scholarship, were joining the faculty of Tokyo Imperial University. They gradually took over the department, which previously had been dominated by kokugaku scholars. As kokubungaku consolidated institutionally during the final decade of the nineteenth century, there were bursts of new publications, including dictionaries, commentaries, and reprints of classical Japanese literary texts, which made them more accessible to the broader reading public. Perhaps most important, the period saw the publication of some of the earliest modern studies of Japanese literary history. Nineteenth-century literary criticism in Europe is known for the rise of literary history, the establishment of national literature as an object of study, and the theorization of realism/naturalism. Late-nineteenth-century Japanese literary scholarship, especially the literary history produced at the time, demonstrates kokubungaku's rapid adaptation and elaboration of many of these themes.

In 1890, three seminal works of kokubungaku were published one after the other by scholars affiliated with Tokyo Imperial University. Ueda Kazutoshi compiled the first kokubungaku anthology under the title *Kokubungaku*. This collection of prose and verses from the late Tokugawa to the Meiji periods was intended to be the first in the series of anthologies that would provide a broad survey of the nation's literature and history. *Kokubungaku tokuhon* by Haga Yaichi and Tachibana Sensaburō was an anthology of poems and prose all the way from the Nara to the late Tokugawa periods with an introductory section that sketched an outline of national literary history. Finally, Mikami Sanji and Takatsu Kuwasaburō published *Nihon bungakushi*, the first full-length modern survey of Japanese literary history. Mikami and Takatsu wrote in the prologue to the text that reading literary history written in the West had made them aware of the absence of a comparable work on Japanese literary history. *Nihon bungakushi*, in other words, self-consciously aimed at applying in the Japanese context some of the theories and structures of literary history developed in the West.

These works from early 1890s forged the disciplinary identity of kokubungaku largely in reaction to what was perceived to be the obsolete model of kokugaku. One of the major effects of the transition to the modern discipline was the enlargement of the literary canon.[3] Meiji kokubungaku criticized kokugaku for the narrowness of its scope, as it focused primarily on classical poetry from the Nara and Heian periods.[4] The interest in a broader historical time span and more diverse literary forms (including not only poetry and prose but dramatic texts and types of literature that would have been considered vulgar by Tokugawa scholars) points to the specific perspectives and assumptions held by kokubungaku. What was considered appropriate *and* worthy of scholarly engagement was transformed as "national" became the defining concept underwriting kokubungaku.

To put it simply, nationalism rather than nativism emerged as the linchpin of disciplinary identity. The nation, or more precisely the nation understood as a historical entity—that which expresses itself through a historical development—called for a more inclusive canon, incorporating varied forms of literary texts produced through temporal trajectory now understood as "national history." Mikami and Takatsu write: "Literary history is a form of history that records the origin, development, and transformation of literature. Just as there are world history and national history in history proper, there are the history of world literature and the history of national literature in our field. The former studies the evolution and progress of human wisdom through literature, and the latter examines historically the literary phenomena that appeared in one nation."[5] We see in *Nihon bungakushi* the strong influence of the nineteenth-century European literary historiography and in particular the work of Hyppolite Taine, to whom Mikami and Takatsu directly refer. Defining the nation as a subject of history, literature was posited as an expression of its historical progress through time.[6]

Kokugaku, Kokubungaku, and Heian Literature

In Meiji kokubungaku, Heian literature was understood as a moment in the evolutionary unfolding of Japanese literary culture. It was deemed the pinnacle of the classical period in Japanese cultural history, the culmination of the process through which national literature came into its own. The Tokugawa period was thought to be the second peak, topping the achievements of the Heian through the diversity of its literary forms and the types of people who participated in literary production, including not only aristocrats and warriors but commoners.[7] The Kamakura and Muromachi periods were perceived to be the dark valley between these two great periods, the era during which literary culture languished under wars and continual political unrest. These three main phases of literary history laid out by Meiji kokubungaku corresponded to the standard Western historiographical division among the classical, medieval, and early modern periods. The pat teleological and organistic trajectory of the birth, death, and resurrection implied by this trichotomy, furthermore, posited Japanese literature's path to its full realization in the present and future.

We may pause here to compare kokubungaku's perspective with those of Mabuchi and Norinaga, who located aesthetic ideals in the archaic or classical past. As I pointed out in the last chapter, kokugaku thought cannot be reduced to simple (or unreflexive) traditionalism in that its invocation of the past served as a means to question the reigning orthodoxy in poetic theory and practice. Nevertheless, an eternal or unchanging past served as its crucial point of reference for legitimating the rejection of the empty and misguided norms seen to be pervading contemporary waka poetics. Kagawa Kageki's view that poetry expresses the changing spirit of time, using themes and forms appropriate to the specific historical milieu, has some resonance with modern historicism. Even so, we need to note that his ideas presupposed the consistency of a cosmic rhythm that was ultimately cyclical (unchanging) rather than open-ended. Kageki insisted that different historical periods produced their own forms of poetry and that none was better than the others. Yet this claim did not signal relativism but a belief that different periods of poetic history all equally drew on the cosmic principle. The concept of "progress," for instance, would have been no more compatible with Kageki's thought than it would have been with Norinaga's or Mabuchi's. What distinguishes kokugaku and kokubungaku's notions of temporality is not so much the former's privileging of the archaic or classical past. More important, kokugaku temporality precludes a radical differentiation among the past, present, and future. As I pointed out in the previous chapter, for Norinaga the authenticity of the ancient world was no different from that of the present. The evolutionary temporality of kokubungaku, in contrast, would not admit such a coincidence between the past and the present. The consistency of the nation as the subject of history is sustained paradoxically by its capacity to undergo radical changes, and the past, grasped through the national narrative, turns into the proof of the nation's becoming (the transformation of itself and the world). We will return to this structure when we examine the dialectical model of literary history presented in Fujioka's work.

One of the most significant epistemological breaks between kokubungaku and kokugaku, therefore, is found in the modern discipline's embrace of linear temporality, the understanding of literary history as an evolutionary process. The approach, furthermore, implicated human agency as the driving force behind the historical transformation of literature. This is why the tripartite schematization among classical, medieval, and early modern was understood, in part, through the shifts of the principal social group that supposedly shaped each epoch: aristocrats, warriors, and commoners. And in an era of nation building that required the massive economic and military mobilization of the population, Heian court society and its culture were shunned more for their aristocratic exclusivity than for their effeminacy. The Heian cultural world deviated from the doctrine of literary egalitarianism such as the one espoused by Haga and Tachibana: "Literature draws people's interest by appealing to the common sentiment and knowledge that make man a man, regardless of one's social status or whether one possesses specialized knowledge."[8]

This is not to say, however, that kokugaku's description of the Heian left no traces on kokubungaku discussions on the topic. Mikami and Takatsu describe Heian society and culture as effete, decadent, and corrupt in a language that echoes Mabuchi's. They argue that the growing Chinese influences on Japan turned simple and rustic native ways more ornate and lavish.[9] Adopting the frivolous glamour of continental culture and Buddhist pessimism, the virility of Japanese men was sapped, turning them effete both in mind and in appearance. The aristocrats willfully feasted on luxury and a dreamlike life of pleasure, ignoring the suffering of the people, and the degeneration of Heian culture and society culminated in the Fujiwara clan's usurpation of imperial power.

While pointing out many deficiencies of the era, Mikami and Takatsu acknowledge the vital importance of the Heian period for national literary history. In particular, the Heian is valorized as the birthplace of the phonetic writing system, kana. Here we find another major difference between kokugaku and kokubungaku's discussion of Heian literature. Phoneticism (i.e., the privileging of phonetic script over characters borrowed from Chinese) was an idea that already existed in kokugaku discourse. Eighteenth-century phoneticism sought to revive the authentic voice of the ancients (and thus become one with them) through their recorded words. In this context, figures such as Norinaga and Mabuchi argued for the superiority of phonetic native scripts over Chinese characters. Despite the privileging of kana, however, the concern of kokugaku discourse ultimately rested not with the scripts but with the voice of spoken words that kana supposedly conveyed.[10] Meiji kokubungaku, in contrast, placed far greater significance on kana as a native invention and affirmed its active contribution to the development of Japanese language and literature.[11] Mikami and Takatsu point to the invention of kana as an epochal event, a remarkable sign of progress in Japanese history. It signaled the growing independence of the Japanese language from the Chinese *shōkei moji* (pictograph) by means of phonetic kana, which was deemed a more advanced form of writing.[12]

The development of kana was considered to be the primary catalyst in the flourishing of Japanese literature in the Heian period: "Once hiragana was created, by knowing only forty-seven scripts one could write anything with the words and grammar of one's own national language. Compared to the fact that they couldn't write exactly what they had in mind even after studying several thousand kanji (Chinese characters) this made a tremendous difference."[13] It was claimed that through kana, the Japanese obtained the means to freely express their thoughts, imaginations, and feelings in their native tongue, stimulating the development of numerous prose genres, including fiction, diary, travelogue, essay, and poetic treatise. Kokubungaku's celebration of the Heian period as the birthplace of a genuine national prose literature written in kana resonated with the modern conception of literary genres taking shape in the Meiji period. Increasingly, the novel was regarded the emblematic form of modern literature, encroaching on the traditional privileges enjoyed by poetry. Kokubungaku's perception that the birth of kana represented an advancement in writing systems was complemented by a belief in the generic evolution from verse to prose, from poetry to narrative fiction.[14]

Meiji kokubungaku's interest in the development of kana writing during the Heian period had as its background the extensive debates over writing systems and styles in the Meiji period. From the mid-nineteenth century onward, the standardization of script and writing style was promoted as an important facet of the project of nation building. The language reform of the Meiji period is commonly known by the slogan *genbun itchi* (the unification of speech and writing) understood as the call to create a written Japanese that is closer to spoken, colloquial language. This conventional understanding of genbun itchi, however, underplays the fact that the very sense of Japanese as a singular national language, whether spoken or written, had to be actively invented through the national education system, new technologies and infrastructures of communications, and the emergence of modern mass media. The creation of standardized and standardizing written Japanese was foundational to the invention of the national language rather than the other way around. Thus Karatani Kōjin and others have argued that *genbun itchi* was not so much a movement to create writing that resembles existing speech as an attempt to fabricate a new form of writing evocative of imaginary national speech. Karatani points out, therefore, that some of the earliest proposals in the genbun itchi movement were in the area of script reform, exploring the possibility of eliminating or radically decreasing the use of kanji so that Japanese would write mostly in kana or even in the Roman alphabet.[15] If kokugaku developed a new mode of reading that posited the original purity of the archaic voice, the genbun itchi movement developed a new mode of writing that forged the phantasmatic identity of a national language.

Kokubungaku's approach to kana (and hybrid kana) writing, therefore, dovetailed the nationalization of language that was going on at the time. Kokubungaku identified kana as a national script and classical prose written in kana as the precursor to national writing. The significance that kokubungaku attributed to kana and kana texts draws our attention to the fact that the broadening of the national literary canon by the modern discipline operated under some strict limitations. Most notably, *kanbun* and *kanshi* (Chinese poetry and prose) produced in Japan, which epitomized the written discourse of high culture up to the Meiji period, were excluded from the category of "national literature." Kana writing served as one of the crucial criteria for what passes as the proper object of study for kokubungaku and hence what could be labeled "national literature." It was through the identification of Japanese texts with kana (or kana and kanji mixed) writing that modern kokubungaku could appropriate kokugaku's canon, invested with the specter of native voice, while at the same time expanding and updating it in manners consonant with modern national identity (e.g., incorporating into the canon highly hybrid literary forms that developed during the Tokugawa period).

Despite the association of national literature with kana writing and the exclusion of kanshi and kanbun, kokubungaku's perspective needs to be differentiated from the anti-Chinese rhetoric of kokugaku. In fact, one of the common critiques of kokugaku launched by kokubungaku involved the perceived xenophobia of the earlier scholarship. In other words, kokubungaku denounced what it saw as kokugaku's desire to purge native culture and language of all foreign elements. Literary historiography of the 1890s readily admitted to powerful continental influences on Japanese literature in the form of Buddhist thought, Confucianism, and a broad array of classical Chinese literature. While traces of kokugaku rhetoric can be found in Mikami and Takatsu's association of Chinese influences with the degenerate tendencies of Heian culture and society, they also acknowledge the significant and positive influences that continental culture had on Japanese literary history.

Kokubungaku's more positive attitude toward Chinese influences on Japanese cultural history can be explained by the shift in the comparative framework against which the native literary tradition was defined. Mikami and Takatsu write, "In the past, when kokugaku scholars sung the praises of Japanese letters (*wabun*) they were merely comparing our classical literature to Chinese literature. This was a limited form of comparison. Now we are bringing together all forms of literature that appeared in our country in the last twenty-some hundred years, comparing them with Western literature. There are areas in which we are inferior to them, but there are also many unique merits in our literary tradition."[16] The rivalry with the Chinese literary tradition was overridden, as Japanese literature was increasingly posited through a comparison with European literary history. Furthermore, in order to constitute Japanese national literature with a temporal breadth and formal diversity that rival those of Western nations, kokubungaku could not afford to disavow the developments in Japanese literary history shaped by the continental influence (and by Chinese writing as practiced in Japan). Again, the central preoccupation of Meiji kokubungaku was not with the primordial purity of the native voice nor the uniqueness of waka but the national expressed through literary history.

Haga Yaichi and Kokubungaku as the Study of National Unity

Although the pioneering works of Japanese literary history were first published in early 1890s, it was in the latter part of the decade that more mature studies began to appear. During the decade or so between the Sino-Japanese War in 1894 to Japan's victory in the Russo-Japanese War in 1905, the nationalistic fervor of the Meiji period reached its height. Important works of literary history published in this period sought to weave together nationalism, the national past, and literature and were eager to establish literary studies as a discipline that promotes powerful national identity. In particular, the works by Haga Yaichi and Fujioka Sakutarō were standardbearers in the field, articulating their distinct perspectives on Japanese nationhood through the ways in which they evaluated various periods of Japanese literary history and organized them into a coherent structure.

Haga Yaichi was born in 1867, the son of a kokugaku scholar. He belonged to one of the first classes to graduate in kokubungakuka from Tokyo University, and shortly after joining its faculty he was chosen to be the only state-sponsored student to be sent abroad in the field of Japanese literature. He returned to Tokyo Imperial University after two years in Germany (1900–1902). In his subsequent career, he reigned over Meiji kokubungaku as a prominent academic-bureaucrat. Haga considered kokubungaku the modern heir to kokugaku to the extent that they shared the ultimate goal in common: the illumination of *kokutai*, the national body/structure.[17] What he was critical of was not so much kokugaku itself but the perceived state of contemporary kokugaku, which had dissipated into a fragmented and conservative discipline, deviating from its original vision. His ambition was to re-create in kokubungaku a modern and scientific version of kokugaku as a general study of national character, presiding over and bringing together diverse academic disciplines as *the* field that takes the essential nature of the nation as its primary object of study.[18] Thus, he proclaimed, "National literature naturally expresses national temperament, thoughts, and sentiments. . . . Political history only studies the external matters. To learn about the true inner life of the nation—how people lived and in what circumstances they were in—literary history is the best source."[19]

Throughout his career, Haga sought to define the unity of the Japanese national character through the study of the literary tradition, producing some of the precursors of the *nihonjinron* (theory of Japaneseness), culturalist tracts on the unique characteristics of the Japanese. The *Kokubungaku tokuhon* of 1890 (which Haga cowrote) had defined the essence of Japanese literature in terms of its elegance in contrast to both the exquisite precision and detail of Western literature, and also to the strength and dynamism of Chinese literature.[20] In *Kokubungaku jukkō* (hereafter *Jukkō*), published in 1899, Haga both elaborated on and explained this characterization of Japanese literature. To begin with, he turned to language to account for the particular aesthetics of Japanese literature: an agglutinative grammatical structure that uses a wide range of particles and postpositions, morphemes rich in vowel sounds, and the relaxed and indirect forms of expression. Calling language the "outer form" of literature, Haga referred to linguistic attributes in order to naturalize (and also invoke the scientific basis for) his discussion of Japanese literary culture. Language and literature come together in Haga's thought, furthermore, through their shared status as expressions of the perpetuity of Japanese nationhood, centered on the unbroken lineage of the imperial dynasty.[21]

Haga's characterization of Japanese literature in terms of soft and elegant aesthetics closely matched the attributes conventionally associated with Heian literature. Furthermore, Haga subscribed to the mainstream Meiji kokubungaku's view, which invested much significance in the development of kana and the rise of prose literature written in the script during the Heian period. The Heian was "the era during which literary prose first blossomed in our nation, and the texts from the period have become models for posterity."[22] However, Haga does not explicitly elaborate on the implied paradigmatic status of the Heian in his version of Japanese literary history. His reluctance to give it too much centrality may be understood, at least in part, in light of his ambivalent attitude toward the role of women writers and their practices in the literary history of the period: "The delicate tendency of Japanese literary prose is rooted, at least in part, in the nature of its language. This is why prose literature in our country first developed in the hands of women. During the Heian period, there were many literary texts written by women. This was, however, a circumstance specific to this historical period — *not [evidence] that the nature of Japanese language was best suited to women.* The fact that our literature in general is superior in its elegance but tends to be weak and monotonous is due to its exterior [i.e., linguistic] factors" (emphasis added).[23] While he suggests that the property of Japanese language accounted for the fact that women pioneered Japanese prose literature, he seems wary of suggesting too strong an association between Japanese language/literature and women. Haga casts Heian women writers as passive media that served as the conduit for the soft quality of Japanese language to realize itself in delicate and elegant literary prose.

Feminization of the National

Despite his affirmation of the effeminate qualities of Japanese language and literature, therefore, Haga was clearly ambivalent about attributing formative functions in Japanese literary history to women.[24] The femininity of Japanese aesthetics was celebrated as long as it is grasped in an abstract, symbolic sense, remaining disassociated from concrete figures of women. It is nevertheless surprising to note the lack of discomfort with which he combined an assertion of an effeminate image of Japanese literature (and by extension its culture in general) with the modern nationalistic rhetoric. How do the soft and elegant aesthetics of Japanese literary culture mesh with the active and dynamic agency demanded of a nation in the self-civilizing mission or its bid to compete with Western imperialism?

A part of the answer to this question may be found in the crucial role that the imperial dynasty plays in his construction of national culture. For Haga, the imperial institution was the cornerstone of national unity—the source of ethics, literature, and "all things beautiful."[25] When Haga defined the core identity of Japanese national culture in terms of soft and elegant beauty, he invoked the traditional concept of miyabi, understood as the aesthetics of the imperial court.[26] Haga argued that waka, closely associated with the imperial court, was the very source of Japanese literature, remaining constant through the ebb and flow of various literary fashions—for example, functioning as the point of contrast against the flourishing of Chinese poetry or the popularity of the vulgar literature of commoners.[27] What we need to note, furthermore, is the specific nature of Haga's imperial doctrine. For instance, he conspicuously refrained from the obligatory condemnation of the usurpation of imperial power by aristocratic clans during the Heian period.[28] Instead, he pointed out that even the powerful Fujiwara family never tried to overturn or overtake the imperial throne—it merely wished its daughters to marry emperors and produce imperial heirs. Fujiwara rule, in other words, was proof that imperial authority or prestige served as the ultimate basis of legitimacy in the Japanese polity. That is to say, the imperial dynasty served as the perpetual basis of Japanese nationhood, regardless of whether the emperor actually functioned as the sovereign at all times. Japanese national unity and the timeless, unbroken imperial lineage were thus mutually constituted outside of history (and politics).

As we have seen in Haga's handling of Fujiwara rule during the Heian period, emphasis on the unbroken imperial line implies the abstraction of the imperial institution from political agency (as the emperor and the imperial court were politically marginal for long periods in Japanese history). The image of the emperor (and his lineage) as spiritually and culturally potent but politically empty and passive, embodying the national identity independent of any active function, complemented Haga's essentially effeminate characterization of national culture. To *be* the incarnation of nation while at the same time being removed from active engagement in creating and developing it — this was the role consistently assigned to women and femininity by modern nationalist discourses in Japan and elsewhere.[29] George Mosse argued that in modernity the combination of bourgeois mores and the reactionary tendencies of romanticism helped constitute femininity as the guardian of continuity as well as the moral superiority of the nation. The feminine embodied the counterpoint to the perceived threat of instability and moral disorder brought on by modernization.[30]

Haga's construction of the imperial dynasty paralleled the ideological functions typically assigned to feminine symbols in modern nationalist discourse. In linking Haga's feminization of national culture to his emperor ideology, however, we cannot ignore the fact that Meiji leaders created an increasingly masculinized image of the emperor, promoting the notion of "direct imperial rule." Takashi Fujitani pointed out that an active and militarized image of the emperor, fully engaged in the state governance and military planning, was orchestrated by the state in order to exploit the imperial institution so as to prop up its own legitimacy.[31] Japan's increased involvement in military ventures in Asia also reinforced the masculine and militaristic image of the monarchy. Nevertheless, the spiritual and nativistic portrayal of the imperial lineage did not disappear from nationalist discourses, persisting especially in combination with the claims of monoethnicity or the common (sacred) ancestry of the Japanese. As suggested earlier, the Japanese imperial institution played a powerful ideological function similar to those of feminine symbols found in modern nationalist rhetoric precisely because its identity was not solely dependent on the active exercise of power over the state. The femininity of the emperor in this sense was rooted less in the psychosocial characteristics attributed to women/mothers in modern social organization (i.e., as nurturing, loving, and affective maternal figures in modern bourgeois domesticity) than in the structural function of the feminine as the counterpoint to the public order of secular and disenchanted modernity.[32] This would help explain how the spiritual and nativistic construction of the imperial institution in Japanese modernity can portray itself as being both feminine *and* patriarchal (the emperor as the patriarch of the family-state).

The interrelations between the feminization of Japanese culture and the emperor ideology in Haga's work shed light on the specific manner in which he conceptualized national unity. Haga, like other early kokubungaku scholars, embraced the notion that national literature evolves through time. Although he celebrated traditional Japanese literary aesthetics, he also exhorted Japanese literature in the present to develop a set of qualities it had previously lacked, incorporating elements of Western literature (e.g., lofty themes and grandeur of scale). Despite this endorsement of an evolutionary narrative, Haga's conception of Japanese culture and his delineation of Japanese literary history were fundamentally nonhistoricist in some respects. He construed the history of Japanese literature as a process in which greater variation of literary modes and aesthetics was achieved without altering its essential character. He did not worry, for instance, whether the absorption of Western literary influences would in some way adulterate the core identity of Japanese literary and cultural traditions. In his view, different forms of literature produced in different temporal contexts related to the national essence without any tension. New facets simply added to the old, enriching and expanding Japanese culture without impinging on its fundamental nature. The key to this frictionless additive process was the passive and effeminate principle of unity. By feminizing the national via the emperor system and classical aesthetics, Haga circumvented the intractable problem of how to constitute a singular national subject out of its historical transmutation. This property of Haga's work will be further clarified through a comparison with the more historically inflected notion of national literature provided by Fujioka Sakutarō.

Women, History, and Heian Literature

Fujioka Sakutarō was trained at Tokyo Imperial University and joined its faculty, filling the vacancy left by Haga Yaichi, who took a leave in order to study in Germany. Although he died in 1910 at the young age of forty-one, Fujioka was a key figure in the development of Meiji kokubungaku. His *Kokubungaku zenshi: Heianchōhen* (*A Complete History of Japanese Literature: The Heian Period*, hereafter *Heianchōhen*), published in 1905, was the first full-length study of Heian literary history in Meiji kokubungaku. *Heianchōhen* influenced subsequent scholarship in the field, for one thing, by taking the historical analysis of literature to a new level of sophistication. In the afterword of the 1971 reprint of the text, Akiyama Ken, one of the representative scholars of postwar kokubungaku, insisted on the continued relevance of Fujioka's contribution, asking whether any study of Heian literary history has surpassed it.[33]

Unlike Haga's blanket assertion of the unity of national culture (literature), Fujioka suggested the possibility of locating in it diverse and perhaps even conflicting characteristics. Published immediately after the Russo-Japanese War, the text begins with praise for Japanese military triumph. It claims that the warrior spirit of Japan, Bushidō, is the very essence of national thought, religion, and morality, leading the nation to victory. This, he claims, is a story greater than any found in fiction.[34] A disclaimer of sorts, however, immediately follows the zealous celebration of Bushidō. Fujioka muses on whether Bushidō, as significant as it is, can capture all that is unique about Japan or explain the whole span of its history.

Taking this question as a point of departure, *Heianchōhen* raised more general problems of studying the literature and culture of distant pasts. Fujioka asked: if it is extremely difficult for a Japanese person to grasp the subtle nuances of Western literature, regardless of the amount of relevant training one may have received, do we not face a similar difficulty in studying a work of one's own culture produced a long time ago? The possibility of profound epistemic dissonance arising between the subject and object in the study of classical literature underwrites Fujioka's critique of Tokugawa scholarship, that is, its anachronistic imposition of contemporary values and assumptions onto Heian texts. Furthermore, he chided Meiji kokubungaku for not having outgrown Tokugawa influences, remaining mired in the old prejudices and preconceptions.[35] He cautioned that in studying literature from the remote past a critic should strive to keep an open and unprejudiced attitude, detaching himself from the present and trying to view the era from the perspective of a Heian person. This was one of the primary goals of Fujioka's *Heianchōhen*—to free the study of Heian literature from the bias of Tokugawa scholarship (and its traces in Meiji kokubungaku) through a critical perspective underwritten by a rational historical consciousness.

What is most notable in Fujioka's discussion of Heian society and culture is the amount of attention he devoted to the condition of women in Heian society. His analysis goes much further than mere

references to Fujiwara dominance over court politics and the flourishing of the rear court, which nourished female literary talents. Fujioka
pointed out, for instance, that the status and social agency of Heian
women were much greater than those of women in other historical periods. Although women in Heian society were not treated as
men's equals, they were less constrained than their counterparts in the
buke shakai (warrior society) that emerged in the wake of the aristocratic era.[36] The relative freedom of Heian aristocratic women, however, came with its own hazards: the polygamous marriage practices of
Heian society were a major source of women's vulnerability and suffering. While women commanded greater agency in choosing a lover
or a husband, they also faced the possibility of neglect and abandon-
ment by men. Fujioka argued that this contributed to the particular
mixture of passion and pathos, happiness and despair, that characterizes Heian narrative literature.

Fujioka also analyzed the reasons why Heian society and culture
in general were so preoccupied with matters central to the female
experience (romance, marriage, family relations, and so on). He explained how in the Heian period male courtiers, too, were disengaged
from more public (masculine) concerns. The Heian was an era of
relative peace in which politics stagnated under the domination of
the Fujiwara family and the aristocrats in the capital were increasingly detached from their ancestral homelands despite their continued
dependence on these outlying regions for material resources. In the
monotonous world punctuated by court rituals and seasonal events,
animated only by petty jockeying over rank and status at the court,
marriage and childbirth were occasions of cardinal importance. These
events forged alliances among families and secured the perpetuation
of lineage, often sealing the fate of individuals and their clans. Thus,
romantic and marital relations stood out as one of the central dramas in the ideal and uneventful world of the Heian aristocracy, providing the focal point of its literary expression.[37] We see here how
Fujioka subtly wove together the specificity of female experience and
the broader tendencies of Heian society, relating them without simply
collapsing one into the other and not taking for granted the supposedly effeminate tendencies of the Heian aristocracy. Although the
accuracy of Fujioka's portrayal of Heian society and the condition of
aristocratic women therein may be disputed, his commitment to ap-

proaching Heian women and their writing historically was ground-breaking.[38]

The emphasis on female experience both psychologically and socially also underwrites Fujioka's analysis of *The Tale of Genji*. He famously stated that the principal theme of the *Genji* is in *fujin no hyōron* (the critique of women).[39] Shifting the center of attention from the main male character, Genji, to the host of female characters, he argued that the amorous hero served as a *hōben* (expedient device) for bringing together a wide variety of heroines. The *Genji*'s depiction of varied female characters has attracted attention throughout the history of its reception. The earlier commentaries, however, dwelled on the relative merits of the characters themselves (one of the earliest examples of this may be found in the thirteenth-century commentary in the *Mumyōzōshi*). Fujioka, in contrast, identified in the *Genji*'s treatment of female characters a more structural function—providing a thematic coherence to the text. In his view, the text's careful depictions and analyses of numerous female figures express profound insights into female virtues and destinies. It shows how to fulfill a variety of female roles, comparing the ways in which different strengths and weaknesses of the various female characters measure up. Fujioka's female-centered reading of the *Genji* was one of the most original and influential interpretations of the text to emerge in Meiji kokubungaku.

The *Genji* and the Didacticism of Kokubungaku

In Fujioka's study of Heian literature, historiography and literary analysis mutually informed each other. It is worth noting, however, that his attention to the historical condition of Heian women did not lead him to reduce the text to its external contexts. In fact, Fujioka was hostile toward a mechanical sort of realism and the reflection theory of literature. He denounced the view that the *Genji* was a prototype of the modern *shajitsu shōsetsu* (realist novel)—that is, an unadorned representation of Heian aristocratic society. It was in the seminal work of Meiji literary criticism, *Shōsetsu shinzui* (*The Essence of Novel*), by Tsubouchi Shōyō (1885–86), that the association between the *Genji* and the newly introduced realist view of literature was first proposed. Tsubouchi drew on Motoori Norinaga's attempt to dissociate the *Genji* from moral doctrines, while at the same time transplanting the notion of mono no aware from poetics into a modern theory of the novel. Like Norinaga, Tsubouchi argued against judging a work such as the *Genji* on the basis of moral values, insisting instead that the essence of the novel is to be found in the expression of human reality as such. It is important to note that what Fujioka objected to was not so much Tsubouchi-Norinaga's arguments and the concept of realism itself but the ironic ways in which they were appropriated into the didactic tendencies of Meiji kokubungaku.

The critique of the *Genji* for its moral failings—according to Confucian and Buddhist doctrines—is a view that dates back at least to the late twelfth century.[40] The issue attained a new resonance in the Meiji period because of kokubungaku's concern for establishing the educative value of literature and literary studies (e.g., the utility of literary studies for advancing human knowledge as well as fostering nationalism). Although Tokugawa theories of poetry had a strong didactic orientation, which kokugaku contested, the didacticism in kokubungaku was founded on new conceptions of education and its purposes—conforming to the Meiji state's policies on education and the self-civilizing mission. The 1890s, during which kokubungaku took shape as a discipline, coincided with the period in which the Meiji state consolidated its political infrastructure (including the promulgation of the Meiji Constitution and the opening of the Diet), paying increased attention to the ideological mobilization of the population primarily through the national education system. Many scholars of Meiji kokubungaku, such as Haga, actively constructed literature and literary education as a means of disseminating patriotism and promoting ethical attitudes befitting a national subject.[41]

Treating texts such as the *Genji* in a manner consonant with the official views on moral education was not a straightforward task, however. The Imperial Rescript for Education of 1892 spoke of the moral duties of the national subject with strong Confucian overtones (together with the Shintoist notion of divine imperial lineage and Western-style civic doctrines), prescribing loyalty to the emperor and filial piety as constituting the fundamental character of the Japanese nation. The regulation of sexual practices through moral education (as well as juridical and medical apparatuses) was also of particular interest to the state. The Meiji government's decades-long mission to civilize the nation (giving it respectability vis-à-vis the West) turned sexuality into a significant agenda in public policy central to the state's control of the moral and physical hygiene of the population.[42] The *Genji*'s depictions of numerous amorous affairs, including the illicit liaison between Genji and Fujitsubo (his father the emperor's consort), which ends up affecting (distorting) the imperial line of succession, transgressed the state-endorsed mores at a number of levels.

Earlier we noted how Haga feminized Japanese literary culture — identifying its unifying characteristics in soft, delicate, and elegant aesthetics — without displaying much sense of unease. More visible internal tension appears, however, in his discussion of the "moral laxity" of the *Genji*. Haga explicitly deplored the fact that the *Genji*, with its morally degenerate characters, is upheld as the masterpiece of national literature. At the same time, he defended the historical and literary worth of the text.[43] One of the ways in which he attempted to evade this contradiction is through the theory of mono no aware: "The prestige of *Genji monogatari* has given rise to the views that it is a story of good triumphing over evil or that it can be read as a Buddhist parable. Norinaga's perspective that it was written to convey mono no aware — that the tale is centered on human sentiment — is highly insightful. This means that the *Genji* is a novel that accurately depicted the conditions of its contemporary society."[44] We may detect here a slippage in Haga's rhetoric from the theory of mono no aware to a superficial brand of realism. He conflates mono no aware as aesthetics based on the authentic expression of human sentiment (as opposed to moral prescriptions) with the notion of literature as an unfiltered reflection of sociohistorical reality.[45]

Rereading mono no aware via the theory of realism, Haga ignored Norinaga's thorough rejection of interpreting literary aesthetics through normative values. Mono no aware instead was invoked as a convenient means of transferring the locus of "transgression" in the *Genji* from the authorial intent to the decadence of Heian aristocracy. In other words, if Murasaki Shikibu was simply depicting the social reality of her milieu, the author (and thus the text itself) is not to be blamed for inventing — much less endorsing — the morally reprehensible characters and their lustful behaviors found in the text. He approvingly cited a Tokugawa Confucian apologia of the *Genji*, *Shika shichiron* (1703), by Andō Tameaki that defended the author's moral rectitude.[46] Through a seemingly contradictory mixing of Norinaga's poetics and kokubungaku didacticism by way of realism, Haga sought to sidestep the inconsistencies between the educative versus aesthetic functions ascribed to literature. Thus, he attempted to recuperate *Genji*'s prestige, which helps anchor the stature of the Japanese literary canon as a whole, while affirming a facile compatibility between literary merits and the moral doctrines dispensed by the state.

In contrast to Haga, Fujioka praised Norinaga's theory of mono no aware precisely for refuting once and for all the imposition of moral values on the *Genji*. He explicitly dismissed *Shika shichiron* as a wrongheaded attempt to rehabilitate the text's respectability without questioning its own anachronistic standard of judgment.[47] He did not stop there. Fujioka questioned the contemporary application of the theory of mono no aware in ways that reduce the text to an objective representation of Heian aristocratic society. He argued instead that the text, despite its seeming "amorality," might convey some kind of *ideal* (i.e., values and purposes).[48] He pointed out that the characters in the text, despite their appearance of moral corruption (from the contemporary vantage point) possessed many attributes highly valued in Heian aristocratic society, including its cardinal virtue of *dōjō* (empathy). He also drew our attention to the philosophical depth of the text, supplied by its growing engagement with Buddhist thought as the plot unfolds. Through its insights into the flaws of characters and the disappointments that they face in their lives, the text conveys the Buddhist perspective on the ephemeral nature of life and the unavoidable suffering of human existence.

While contesting didacticism, Fujioka's analyses of the *Genji* nevertheless defended the text against critics who might condemn it as a frivolous tale of lust. By explaining why amorous affairs and their consequences in matrimonial ties or the reproduction of offspring were so significant for Heian aristocratic culture, Fujioka *rationalized* the text's focus on romance (i.e., as not merely a result of moral decadence). Also, by discussing the text's thematic underpinning through the female perspective—the ways in which romance and romantic relations had particularly grave consequences for women—Fujioka moved the critical focus away from the amorous adventures of the male protagonist (Genji's debauchery) to the suffering of the female characters. Leading female characters, we should note, are generally not depicted as active agents of erotic desire, though they often pay a heavier price for love affairs gone awry. The *Genji* is presented as a somber and even meditative text by recasting the male protagonists' amorous escapades as a device for engaging in a *serious* meditation on female destiny. Thereby, he secured for the text, if not a moral respectability, at least an aura of depth and dignity commensurate with its status as a literary masterpiece. Thus, Fujioka suggested that the "ideal" of a literary masterpiece such as *Genji* was to be understood through both the accurate grasp of the social context of the text *and* philosophical and aesthetic visions that cannot be reduced to historically contingent codes of moral behavior. The critical difference between Fujioka's rejection of conventional mores in his approach to the *Genji* and that of Norinaga lies in his affirmation of an overarching or transcendent meaning in the text. The consequences of this difference are examined later in the chapter.

Fujioka's Methodology

The combination of perspectives that intersect in Fujioka's scholarship testifies to his methodological self-consciousness, which was unparalleled in the field of kokubungaku at the time. In *Kamakura Muromachi jidai bungakushi*, Fujioka enumerated different approaches to literary studies, organizing them in a hierarchical order and placing the greatest emphasis on what he calls *hihyōteki hyōron* (critical studies). In particular, he pointed to aesthetic and philosophical analyses as the most important elements in critical studies—the means by which one grasps the form and content, respectively, of a literary text. Aside from critical studies, Fujioka discussed a category, *setsumeiteki hyōron* (explanatory studies), which *explains* rather than evaluates literary work through its historical context and the biography of an author. Although Fujioka considered the explanatory approach to be supplementary to the critical one, he cautioned against dismissing it. He suggested that the contextual study of literature serves as an important support for studying literary texts, particularly because of the difficulties involved in establishing the genuine (i.e., not merely subjective) bases for measuring the worth of a literary work. This consciousness of the opacity of a critical standard was derived in part from his reflexive awareness that even the most widely accepted assessment of an individual or a group of literary texts may change over time. Thus, he consistently cautioned against taking the received views of critical tradition for granted, seeking to systematically flush out the biases and mistaken assumptions of past scholarship. Fujioka grappled with the fact that not only the literary text itself but critical standards and perspectives are shaped by their historical contexts.

It was precisely because he seriously engaged with the historicity of literary texts (and criticism) that the question of how to devise an autonomous methodology of literary studies arose as a major intellectual challenge for Fujioka. Compared to Haga, Fujioka was more insistent about the independence of literary and aesthetic values from extrinsic standards while at the same time paying much more careful attention to the issue of historical contextuality. This is why he could not be satisfied with the superficial compromise struck by Haga between the moral/educative versus aesthetic values of a literary text. Although his outline of methodologies is crude and inconsistent at times (perhaps partly due to the fact that *Kamakura Muromachi jidai bungakushi* was published posthumously based on his lecture notes), it demonstrates his attempt to theorize the division as well as the relationship between intrinsic and extrinsic modes of criticism.

As we saw in the first chapter, eighteenth-century kokugaku poetics proposed a theory of authenticity based on the immanent experience of affect that challenged ready-made critical standards (e.g., based on neo-Confucian doctrines on ethics and rationality). Nineteenth-century kokubungaku introduced a perspective distinct from both neo-Confucian and kokugaku poetics. Deeply informed by historicism and literary realism, scholars such as Fujioka identified the truth in the diverse and ever-changing dynamics of social reality, and narrative prose, rather than poetry, was designated the foremost embodiment of such truth. In Meiji kokubungaku, therefore, the social diversity manifested in the perpetual historical transformation became the most significant counterpoint to the normative and static forms of knowledge and values. Literature that supposedly depicts "human reality," in turn, was considered to be one of the most exemplary sites of such authenticity. The crucial question for the discipline, then, was how literature, which is deemed to be free of moral prescription and reflective of ever-changing flux of history, nevertheless has a transcendent value: articulating the purposefulness of national history and the cultural identity that support the nation's civilizational status defined in terms of modern humanism. If Norinaga responded to the anomie of affective experience by positing the communal nature of poetic practices, Fujioka, as we will see, responded to the problem of historical relativity by invoking the unity of the nation as the subject of history.

Native Essence, National Progress

Fujioka's critique of kokubungaku didactism in *Heianchōhen* should not be equated with rejection of the national ideological project in literary studies. Haga's approach to literary history, deeply colored by emperor worship and official mores, contrasts with the more nuanced ways in which Fujioka brought together the national and literary. In *Kokubungakushi kōwa* (1908) (hereafter *Kōwa*), a survey of national literary history, Fujioka constructed Heian literature in relation to a broader vision of national cultural identity. While *Heianchōhen* celebrated Heian aristocratic culture as centered on passion, sentiment, and aesthetic refinement, his discussion of the same subject in *Kōwa* took a markedly different tone. There he repeated the cliché about the decadence of Heian society, condemning its moral corruption and the oppression of common people. What I would like to shed light on, however, is not the difference but the continuity underlying Fujioka's treatments of Heian in the two studies.

In an apparent divergence from *Heianchōhen*'s avoidance of reducing national character to a monolithic set of attributes, in *Kōwa* Fujioka stressed the unity of the Japanese character, which he likened to the singularity of an individual personality.[49] He asserted that Japanese culture is centered on a strong sense of collectivity, which on a small scale creates the solidarity of family and on a large scale national unity. Japanese families are so close, he argued, that all the members act in unison, and the nation is as harmonious as if it were one big family. We may detect in this discussion an echo of the kokutai ideology that was spreading at the time, fashioning Japan into an extended family nation with a common ancestry that could be traced back to the sacred lineage centered on that of the emperor. Furthermore, his assertion that national literature is the expression of national thought suggested that such overarching unity was operating in Japanese literature as well.

Up to a certain point, Fujioka's discussions of the Japanese national character in *Kōwa* seem indistinguishable from Haga's writing on the same topic. We begin to detect a difference between them, however, in Fujioka's sharper and more direct critique of the attributes that supposedly define Japaneseness. For instance, he pointed out that social solidarity and familial ties may, in some contexts, calcify into unyielding class stratification. The most notable examples of the ill effects of familism were located in the Heian period, during which aristocrats controlled politics and made many official positions of the state bureaucracy hereditary.[50] This degeneration of the sociopolitical structure rubbed off on the literature as well. So even a great masterpiece such as the *Genji*, suffered from a lack of dynamism.[51] We need to note here that for Fujioka what was blameworthy about the rigidly stratified society was not so much the unequal and unjust distribution of wealth, resources, and power that it fostered. Rather, he sounded the alarm against its suppression of individual talents and abilities, which in turn inhibited national advancement: "The nation stands on the footing of collective support, but it progresses by allowing individual talents to thrive."[52]

One of the central theoretical projects of *Kōwa*, therefore, was to locate the compatibility between the cultural essence of Japan and the nation's historical progress envisaged via the ideals of liberal humanism. Fujioka's approach to this problem is apparent in his discussion of another central characteristic of Japanese culture: its deep regard for nature. The diverse, beautiful landscapes, temperate climate, and bountiful resources of Japan have allegedly nurtured the nation like a benevolent mother. Japanese, living in such a physical environment, developed peaceful and aesthetically sensitive personalities with unsurpassed love for nature equivalent to a child's love for a parent. While praising Japanese culture's appreciation of nature, Fujioka turned to the shortcoming of what he referred to as the "nature-centered" outlook found not only in Japan but in Asia in general. Rather than simply fostering the appreciation for nature, the Asian mentality has inhibited or even suppressed the effort to fully awaken human potential. Unlike the West, where the will to challenge the forces of nature has cultivated knowledge and technology, naturecentrism in Asia has promoted passivity, fatalism, and withdrawal from the world, seeking to adapt human existence to the external environment.[53]

Having established this East-West binary, however Fujioka insisted that the uniqueness of Japanese culture set it apart from the rest of Asia. He argued that although Japanese people love nature deeply they are not terrorized by it or enslaved to it. Japanese reverence for nature does not signify passive subordination but joyous and active love. If nature is thought of as an awe-inspiring master in other parts of Asia, Japanese regard it as a loving mother. Fujioka's use of the familial (particularly maternal) metaphor, therefore, helps to distinguish the Japanese relationship with nature from what he posits as more general Asian tendencies. Asian passivity, then, is not native to Japan but an attitude that entered it from the continent, affecting (dampening) its indigenous spirit.

By characterizing Japanese culture as active, optimistic, and more humanistic compared to those of other Asian nations, Fujioka depicted Japanese history as a dynamic, developmental process.[54] According to him, the history of Japan was shaped by the tension between and intermixing of native and foreign (i.e., continental Asian) influences. During the Kamakura and Muromachi periods, when the Buddhist faith dominated cultural life, fatalistic tendencies in Asia overwhelmed the active native spirit. The lively poetry of *Man'yōshū*, and the reawakening of native cultural forces during the Heian and Edo (or Tokugawa) periods, however, displayed the irrepressible native spirit. In the era of the Meiji Japan's indigenous characteristics were being reinforced by the importation of the *katsudō shugi* (active tendencies) of the West. He predicted that Japan in the future would depart even further from the Asian passivity that clouded some of its past.[55]

The triadic model of comparison among Japan, Asia, and the West was a frequent theme in early kokubungaku discourses. Fujioka, writing in the wake of the Sino-Japanese and Russo-Japanese Wars, which launched Japan's imperial and colonial expansionism, gave this structure an explicitly hierarchical cast, with Japan vying for the equality with the West through its superiority vis-à-vis Asia. Through rhetorical maneuvers that anticipate works such as Watsuji Tetsurō's *Fūdo*, Fujioka set up Asia as an intimate Other that carries negative properties attributed to Japan more emphatically. Japan as the unique hybrid of Asian and non-Asian characteristics is imagined as a privileged site of East-West synthesis and the nation most suited to lead Asia in the modern age.

What underwrote Fujioka's construction of Japan was his use of the dialectical model of history, in which competing forces collide and catalyze the development of the national subject. Native identity was rendered as singular yet fluid, having different effects according to specific historical contexts and complementary/antagonistic forces at work. Thus, native collectivism may degenerate into static social hierarchy in one context while serving as a cornerstone of powerful and benevolent national solidarity in another. Similarly, the native attitude toward the external environment may turn passive and pessimistic under Asian influences but may reaffirm its active potential when mixed with Western humanism. The elasticity of native character enabled Fujioka to critique some of its local manifestations while valorizing it in essence.

Gendered Dialectics

The dynamics of national history, furthermore, did not rest on a single set of dialectical relations between foreign and native. In the rest of *Kōwa*, Japanese literary history was discussed as a process in which the classical culture that came to maturation in the Heian period was sublated by the emergence of a new trend, which reached its apogee in the Edo period. As we saw earlier, the notion that the Edo and Heian represent the two greatest moments of traditional Japanese literature was a standard view of Meiji kokubungaku, but Fujioka fleshed out this narrative from a new perspective.

Highlighting the profound difference between the Edo and Heian cultures, he wrote: "It is quite incredible that two distinct mountains [Heian and Edo] stand against each other with only a valley [the medieval period] between them."[56] Here the medieval period was reduced to a partition between old and new. Yet on closer examination we see that the medieval, precisely because of its purported social disorder and cultural decline, not only separated but also mediated the transition from the old to new.

While courtiers are characterized by their strict adherence to traditional rules and passive conservativism, warriors tend toward revolutionary changes and the willingness to lay down their lives for their goals. . . . New cultural currents [of the medieval period] valued simplicity and freedom, breaking up everything rooted in past history and customs. We cannot help but marvel at their active and resolute stance. Regrettably, however, as warriors were singularly focused on military affairs, they had no time to engage in other activities. Thus, the literature of the period was not much influenced by them. Literary art, rather than turning to this glorious new development, held on to the old ways and continued to deteriorate.[57]

What was significant about the medieval period for Fujioka was the emergence of the warrior class, which developed into a genuine cultural agent in the Edo period. During the tumultuous medieval period, the revolutionary and active warrior class disrupted the social hierarchy of the classical era. It thus inaugurated the process in which more segments of the population began to participate in cultural and social developments. The rise of the warrior class, therefore, prepared commoners to move to the center stage of history in the Edo period and beyond.

Having established the principal role of the warrior class and its mentality in postclassical culture, Fujioka analyzed Edo culture in terms of Bushidō, "the way of the warrior" (i.e., military valor, loyalty, adherence to ethical codes overriding personal interests and sentiments, and so on). In Fujioka's discussion, the culture of Edo became strongly linked to masculinity and masculine principles. Together with old versus new, or conservative versus dynamic, the gender binary served as a central organizing metaphor through which Fujioka contrasted Heian and Edo: "In all aspects of society, the Edo period was masculine while the Heian period was feminine. One prioritized principles and reasons while the other valued affect and taste."[58] To posit the Edo period as the epitome of masculine culture was not as widespread a notion as the feminization of the Heian was. Fujioka himself concurred with the long-standing association between Man'yō poetry and valiant masculinity proposed by eighteenth-century critics such as Mabuchi. He repeated the standard line that Man'yōshū and its milieu expressed the masculine spirit of native culture, which was displaced under continental influence and supplanted by the effete style of poetry in the Heian period represented by *Kokinwakashū*.[59] His main argument, however, was that, although the fundamental spirit of Bushidō had been with the nation since its very origin, it came to the surface through the social and political turbulence of the medieval era and the attendant ascent of the warrior class, becoming fully established as the core cultural principle in the Edo period.[60]

Fujioka placed a greater emphasis on the masculinity of Edo, in part, because he did not insist on preserving or recapturing the purity of native culture. Edo was privileged not so much as the inheritor of an originary native spirit but as the embodiment of Japanese culture's ability to create something new and unique from diverse and possibly competing influences. For one thing, he argued that Bushidō developed out of the melding of Buddhism and Confucianism in a distinctly Japanese way. If the virility of *Man'yōshū* signified the masculinity of the primordial native spirit, Bushidō expressed Japanese culture's capacity for incorporating the foreign and making it its own.

The full force of Bushidō, however, was apparently not yet fully realized in the Edo period. Fujioka argued that at the time Bushidō had not spread throughout the nation and that it remained fragmented under the feudal order. Furthermore, Bushidō in the Edo context was elitist (i.e., the prerogative of the warrior class) and lacked an egalitarian, public spirit. He also suggested that during the Edo period the warrior class itself retreated from its earlier dynamism and became more conservative. It was not the warriors but the other primary cultural agent of the period, townspeople, who became the foremost innovative force. Fujioka lamented the fact that the dignity and propriety of the warrior class and the new creative energy of townspeople failed to influence each other.[61]

We can now understand why *Kōwa* does not refer to Bushidō as the core feature of the indigenous Japanese character. Bushidō represented not so much the "native" as it did the active and transformative energy of the nation as a historical entity. Extending beyond the feudal era and warrior society, it had propelled Japan into modernity and continued to fuel the nation's advancement in the era of military expansionism, buttressing Japan's status as a player in global history. We have seen that kokubungaku emerged in the early 1890s, upholding the historical nature of the nation as the kernel of its disciplinary coherence. Yet, as we saw in the case of Haga, kokubungaku's rhetoric of progress and transformation often remained superficial, not structurally integrated into the concept of the national. It is only in Fujioka's work in the early 1900s that we begin to see a kokubungaku scholarship that promotes the notion of national unity based on a properly historicist and developmental framework. Here, the native is subsumed under the national as the internal essence that persists through sublation (suppression/conservation) in a Hegelian sense. This is another way to speak of the "elasticity" of the native in Fujioka's discussion referred to earlier.

Fujioka's use of the gender metaphor in delineating Japanese literary history also needs to be understood through this dialectical relation between national and native. *Man'yōshū* epitomized native masculinity, which was displaced by foreign influences and supplanted by the femininity of mature classical culture. The feminine classical culture, in turn, was subsumed by the new cultural force that crystallized in Edo. The virility of Edo was both related to and distinct from archaic native culture, prefiguring the full masculinity of Japan as a modern nation. Masculinity, therefore, appeared to be an attribute of the originary native spirit *and* the national subject. Masculinity in the second sense functioned as the "negation of negation" that drove the nation out of feminine stasis. The doubling of the masculine suggested that it was not only the opposite of the feminine—instead it figured the transcendence of the gender binary itself. The feminine, in turn, was understood to be a passive medium linking the prehistoric masculinity of the native and the transcendent masculinity of the nation.

The function of the gender binary in Fujioka's literary history, however, was not completely exhausted in the transition from the classical to the early modern period. In *Heianchōhen*, Fujioka drew a link between the Heian and the contemporary vogue of aestheticism (art for art's sake). He wrote that Heian aristocrats "privileged romance and ignored duties, valorized beauty and failed to speak of virtues. The 'aesthetic life' has been a popular phrase in recent years. Yet if there was ever a time and place when this idea was actually put into practice we need not look any further than the everyday life of Heian aristocrats."[62] The *Biteki seikatsu* (aesthetic life) was a term coined and made famous by Takayama Chogyō, an influential romantic nationalist critic. In an essay entitled "Biteki seikatsu o ronzu" (Discussing the Aesthetic Life), published in 1901, Takayama, allegedly under the influence of Nietzsche, argued for the intrinsic value of fulfilling basic human desires and instincts as opposed to the extrinsic value based on morality and rational thought. Although Fujioka argued that the cutting-edge vision of Takayama had been realized in the Heian nearly a millennium earlier, Fujioka's construction of the Heian as an aesthetic paradise was greatly influenced by this turn of the century cultural theory.

Harry Harootunian's analysis of Takayama's perspectives sheds light on the broader implications of the late Meiji aestheticism through which Fujioka saw Heian culture. Harootunian points out the continuity underlying Takayama's seemingly abrupt "conversion" from his passionate support of Meiji's state's imperialism to the seemingly apolitical advocacy of aesthetic life: "In both cases, the leitmotif was an aggressive, indeed Darwinian, egoism. A nation following its own impulses and defining, by force, its own stature in the international community was really no different from the individual acting on his own instincts and the authority of personal feelings."[63] According to Harootunian, Takayama's aestheticism, despite its seemingly apolitical affirmation of beauty and sensuality, did not stray very far from the national narrative in some respects. His analysis suggests, furthermore, that contrary to its putative defiance of bourgeois morality Takayama's aesthetic life remained inextricably bound to the tenets of liberalism, including individualism, utilitarianism, and developmental narrative of self-fulfillment. Fujioka's earlier celebration of Heian as the Arcadia of affect and art and the subsequent devaluation of it in the context of national literary history can be understood as the inverse of Chogyū's intellectual itinerary. The Heian is romanticized from a perspective that valorizes the narcissism of self and its private enjoyment while it is subordinated and debased under the framework of the collective narcissism of the nation, centered on the historical destiny of Japan. Feminine aestheticism is thus the complementary Other to the masculine principles that allegedly drive history (ethics, rationality, innovation, and so on). Although the Heian period is constituted as its most exemplary embodiment, the function of this feminine principle as a structural negative in opposition to the positive masculine principle persists, continually sublated and resublated through the evolutionary advancement of the nation.

Totalized Order of Gender

Meiji kokubungaku nationalized the literary discourses of the past by grafting them onto the narrative of national history. This process, however, harbored a profound contradiction between the alleged unity of national cultural identity and the diversity of literary discourses that the historicism foregrounded. While historicization helped unmoor literary discourses from older, prenational interpretative conventions, it also posed potential threats against the integrity of national culture. Fujioka's study of Japanese literary history attempted to overcome this tension by invoking the very autonomy and heterogeneity of literature (i.e., its irreducibility to ready-made moral values and fixed sociohistorical locations) as a means of understanding the dynamic identity of the national subject evolving through time. The thorny issue of "unity in diversity" was resolved by constituting the national as the reified subject of historical dynamics.

The significant effects that this theoretical strategy had on the discussion of gender in kokubungaku can be seen in Fujioka's analyses of Heian literature. The introduction of historicism in Japanese literary scholarship fundamentally transformed the nature of the association between Heian literature and femininity. It redefined the effeminacy of Heian literature not simply as a matter of aesthetic/affective inclinations attributed to Heian culture in general but as a matter to be discussed in relation to the condition of aristocratic women at the time. The specific positionality of women and the workings of gender relations in Heian society were invoked as the empirical bases for understanding the literary styles, topics, and themes of the period. The rational and historical approach to Heian literature also enabled Fujioka to analyze texts such as *Genji* against the grain of parochial mores (including those advocated by the Meiji state) as well as (male) hero-centered readings of the text.

Fujioka's recognition of the historical specificity of Heian literature through the investigation of female experience and agency, however, was ultimately subsumed by the imperatives of nationalization. In the context of national literary history as a whole, such as his discussions in *Kōwa*, the focus on a historically and socially inflected understanding of gender difference and gender relations gave way to the abstract, disembodied schema of the gender binary. Rather than tracing the effects of gender difference on the process of literary production, as he did in *Heianchōhen*, he discussed the "feminine" as a ready-made trope that *represents* the characteristics of Heian literary culture. It thereby mechanically performed the predetermined role of the symbol of negativity. In this narrative, the Heian-feminine figured the new level of sophistication and self-consciousness of Japanese literature, only to be superseded by properly masculine and humanistic forces.

Fujioka's dual approach to the Heian explains why, despite his positive assessment of literature shaped by the experience and perspectives of women, he was at times critical of the feminine tendencies in Japanese culture. It is worth noting that the call to overcome the limitations of the feminine through masculine agency is found more forcefully in the seemingly more progressive work of Fujioka than in the explicitly reactionary rhetoric of Haga. It was not by an accident, then, that anxiety over the alignment between national and feminine that we detect in Fujioka's literary history resurfaced in the works of so-called Taisho liberals such as Watsuji Tetsurō and Tsuda Sōkichi.

Watsuji's essay, " 'Mono no aware' ni tsuite," published in 1922, drew much from Fujioka's study of Heian literature and extended some of its implications in a highly instructive manner.[64] The essay refers to Norinaga's concept of mono no aware as a momentous event in Japanese intellectual history, a seminal statement of the autonomy of literary art from extrinsic standards of judgment. For Watsuji, the notion of mono no aware defined the essence of literary aesthetics through man's longing for the timeless origin of being—the yearning for the eternal and transcendent through the ephemeral and phenomenal experience. Watsuji objected, however, that Norinaga's concept, which was developed through his reading of Heian literature, was flawed by the historical limitations of the sources. He contended that mono no aware falls short of the universality ascribed to it, trapped in hedonism, sensuality, and pathos endemic to Heian culture. Approaching aesthetics via mono no aware, Norinaga identified *memshiki hakanasa* (effete and insubstantial qualities) at the depth of the human heart. Watsuji countered that transcendent longing can be found in other, less effeminate, forms of literature (e.g., the ferocious and optimistic expression of passion in Man'yō poetry or the cries of blood-drenched warriors in medieval tales).[65]

Watsuji attributed the parochialism of mono no aware to the femininity of Heian aesthetics. This femininity, in turn, could be explained by the prominent roles played by women in the development of Heian literature. Through a grasp of Heian society and culture clearly indebted to Fujioka's study, he suggested that because the zeitgeist of the Heian era was shaped by women its aesthetics must be also understood in relation to the *onna no kokoro* (female heart):[66] "Because mono no aware is the flower that blossomed in the female heart, it saliently bears all the features of female sensitivities and weaknesses. . . . From this, we can understand our own dissatisfaction with the mono no aware of the period and with Heian literature itself. As has been often said, this literature and the very environment that produced it can be defined by the lack of masculinity. We must discern the source of our discontent in the very font of what allures us [about Heian culture and literature]."[67] Watsuji, therefore, *explicated* the femininity of Heian literary aesthetics in terms of the historical function of Heian women writers. Heian women's social conditions and perspectives, which were identified through attention to the historical context of literature in Fujioka's study, were made to justify the negative assessment of Heian literature and its aesthetics. Watsuji's seemingly positive reference to *fujin no kōseki* (female accomplishment) immediately turned into ammunition for devaluing Heian literature from the standpoint of truly pure and universal aesthetics: "If women represented the most highly realized spirit of the time, then it is inevitable that the spirit of the (Heian) era is characterized by effeminate mono no aware."[68]

To say that the aesthetic culture centered on female agency cannot help but fall short of genuine universality due to its effeminacy suggests that the transcendent aesthetics must be nonfeminine. Given that Watsuji did not make equivalent qualifications about the parochialism of aesthetic culture dominated by men or characterized by the "male heart," we may suspect that the charge of particularity did not apply equally to both poles of the gender binary. The feminization of Heian literature and the negative assessment that followed from it enabled Watsuji to postulate elsewhere *nonfeminine* (i.e., masculine) aesthetics that is truly universal. We may detect here a gesture similar to the dialectical construction of Japanese literary history by Fujioka: literary aesthetics, which is discovered through the "feminine," must be superseded because of its "lack" of masculinity, making way for the transcendent principle figured by the Masculine with the capital *M*. Once placed in the register of generality (in Fujioka's case this was explicitly signified by the national), the Heian-feminine fills a predictable role as the embodiment of lack, an Other opposed not only to the masculine, in the ordinary sense of gender dichotomy, but to the transcendent masculinity in the dialectical schema.

We need to note that Watsuji made a rhetorical move that Fujioka himself did not make, explicitly postulating a causal link between female agency and feminine aesthetics. On this basis, he projected the characteristics structurally assigned to the feminine in the abstract gendered dialectic onto Heian women as their essence. The negativity of abstract feminine value and the alleged attributes of concrete women (weakness, sentimentalism, sensuality, etc.) were made to mutually reinforce each other. Thus, Watsuji extended the gendered structure in Fujioka's work by creating a closed circuit between gender conceived at the empirical and speculative levels.

The treatment of Heian literature by Fujioka and Watsuji reminds us that the regime of gender in modernity is not simply a dimorphic construction that effects meaning in relation to the binary Other — that is, men versus women or masculine versus feminine. It also operates as an epistemological order in which gender differences conceptualized in diverse frames of reference — scientific, aesthetic, economic, political, and so on — are integrated into a complex network of knowledge. Gender categories function in the modern organization of power through the naturalization not only of binary division of gendered values but of the connections among these distinct levels and forms of knowledge, creating a specter of generalized coherence. Between Fujioka's and Watsuji's discussions of Heian literature and literary production, we see the connections drawn and feedback loops created among abstract and concrete, particular and general, and empirical and speculative constructions of gender. This interconnected formation of gendered discourses supports the seemingly unlimited dispersion and a priori status of the sexist order. So, regardless of how one may organize the relations among these various epistemic frameworks — say, privileging empirical over speculative knowledge and vice-versa—the naturalization of the sexist order remains unchallenged. In this sense, modern gender ideology finds more complete articulation and totalized form in Fujioka and Watsuji's perspective than in Haga's overtly misogynistic reluctance to recognize women's contribution to the development of Japanese literature.

Sexism and National Unity

It has been said that, compared to Haga, Fujioka was not a rigid nationalist, refusing to subject literary texts such as *Genji* to moral judgments dictated by the ideological agendas of the state.[69] Such an assessment of Fujioka overlooks the fact that neither the attention paid to the historical contextuality of literature nor his reluctance to evaluate literature through extrinsic standards precluded him from conforming literary history to the nation form. In fact, as we have seen, those very arguments and perspectives that appear to support the autonomy of literature from nationalist projects were instrumental to the ways in which Fujioka forged a powerful alignment between literary history and national destiny. History was conceived as a process through which discrete conflicting elements and forces are continually absorbed into the dialectical dynamics. The integrity of national culture was construed not as a simple unity that cannot tolerate divisions but as a synthesis growing out of diversity and tension. This developmental organization of national culture, furthermore, constituted the national subject, claiming its centrality and agency precisely by virtue of its ability to subsume these fragmenting forces. It is in this formation of the abstract, rational, and masculine national subject of history that we locate the modern regime of gender in Fujioka's work. The understanding of Heian literature through specific conditions of women, on one hand, and a more abstract characterization of the Heian as the feminine moment in national literary history, on the other, were brought together via the national synthesis.

Thus, in Fujioka's work the subject of national literary history emerged out of the subordination of divisions within (sociohistorical diversity marked by the sexist organization of gendered attributes) and without (ethnocentric and racist differentiation of Japan from other Asian nations). Japanese identity was thereby constituted in a manner commensurate with the imperial ambition of the state—

capable of containing the ever-increasing variety of language, ethnicity, and histories that must be integrated. If the simplicity of national unity (centered on the emperor) conceived by Haga was conceptualized primarily in relation to the demands of nation building and a defensive posture vis-à-vis Western imperialism, Fujioka's synthetic nation responded to and anticipated the identity formation called for in the process of empire building. However, a rigid chronological ordering of Haga's and Fujioka's perspectives would be misleading. The different approaches to national unity that they represented—for example, ahistoric integration revolving around the emperor as the passive embodiment of national essence versus dialectical synthesis of heterogeneity that tends toward the national teleology—continued to coexist in imperial Japan and even supplemented each other.[70] As I suggest in the next chapter, some traces of Haga's feminized nation return to the foreground in postwar kokubungaku.

Fujioka's work, examined against the history of Meiji kokubungaku, reveals a paradoxical development. A critical engagement with the contradiction endemic to the modern concept of national literature paved the way for the higher order of integration and a new paradigm of disciplinary identity. The recognition of female agency in Heian literary production contributed to the fuller nationalization of literary discourses in which the feminine was ultimately detached from concrete history, performing the ghostly functions of the Other preassigned to it. This process, furthermore, helped to incorporate the totalizing structure of modern sexist epistemology in kokubungaku scholarship. We find here a familiar pattern in the modern history of gendered discourses—a history that oscillates between the progressive opening and reactionary closure. Thus, the critique of gender ideology inscribed in the modern construction of Heian literature must go beyond inquiries into the valorization/denigration of women's literary practices or the recognition/erasure of the ways in which gender difference informed literary production. We need to contextualize these questions by paying attention to the mutual construction of literary and social formations in modernity and the ways in which women's literary production, or feminization of certain literary modes and historical periods, was constituted therein. Otherwise, we cannot come to terms with the multiple facets of gender ideology embedded in kokubungaku or in the national narrative that has served as the basis of the discipline—how it gave ground to the historicity of women's literary practices while foreclosing their disruptive implications.

In chapter 1, I discussed the feminization of Heian literature and the use of gender metaphor in relation to transformations in the eighteenth-century cultural and intellectual world that continued to resonate in modernity. The assessment of Heian literature by Meiji kokubungaku was influenced not only by concrete discussions of Heian texts in kokugaku poetics. Just as important are the ways in which kokugaku poetics set the stage for gender metaphor to play a vital role in the mutual construction of the literary and the social. In other words, the gender binary helped articulate the hierarchical consistency of the world, countering the perceived threat against the integrity of the social body by the diversity of human experience and interests, the erosion of self-evident and static norms, and the loss of transparent means of communication.

This is not to say, however, that kokubungaku somehow fulfilled and completed the kokugaku project, that nativist poetics culminated in the nationalist literary history of kokubungaku. The relationship between the eighteenth- and nineteenth-century approaches to literary discourses is neither one of progress nor simple discontinuity. In some sense, Norinaga's poetics appears to be more subversive than Meiji kokubungaku scholarship from our present vantage point. Instead of positing a transcendent aesthetic community, he articulated the authentic sociality at the level of negativity inscribed by the feminine, marginal, and affective. The possibility of a genuine human community, in other words, was defined in a parasitic relation to and against the dominant official order that rationalized the principle of social organization and unity imposed from above. The ideal communality envisioned by Norinaga, of course, could not coincide with the official, prescriptive codes. This was not so because a genuine community was to be sought "elsewhere" (e.g., in the future, as the teleology of evolutionary history would have it) but because it was thought to already exist in the interstices of regulatory forces. As I suggested earlier, temporality in Norinaga's thought precluded a radical rift among the past, present, and future. This also means that Norinaga's poetics was not only antinormative but antitranscendent.

Watsuji misread Norinaga from an emphatically modern perspective when he defined *mono no aware* as a yearning for the genuine universal that became trapped in the parochial aesthetics of effeminate Heian aristocratic culture. He explained this failure by Norinaga's Heian/*Genji* fetishism and the proclivity for the passive, feminine, and weak. Watsuji's objection with mono no aware resonates with the common critique of Norinaga's stance for its conformity, its refusal to posit the ideal that goes beyond and clashes directly with the existing order. Before we rush to charge Norinaga with settling for the status quo, however, we may pause to ponder where the "transcendent yearning" of Meiji kokubungaku takes us.

Indeed, Meiji kokubungaku discourses on literature posited the autonomous aesthetic ideal that transcends the given historical condition (it is more than native, more than conventional morality, going beyond the incessant permutation of society through history). The result, however, was the subordination of the literary, social, and aesthetic in the national frame. Moreover, we need to note that this maneuver supported the subsumption of the literary under the *state*, which assumed the role of exemplifying the national subject. If, as I have suggested, the national is constructed as the reified subject of diverse and dynamic historical processes, the state (if not the actual regime in power) is typically construed as that which *represents* the nation to itself.[71] This multileveled logic, in which heterogenous and concrete phenomena are continually subsumed into a progressively abstract and singular unity, operates at the heart of modern nation-state ideology. The specter of transcendent aesthetics constituted through the dialectical overcoming of the binary (e.g., masculine/feminine or native/foreign) underwrites the singularity of national literature abstracted from history. This empty ideal (the identity of national literature), in turn, becomes a convenient support for the notion of the national destiny that state invokes to legitimate itself and its policies. We saw that in Fujioka's work the construction of authentic literary aesthetics autonomous of normative values became a basis for positing a transcendent national subject. This subject (imperial Japan), which allegedly developed through the sublation of the feminine and Asian elements, continues its path toward self-realization, most importantly by means of its imperial expansion.

I should hasten to add, of course, that Norinaga's formulation of a feminized aesthetic community was hardly less problematic than the sexism of modern kokubungaku. His valorization of the abject feminine was entirely disconnected and most likely inimical to any form of challenge against the existing gender hierarchy. As I argue in chapter 4, Norinaga's identification of literary discourses with the communal reverberation of feelings foreclosed the possibility of approaching them politically—articulating the tension among divergent social positions and interests, including those pertaining to gender difference. It is equally unthinkable, on the basis of Norinaga's schema, to recognize and explore the historical agency of women's literary production. My critique of the literary historiography produced by Meiji kokubungaku is aimed not so much at the historical approach to literary texts per se as at the specific understanding of history that subsumes the literary under the national. If we hope to develop an alternative means of approaching Heian literature and women's literary production during the period, we would have to be critical of both kokubungaku historicism as well as eighteenth-century poetics without conflating the two. In other words, we need to pay attention to the aspects of kokubungaku ideology that cannot be traced directly back to Norinaga or any other eighteenth-century sources. Thus in this chapter I have tried to shed light on the specific manner in which the construction of gender in kokubungaku discourses intersects with that of literature, history, and nation in modernity.

CHAPTER THREE

Women and the Emergence
of Heian Kana Writing

In chapter 2, we saw that Meiji kokubungaku discourses at times explicitly linked literary education with the promotion of nationalism or constructed a literary history that underwrote not only the unity of the national identity but its historic destiny as an expanding empire. During the first half of the twentieth century, the overtly nationalist/imperialist rhetoric of mainstream kokubungaku scholarship waxed and waned. Predictably, it crested during the period between the mid-1930s and the end of World War II in 1945, with many scholars in the field actively supporting emperor worship and Japanese militarism. After Japan's defeat in the war, most members of the kokubungaku establishment disavowed their wartime complicity with the military state, and the discipline began reinventing itself in accordance with the postwar sociopolitical order.[1] In the course of postwar history, many came to regard the disciplinary designation of kokubungaku itself as obsolete, expressing a preference for *nihon bungaku* (Japanese literature). In other words, the ethnocentric self-reference that conjured up the ghost of Japanese imperialism was to be replaced with a more relativistic term that identified itself within the global community of national literatures. Yet, insofar as the nation is assumed to be the natural unit for identifying a social and cultural collectivity (including the unity of literary tradition), we find the basic framework of nation form operating not only in the chauvinism of "national literature" but in a seemingly more neutral "Japanese literature." Étienne Balibar has pointed out that national ideology functions by becoming "an a priori condition of communication between individuals (the citizens) and between social groups—not by suppressing all differences but by relativizing them and subordinating them to itself in such a way that it is the symbolic difference between 'ourselves' and 'foreigners' which wins out and which is lived as irreducible."[2]

The impetus for unifying the diversity of literary history under the national frame therefore persisted in the postwar kokubungaku even though the discipline distanced itself from the wartime, imperial nationalism. In some respects, furthermore, the displacement of the universalist and expansionist aspirations of the imperial state by the particularistic ethno-nationalism of the postwar democratic state *reinforced* the need to demarcate the boundary of national interiority. The insistence on the insularity and homogeneity of Japanese culture, underscored by its unique tradition, helped reconstitute nationhood in a manner commensurate with the status of Japan within the postwar global order. Thus postwar culturalist discourses on national identity both inside and outside of kokubungaku echoed some elements of ahistorical and feminine national unity envisaged in Haga's writing. In the postwar context, however, the fervent emphasis on the imperial lineage as the basis of Japanese national unity was somewhat curbed, supplemented by insistence on the singularity of Japanese ethnicity, language, cultural practice, and so on.

It is not surprising, then, that the postwar discipline inherited more or less intact kokubungaku's valorization of the Heian period as the birthplace of the native writing system, which in turn stimulated the emergence of a distinct native prose. The account of a uniquely Japanese literary and linguistic tradition, emerging out of the social sphere of Heian women sequestered from Chinese influences, clearly resonated with the cultural doctrines of postwar ethno-nationalism. Postwar scholarship, furthermore, took a much more active stance in celebrating the instrumental roles supposedly played by women in the interrelated emergence of native script and native prose. This enthusiasm for highlighting women's contribution to Heian literary history may be related to some of the broader forces at play in postwar Japanese society as well as to more local conditions affecting kokubungaku. For one, establishing the strong presence of women in Japanese cultural history was a view in keeping with the sexual equality promoted by the Occupation regime, which was institutionalized through the new Constitution. Women's contributions at one of the origins of Japanese linguistic and literary history together with the feminine qualities of traditional Japanese literature that Heian literature allegedly embodied were also compatible with the demilitarized and self-proclaimed pacifist facade of the postwar Japanese state.[3] The postwar kokubungaku's tendency to devote greater attention to Heian women writers and their literary practices was also, no doubt, encouraged by the changes in the institutional environment of the discipline. Postwar education reforms and the changing social and economic conditions in Japan contributed to expanding female enrollment in institutions of higher education. Kokubungaku became one of the more popular majors for a new generation of female college students (and students at the women's junior colleges that began proliferating in the mid-1960s). By the 1980s, the increase in female students in the kokubungaku curriculum was compounded by the boom in adult education, where courses on Japanese classical literature were largely subscribed by middle-aged female students. Teaching at these so-called culture centers became a significant source of income for the kokubungaku faculty in top-ranked universities. The celebration of feminized Heian literature and its female literary figures in postwar kokubungaku responded to the growing importance of catering to the female audience both inside and outside of college classrooms.

The Feminine Hand in Heian Literary History

In this chapter, I examine the relationship between women, literary production, national language, and modes of writing presupposed in kokubungaku discourses—the assumptions that have continued to exert powerful influences on postwar discussions of Heian literature and women/femininity. Thereby, I question the roles supposedly played by women and women's writing in the received history of Heian literature and the origin of kana. I rethink some of the key distinctions made in Heian texts—between kana and mana, Chinese and Japanese poetry, and masculine and feminine writing—against the grain of modern conceptions of gender identity and national language/literature. By examining the function of national ideology in the conventional association of women with the evolution of kana and kana literature, I identify the misogynistic logic that it harbors.

According to the conventional literary history of Japan, the tenth century marked a critical juncture in the evolution not only of Japanese literature but of its language and its writing system. The period saw the appearance and rapid development of vernacular (as opposed to Chinese) prose literature while Japanese poetry, which had been eclipsed by the popularity and prestige of Chinese poetry at the court in the early Heian period, was revived, gaining new legitimacy. One of the principal factors that catalyzed this development of native literature is said to have been the appearance of the new phonetic syllabary, kana. In particular, a type of kana called the *wonnade* (feminine hand), considered to be the direct precursor of the hiragana still in use today, became the primary script for the reinvigorated native poetry and newly emerging literary prose. The feminine hand is said to have developed out of an earlier form of inscription in which the Japanese, who did not have an indigenous writing system, began using Chinese characters as phonetic scripts to write in their native language. Scholars have called such scripts *man'yōgana* after the first Japanese poetic anthology compiled in the eighth century, *Man'yōshū*. The feminine hand allegedly evolved from man'yōgana through two major transformations: the standardization and contraction of the pool of graphs used as phonetic scripts and the radical cursification and simplification of Chinese characters. Compared to man'yōgana, Heian kana is deemed a superior form of phonetic writing, providing easier and more efficient means of transcribing the mother tongue. Thus, the development of Heian kana is thought to mark the Japanese acquisition of a distinct form of writing, well suited to the native language.

This argument about the history of kana is often accompanied by claims regarding women's role in the development of the feminine hand. Excluded from training in Chinese writing, which was a required skill for male courtiers, aristocratic women helped to create and popularize the expedient phonetic script. Their distance from the masculine domain of Chinese language, literature, and culture, furthermore, kept them more anchored in the spoken Japanese and its oral literature. Many aspects of the new kana literature supposedly germinated in women's everyday linguistic activities: their oral storytelling, private letters, diaries, and informal exchanges of poetry. The literary legacies of these anonymous women laid the groundwork for the rise of vernacular masterpieces by illustrious women writers after the late tenth century, including *The Tale of Genji* by Murasaki Shikibu (written in the early eleventh century), arguably the most celebrated text of premodern Japanese literature.

The above is a composite of textbook versions of Heian literary history. There are, of course, more nuanced and sophisticated representations of the history that are cautious about drawing broad inferences from limited evidence, avoiding simplistic causal explanations and excessively rigid binarism between Japanese and Chinese language and literature. The link between kana script and native speech (as well as oral literature) and the central role of women in the development of kana and literature in kana to which my outline points, however, are powerful assumptions in the field. The prevalence of these views is even more striking when we consider the lack of historical material that proves, for instance, women's contribution to the development of kana or locates traces of the informal writing that supposedly laid the basis for refined kana literature. Before the late tenth century, there are very few texts (in kana or otherwise) that can be attributed to women with relative certainty.[4]

Among the existing early kana texts, a work that is often held up as proof of the ties between women and the emergence of kana literature is *Tosa nikki* (ca. 940). In this journal/travelogue filled with poetry, a female narrator records the journey of an ex-governor of a remote province returning to the capital at the end of his term. It is considered to be the first known sample of a *nikki bungaku* (literary diary) in kana, a genre that includes many of the most renowned works of Heian literature by women. Furthermore, it is thought to be the earliest surviving kana text that explicitly deploys the female voice in its narration. *Tosa nikki* opens with the line "Men are said to write such a thing as a diary; perhaps a woman may also give it a try" (をとこもすなる日記といふものを、をむなもしてみむとて、するなり。). Modern commentators have often read this opening passage as a self-referential gesture through which *Tosa nikki* highlights its status as a vernacular text written in the native script. The men's diaries, against which the text contrasts itself, are presumably semiofficial records of court rituals and events that Heian courtiers wrote in Chinese. Self-conscious identification with vernacular writing is a stance that accords with the established persona of Ki no Tsurayuki, to whom the text has been historically attributed. Tsurayuki was an important *male* poet and critic, most famous for his work as a chief compiler of *Kokin-wakashū* (from the early tenth century), the first imperial anthology of Japanese poetry, which is credited with elevating the status of waka in court culture.

It may seem odd that a work by a man initiated a genre identified with *heian joryū bungaku* (Heian female literature) or that his writing supports the link between women and the development of kana literature. Yet the very fact that a man apparently chose to speak as a woman in order to write a diary in the mother tongue is said to demonstrate the gendered division of language at the Heian court and the strong identification between women and kana writing. According to a classic interpretation of the text, it would have been improper for Tsurayuki, a male aristocrat and court bureaucrat, to write a personal diary in the vernacular language touching on topics such as the voyagers' longing to return to the capital or the description of a mother who laments the loss of a young child. Some have argued, therefore, that he took a fictional female persona, adopting the form of personal diaries written by women at the time.[5]

The hypothesis that Tsurayuki *imitated* diaries kept by women remains speculative, for we have no reliable sample of a woman's diary that predates *Tosa nikki*.[6] Furthermore, some scholars have questioned whether Tsurayuki earnestly tried to simulate a female mode of writing, arguing instead that his female impersonation was halfhearted and intended to achieve a parodic effect. The text's humorous comments with erotic innuendoes or sarcastic critiques of the corrupt practices of provincial officials are thought to reflect masculine sensibilities, revealing the true gender of the writer. It has been pointed out, furthermore, that the text's prose style differs significantly from existing Heian diaries and tales authored by women in later periods. *Tosa nikki* uses sinified vocabularies and expressions that do not appear in the Heian texts attributed to "real" women.

In recent studies of *Tosa nikki*, we find more nuanced analyses of the text's narrational gender. Fujii Sadakazu argues that in *Tosa nikki* Tsurayuki experimented not with a feminine mode of writing but with a new form of Japanese discourse that was closer to everyday speech.[7] Although this new vernacular style of writing was more masculine than feminine, simulating in kana men's diaries written in Chinese, Tsurayuki neutralized its gender association by setting up the narrator as a woman. He thus made it appropriate for use by both sexes, similar to the genbun itchi style of writing developed through the modern vernacularization movement in Japan.[8] Kojima Naoko supports Fujii's objection to the facile identification of kana writing with women and femininity in the Heian context. She suggests that in *Tosa nikki* the authorial (gender) identity is erased as the man disguises himself as a woman and then adopts a more impersonal (i.e., neither feminine nor masculine) narrative voice, creating a world of "fiction" where the discursive gender is divorced from the authorial gender.[9] From a somewhat different perspective than that adopted by Fujii and Kojima, Lynn K. Miyake acknowledges masculine themes and forms present in the text, but she also calls our attention to the unmistakably feminine framework supplied by the female narrator. Instead of reducing the text to monolithic categories of male, female, or even androgyny, she proposes that *Tosa nikki* be read as an innovative "gender-bending text" that subverts binarism by bringing male and female voices together in a rich interplay.[10]

A fundamental problem that tends to be underplayed in this panoply of both traditional and more recent hypotheses concerning Tsurayuki's female masquerade is the difficulty of knowing what passed for overtly feminine attitudes, topics, and modes of writing at the time the text was written (and for that matter the accepted forms and content of men's writing in that milieu). Although we have some sense of what men wrote in Chinese at the time, there is no evidence that writing a kana diary or kana prose in general was considered feminine; neither do we know for sure that women did not use sinified diction or style at this stage of the development of kana writing. All too often scholars have tacitly read into *Tosa nikki* received views on gender conventions that are derived from their understanding of the later Heian texts by women as well as from modern norms. Even recent scholarship that attempts to reread the text through nonessentialized notions of gender typically relies on established assumptions concerning feminine and masculine attributes in the Heian period, reproducing them not as biologically but culturally determined properties. If, however, we take seriously the notion that gender difference is historically constructed, *Tosa nikki* is one of the few sources from which to explore the possible range of mid-tenth-century kana writing by women. Before we judge whether the text's narratorial discourse and themes are feminine, masculine, neutral, or mixed, therefore, we need to proceed with great caution in determining what we accept as valid gender markers, carefully evaluating them in relation to what we may surmise about Heian aristocratic society as well as to the broader thematic and formal structure of the text.

My study of *Tosa nikki* focuses on a rather narrow set of textual gestures that seem to mark the feminine identity of its narrator, and I analyze how this gendering functions in relation to a theme that runs throughout the text: the evaluation and composition of Japanese poetry. While I do not attribute to the text any active intention to subvert the established gender norms of its society, I do suggest a reading that refracts the expectations about gender and writing that the discipline of Heian studies has persistently projected onto it. I argue that the text's construction of a female narrator does not affirm the conventional notion of female/feminine writing (private, emotional, quotidian, etc.) or the assumption that kana prose was more or less strictly a woman's domain. I hope thereby to highlight the ideological functions that *Tosa nikki*, as a paradoxical forerunner of "Heian female literature," has been made to play in the modern construction of Heian literary history.

Female Literacy and Comparative Poetics

Following the opening phrase, little is revealed about the narrator in *Tosa nikki*. She seems to be cast as an anonymous observer in the entourage of the ex-governor, who was traveling by boat. The narrator is often believed to be one of the female attendants of the ex-governor's household because of her occasional use of honorific expressions when she refers to him and another female character who may have been his wife. On the whole, however, the text does not elaborate on the narrator's identity. As I have mentioned, even her gender identity, which is practically the only thing about her that the text lets the reader know, is considered questionable by some commentators. There are, however, specific moments in which the text seems to draw our attention to the narrator's gender.

After describing a banquet held in honor of a departing governor at which people recited both Chinese and Japanese poems, she writes, "Chinese poems (*kara uta*) could not be recorded, but the new governor composed this Japanese poem (*yamato uta*)" (Twelfth Month, Twenty-sixth Day, 264).[11] Although the reason why the narrator does not record the kara uta is unexplained, the passage is most likely implying that, as a woman, she could not or would not read or write Chinese texts. The text, furthermore, highlights the narrator's gender-based distance from the Chinese poem by showing how other women share this condition.

> The vessel could not be taken out, as the winds were strong and the waves rough. Everywhere people were emitting deep sighs. The men tried to amuse themselves by reciting Chinese poems. A woman composed this poem after having caught the gist of a [Chinese] verse that said something like "Looking at the sun, the capital seems even farther away" (日をのぞめばみやことほし).
>
> ひをだにも　あまぐもちかく　みるものを　みやこへとおもふ　みちのはるけさ
>
> Even the sun looks near the clouds, but so far is the path to the capital for which I long! (First Month, Twenty-seventh Day, 280)

Again the Chinese poems that men recite are mentioned but not written down, and the narrator, together with the woman who composes the poem here, claims to have only a rough understanding of it. This passage also foregrounds the fact that it is Chinese poetry in the written form from which women are most distanced. By the mid-Heian period, Chinese poems, though written according to Chinese grammar and orthography, were often read (instantaneously translated) in a form of sinified Japanese known as "*kundoku* discourse" (*kundoku-tai*). This is presumably why Chinese poems recited by men would be roughly comprehensible to women.

Although such references to kara uta are widely understood as the text's allusion to the narrator's gender, Hagitani Boku and others have argued that the author removes his feminine disguise to discuss Chinese poetry.[12] In other words, the text's references to Chinese poetry are deemed to attribute too much knowledge of Chinese literature to the supposedly female narrator. We may note a paradox here. The way in which Chinese poetry is treated in the text is read as the signature of the narrator's womanhood as well as a revelation of the narrator's gender imposture. The gender of the narrator, then, seems to be fractured between two conflicting impulses of the text: its insistence on referring to Chinese poetry while refusing to commit it to writing. This does not necessarily indicate a confusion or inconsistency on the part of the text if it is understood as a strategy that specifically excludes Chinese poetry presented *in writing*.

What purpose could such handling of Chinese poetry serve? The answer to this question would also enable us to probe further into the function of the female narrator in the text. The absence or presence of kara uta may be related to the other type of poetic discourse, which is mentioned alongside Chinese poetry, the type that *is* written down: yamato uta. As in the banquet scene, the text frequently describes Chinese and Japanese poems recited side by side or it refers to the ways in which Japanese poems borrow words and images from Chinese poems, suggesting a fluid interchange between the two. Furthermore, the text repeatedly suggests the fundamental commonality between Chinese and Japanese poetry. Referring to a poem about a mother lamenting the death of her child, the narrator comments, "Such an outflow of feeling and words is not something one can produce deliberately. *In China as well as in our land, they well up from emotions too powerful to be borne*" (Second Month, Ninth Day, 287–88; emphasis added).

To claim a relationship of equivalence between kara uta and yamato uta in the context of tenth-century Japan most likely functioned as a polemical gesture in support of Japanese poetry. Throughout the Heian period, Chinese poetry was the premier literature of male aristocrats, buttressed by the Confucian ideology adopted by the state and commanding an official status confirmed by a series of imperial anthologies. By the tenth century, however, we begin to see attempts to legitimate yamato uta, a project most famously associated with *Kokinwakashū*, which was compiled by a group of poet-bureaucrats among whom Tsurayuki was a leading figure. Nevertheless, at first glance *Kokinwakashū*'s rhetoric for bolstering the status of Japanese poetry appears to differ considerably from that of *Tosa nikki*. In the Kana Preface of the anthology attributed to Tsurayuki, we do not find an overt claim of equivalence between kara uta and yamato uta. Instead, the preface generally underplays the presence of Chinese poetry and the powerful impact it had on Heian poetic practice.

Discussing the history of Japanese poetry, the preface attributes its decline in the early Heian period not to the dominance of Chinese culture and literature at the court but to Japanese poetry's loss of its true identity—its literary sophistication and public importance.[13] That is to say, some of the very properties of Chinese poetry that anchored its status in court society are claimed to be Japanese poetry's original characteristics. Lamenting the degeneration of Japanese poetry, the preface recalls the glories of the past: "Things were not so in earlier days. During the reigns of ancient sovereigns, an emperor gathered his attendants to enjoy spring blossoms in the mornings and the autumn moon in the evenings, commanding them to compose poems according to the occasion. . . . Looking into the minds of these men [through their poems], the emperors could distinguish between the wise and the foolish."[14] The Kana Preface calls for a "return" to the essence of Japanese poetry, which is in fact an ideal most likely drawn from traditional Chinese poetics and the practice of Chinese poetry in Japan that it inspired.[15] The only time that the preface openly refers to kara uta is when it discusses the *sama* (poetic styles) of Japanese poems. There it mentions Chinese poetry in a matter-of-fact tone: "Now there are six Japanese poetic styles; the same is true of Chinese poetry." The concept of six styles is probably borrowed from the "six principles" discussed in the Great Preface of *Shi jing*, one of the most canonical texts on poetics in the Chinese tradition. The Kana Preface, however, suggests that Chinese poetry conforms to a norm intrinsic to Japanese poetic tradition. The preface neutralizes the powerful influence of Chinese poetry and poetics while tacitly incorporating their elements into its construction and legitimation of yamato uta.

Although *Tosa nikki* compares Japanese and Chinese poetry more directly than does the Kana Preface, there are significant points in common between the rhetoric of the two texts. *Tosa nikki* indicates a close relationship between Chinese and Japanese poetry, but it filters out kara uta at the level of inscription, presumably due to limitations in the narrator's literacy. Because it is in the sphere of writing that the overwhelming prestige of Chinese poetry is grounded, the exclusion of kara uta in the written form helps the text compare and connect the two while glossing over the asymmetry of their status and various other differences between them. *Tosa nikki*'s comparative poetics of Japanese and Chinese poetry, which depends on omission—the avoidance of an unfavorable comparison—parallels the Kana Preface's strategic silence regarding kara uta. Furthermore, we must note that both *Tosa nikki* and the Kana Preface place yamato uta apart from kara uta only to suggest the fundamental commonality and continuity between Japanese and Chinese poetry.

The conflation of Chinese and Japanese poetry in *Tosa nikki* takes an interesting form in the anecdote it tells of Abe no Nakamaro, a renowned poet who was sent to China by the Japanese court as an envoy. At a farewell party hosted on the occasion of his return to his homeland, he composed a Japanese poem.

> あをうなばら　ふりさけみれば　かすがなる　みかさのや
> まに　いでしつきかも

> Gazing far away, I see a moon above the blue ocean. Is this the same moon as the one that rose over Mikasa Mountain in Kasuga?

Nakamaro feared that Chinese people would not understand his poem, but he tried to convey its meaning by writing down its sama (outline) in "male script" and then explained it in speech to a person who knew our words. To his surprise, the Chinese audience warmly praised the poem. Although the words of China and Japan are different, just as the moonlight in both places is the same, there is no difference in the way people feel. (First Month, Twentieth Day, 277)

The term *wotokomoji* (male script) presumably refers to Chinese characters. Thus, Nakamaro wrote out his poem (or at least nominal and verbal stems used in it) in characters so that his words would be comprehensible to the Chinese audience. Commentators have wondered why Nakamaro resorted to such a method of communication if there was a person at the scene who could have translated his oral explanation of the poem.

A key to solving this puzzle may be the term *sama* in the passage, which I have tentatively translated as "outline." Nakamaro used the male script not to transcribe the waka as a whole but rather its sama. As I mentioned earlier, this term is also found in the Kana Preface of *Kokinwakashū*, in its discussion of the six sama of poetry. Although the definition of *sama*, has been widely debated, most contemporary studies of *Kokinwakashū* agree that in its broadest sense it refers to the formal structure of a poem.[16] However we may surmise the precise meaning of the six sama that the preface enumerates, it is likely that they were put in place to underscore the sophistication and diversity of the poetic forms of yamato uta—a gesture that invokes a comparison with Chinese poetry. If we take into account the discussion of sama in the Kana Preface in our understanding of the above passage from *Tosa nikki*, what Nakamaro sketched out in "male scripts" was the formal and tropic organization of his poem. The characters could suggest to Chinese readers the imagery and parallel construction of the poem (the moon in front of the poet and the moon of his homeland in his memory). Parallelism, of course, is a major structural principle of classical Chinese poetry. That Nakamaro first wrote his poem in Chinese characters and then had it explained in speech would not be redundant if such formal and figural features of the poem were deemed to be more effectively expressed visually in writing than through an oral explanation or translation. Overcoming the difference in words between Japanese and Chinese that the narrator proclaims, therefore, is achieved not solely through the commonality of feelings and the poetic effects of moonlight; the shared graphs and poetic conventions also facilitate the communication of Nakamaro's yamato uta to his Chinese friends. *Tosa nikki* thus shows how yamato uta could visually simulate Chinese poetry and move the Chinese audience, presenting it as a written discourse with conventions comparable to those of kara uta.

At the same time, however, the transcription of the Japanese poetry is not reproduced in the text (the text does not show exactly how Nakamaro wrote his poem in the male script). In practice, *Tosa nikki* draws kara uta closer to yamato uta by commenting on and describing it in a textual space monopolized by Japanese poetry. On occasion, *Tosa nikki* takes this one step further, rendering a Chinese poem in kana: "As the thick clouds disappeared from the sky, exposing a delightful late night moon, the crew rowed the vessel out. The sky and the sea looked just like each other, with moons shining in both. It's no wonder a person once said something like this: 'The oar pierces the moon on the waves. The boat presses against the sky in the sea' (さをはうがつなみのうへのつきを。ふねはおそふうみのうちのそらを)" (First Month, Seventeenth Day, 275). The anonymous verse the narrator cites refers to a poem by a T'ang poet, Gu Dao. By introducing the poem as a discourse that the narrator has heard rather than a kara uta, the text circumscribes the conventional mode of inscribing Chinese poetry. We may also note that the text refers to the couplet as being *ifu* (uttered) rather than *yomu* (composed). In general, the narrator describes kara uta being uttered (or recited) by the male travelers on the boat rather than being composed.[17] Thus, while the text emphasizes the literateness of yamato uta through a variety of means, Chinese poetry, which is the quintessential literate discourse at the Heian court, is placed on the register of speech—that which is heard or overheard by women.

Tosa nikki has sometimes been read as a poetic treatise in disguise because of its extensive discussion of Japanese poetry.[18] Although a number of studies on the text have associated the female narrator with the text's polemic in support of Japanese poetry, these discussions take for granted the ties between women, kana, and Japanese poetry.[19] In my analysis of *Tosa nikki*, I have studied the function of the female narrator in relation to the text's complex rhetorical construction of Japanese and Chinese poetry. I suggest that the text seems to exploit the narrator's gender not so much for "feminine" topics and sensibilities, or for her privileged relation to kana writing as a woman, but for her limited access to Chinese poetry. If it were only a matter of writing yamato uta in kana, men, too, could have filled this role. Although Chinese poetry commanded more prestige, aristocratic men were actively engaged in composing Japanese poetry, and men, along with women, wrote their waka in kana. Male aristocrats (who were expected to be fully versed in Chinese poetry), however, could not have mediated the text's subtle strategy for both invoking and repressing kara uta as the parallel and counterpoint of yamato uta. Thus, while the narrator's discourse appears to be inflected by her gender, the text does not necessarily invoke a distinct set of properties that defines female writing as such. By understanding the gender marking of the narratorial agent in negative terms (through what she *does not* write),

I suggest an approach to the text that avoids presupposing a reified link between women and kana or kana literature.

Reading between Mana and Kana

Although my analysis of *Tosa nikki* is premised on Heian women's relative unfamiliarity with Chinese poetry (particularly in the written form), the relationship between women and Chinese writing is itself an issue that deserves more scrutiny. Modern scholarship has generally assumed that in the Heian period there was social censure against women's use of the Chinese language, which drew a gendered division between the Chinese and Japanese linguistic spheres. We do find in Heian kana texts apparent references to the prohibition of women's use of Chinese. For instance, in a famous scene in *The Diary of Murasaki Shikibu* (the early-eleventh-century diary of the author of *The Tale of Genji*) a narrator browsing through the Chinese texts that belonged to her deceased husband is criticized by her female attendants: "Our mistress invites misery by going on like this. Why must a woman read Chinese texts?! In the past, women were told not to read even Buddhist scripture."[20] The comment suggests that reading Chinese texts was considered inappropriate for women, bringing misfortune to those who transgressed this custom. In the original, the Chinese texts are referred to as *mana bumi* (mana texts). *Mana* is a term often paired with *kana* and is generally understood to mean Chinese, Chinese writing, or Chinese script. We need to bear in mind, however, that the term *mana* may refer to characters even when they are used in vernacular writing. In *The Tale of Genji*, a male courtier criticizes women's use of mana in their letters: "It is extremely regrettable when a woman flaunts superficial knowledge of things she has casually picked up, scribbling mana everywhere, inexcusably filling up more than half of a female letter (*wonnabumi*) with it."[21] The meaning of the term *female letter* in the passage is not clear, but it most likely refers to letters written by or for women. It is difficult to interpret this passage unless we assume that such letters were expected to be mostly written not in mana but in kana. If, however, the prohibition was imposed against women's reading and writing of the Chinese language, we need to explain why they had to be discouraged from writing mana in the context of supposedly vernacular texts (female epistolary writing). When women were told to stay away from mana, were they being distanced from the Chinese language or Chinese script?

Such a question has never been seriously entertained in Heian literary studies because women's avoidance of mana script, even in writing Japanese texts, has been deemed an extension of their more basic exclusion from the Chinese language. A widespread belief that women played a major role in developing and popularizing the native phonetic script relies on the premise that women's use of Chinese characters was limited even when there were no other types of script available with which to write Japanese poetry and letters.[22] There is, however, no clear evidence that the avoidance of characters was derivative of linguistic prohibition. Nor can we ascertain that the unfeminineness of mana was based on the graph's association with the Chinese language. The issue at stake here is not only the norms concerning women's writing in the Heian aristocratic society but more fundamental problems regarding Heian aristocrats' linguistic consciousness. How did they perceive the relations between Chinese and Japanese texts or between writing and language? Before we investigate the nature of the mana taboo allegedly imposed on women, therefore, we need to examine the mana versus kana opposition in general and the dualism of Japanese (native) and Chinese (foreign) linguistic spheres in Heian society that this pair of scripts is said to symbolize.

The term *mana* has fallen out of use in modern Japanese, but *kana* is a generic name for the phonetic syllabaries currently used in written Japanese. Thus, *kana* in contemporary parlance is understood primarily as phonetic scripts, in contrast to *kanji*, which represents morphemes in the modern Japanese writing system (the term kanji is often considered a modern equivalent of *mana*). According to the standard etymology, the word *kana* was originally pronounced *kanna* with a root in the expression *karina* (borrowed or provisional name). This etymology supports the modern understanding of the evolution of the kana script — it began in the Japanese "borrowing" of Chinese characters to write down native words and phrases. The word *mana*, on the other hand, is usually rendered with the characters that mean "permanent or true name," marking a clear contrast with *kana*. The term *mana* therefore reflects the fact that the script performs the proper function of logographic characters, which are equipped with both phonetic and semantic values.

It is also well known that Heian kana developed through figural transformations that altered and simplified the shapes of characters through cursification; the emergence of kana cannot be understood apart from the history of calligraphy in Japan. Nevertheless, both contemporary usage of the term *kana* and the accepted etymology place the emphasis squarely on the phonetic function of the script rather than on its formal calligraphic characteristics. Furthermore, because kana has been defined through its phonetic function, its development is closely associated with the evolution of Japanese language from orality to literacy, thus reinforcing the ties between the script and the native language (and by contrast the link between mana and the Chinese language).

Marshall Unger has questioned this etymology of kana, however, observing that the transformation of the word from *karina* to *kana* does not necessarily accord with the known patterns of sound change in Heian words.[23] Furthermore, he points out that as far as their usage in Heian texts is concerned, the terms *mana* and *kana* were distinguished not by their functions of representing morpheme versus phoneme but by their formal differences.[24] Indeed, in what is said to be one of the earliest records of the term *kana*—found in a Heian tale, *Utsuho monogatari*, from the early tenth century—the word appears in a passage that describes a number of writing samples to be used for studying calligraphy.[25] The term is used as a generic reference for various forms of calligraphic styles, including the feminine hand. In *The Pillow Book of Seishōnagon*, when a man is said to be "terrible at writing both mana and kana," the ridicule is launched against his calligraphic skills and not his ability to compose prose or poetry in Japanese and Chinese.[26] Even in later periods, we find evidence that these two terms were understood through the framework of calligraphy. Until the late nineteenth century, it was generally believed that hiragana (or *wonnade*) was *invented* by a single individual, the legendary master of calligraphy, Kūkai. The theory of kana history that links man'yōgana to Heian kana through a gradual evolution of phonetic script did not appear until the mid–nineteenth century.[27] The term man'yōgana itself was coined by modern scholarship, which sought the origin of kana from a perspective that had already defined it as a phonetic system of writing.

In a groundbreaking study that examines Heian society and culture through calligraphic and poetic practices, Thomas LaMarre argues for a nonlinguistic understanding of the terms *mana* and *kana*.

> *Mana*, despite their reputation as Chinese, do not fall in line with contemporary stories of China versus Japan. In ninth-century Heian culture, the category of *mana*, although tied to notions of a Kara or Chinese mode, includes a number of things that would be considered Japanese from our standpoint. *Mana* do not strictly designate Chinese texts written in Chinese characters, nor do they imply characters used nonphonetically as ideographs. *Mana* referred to a mode of writing in which characters were written in their full or perfected forms. It mattered little whether those characters were to be read ideographically or logographically, or whether the grammar approximated Chinese or Japanese. What seems to have mattered most was the notion of *mana* as a mode of style of calligraphic performance.[28]

LaMarre foregrounds the importance of calligraphic performance in Heian literary practices by suggesting that the style of writing, more than grammar and pronunciation, determined the classification of Heian poetic discourse into categories such as waka and kanshi.[29] He points to a Heian manuscript of *Man'yōshū* that presents the same Japanese poem in mana and kana versions side by side with the visual effect strikingly similar to the juxtaposition of Chinese and Japanese poems in the manuscript of *Wakan rōeishū*, a highly influential collection of Chinese and Japanese poems from the early eleventh century. He suggests, therefore, that the difference between Japanese poems written in mana, on one hand, and the Chinese poems, on the other, was not clearly marked in the minds of Heian aristocrats, to whom the archaic mode of transcription employed in *Man'yōshū* had already become largely unintelligible.[30] Redefining *mana* and *kana* through their figural functions, LaMarre points to the diversity of mana and kana calligraphic styles, which coexisted and intermixed, constituting not neatly compartmentalized genres but a field of fluid variations. He approaches Heian discursive space in general as being comprised of multiple styles and variations in which yamato and kara modes overlap, double, and hybridize with each other.

LaMarre's discussion forcefully raises the issue against superimposing the exclusive binarism of Japan and China or Japanese and

Chinese in our understanding of kana and mana or Heian cultural practices in general. The Heian lexicon does not have a term such as *nihongo* (Japanese) or *kokugo* (national language), and scholars have often turned to *kana* as a Heian equivalent of these words. Thus, for instance, they coined the expression *kana-bun* (kana prose) to refer to vernacular prose in the Heian period. As I have mentioned, however, the general usage of the word *kana* in Heian texts does not explicitly evoke phonological or syntactic systems of Japanese language. The search for the traces of vernacular self-consciousness in the Heian period hits an impasse in the circular definition of *kana* and *Japanese language*. This is because most modern Heian studies fail to consider the historicity of the concept of national language before trying to locate it in the Heian texts.

Contemporary studies on nationalism and the history of the modern nation-state suggest that the widespread identification of social collectivity through a shared language or the positing of language as a basis for ethnic, political, and cultural unity is a relatively novel phenomenon.[31] The term *national language* represents a highly specific understanding of language and its function in the world. It defines *language* as a consistent and unified structure (of grammar, phonology, morphology, etc.) that regulates and brings under its order diverse linguistic practices. In late-nineteenth- to early-twentieth-century Japan, for instance, while the state sought to promote the national language, there was no such thing as *the* language of the Japanese people, only a huge variety of discursive forms practiced within the country's territorial boundaries. The call for the resurrection and reinforcement of a national language therefore led to the reorganization and reduction of such diversity (including regional, ethnic, class, and gender differences) under the hierarchical regime of "standard Japanese." This process established a specter of national language as a unity that cuts across and draws together linguistic practices in different genres and mediums, constructing a singular evolutionary history that can be traced all the way back to the preliterate past.[32]

According to the modern concept, a linguistic system and social collectivity complement and mutually ground each other: the definition of *language* as a closed structure implies a homogeneous body of agents that mediates it. The consistent linguistic system is the basis of linguistic competence in a community (regulating the exercise of

language by each individual) while it is itself constantly being modified by the communal use of language. A complex symbiosis is thus
posited between the everyday linguistic communication in a social
field and the abstract linguistic structure. This explains why the dominant theory of language in the age of the nation-state is phonocentric,
privileging speech over writing and phonetic scripts over other modes
of writing.[33] Writing, despite the appearance of being the more regular
and stable form of linguistic practice, cannot be the principal source
for identifying linguistic systematicity and wholeness because it is associated with distance rather than immanence, linguistic exchanges in
the absence of live agents, and the possibility of words divorced from
their "original" meanings through decontextualization. Speech, on
the other hand, is perceived to be the primary medium of social interaction, constituting immediate connections between subjects sharing
a particular spatio-temporal context. Thus, speech is more fundamental to the underlying unity of language than is writing, as the function
of writing at best lies in the conveyance of speech as faithfully and effi-
ciently as possible. As the new national language was being created in
modern Japan, therefore, political and cultural leaders seriously considered the possibility of eliminating kanji and writing the language
entirely phonetically in kana or even the roman alphabet.[34]

Today's definition of *Heian kana* as a phonetic system of writing
has been deeply inflected by modern linguistic ideology and its reification of the spoken national language. In the Heian period, however, there was no concept of a Japanese language that hierarchically
unifies the diverse practices of speaking and writing; neither do we
find in that context an epistemological basis for valorizing phonetic
writing as a medium of native voice. Heian poetics strongly suggests
that the relationship between sound and script was not grasped in-
strumentally, with writing reduced to the signifier of speech. For instance, in the Heian period the most popular type of Japanese poetry,
tanka (short poems made up of thirty-one syllables), was commonly
referred to as thirty-one *graphs* (*misohitomoji*). In other words, the
poem's syllabic pattern was measured in terms of the unit of writing
rather than sound. Describing the origin of tanka, the Kana Preface
of *Kokinwakashū* remarks that "In the age of gods, poetry did not
have set [numbers of] graphs. In the human era, the composition of
thirty-one graphs began with the poems of Susanowo no Mikoto."[35]

The readers of the preface would have known that strictly speaking there were no graphs with which to write down the first song uttered in their land (the history of a writing system entering Japan from China is mentioned elsewhere in the anthology).[36] The passage suggests that from the point of view of Heian poetics, however, regardless of whether poems were actually written down, graphs served as the conceptual apparatus through which the formal convention of yamato uta was recognized. Writing, as it were, anchored poetic discourses to a proper form.

We have already examined how *Tosa nikki* attempts to legitimate yamato uta by fashioning it into a *literate* poetic tradition comparable to kara uta. In another section of the text, there is a curious anecdote tacked on to the end of a scene describing travelers reciting a few poems to each other: "There was a person who had been listening intently to the others discussing these poems. Then he produced a poem of his own containing thirty-seven graphs. People couldn't hold back uproarious laughs, much to the chagrin of the poet, who grumbled a few objections. The poem was impossible to repeat. Even if it had been written down, I doubt that it could have been read. If it was so difficult to recite it on the spot, one can imagine what it would have been like to try to repeat it later" (First Month, Eighteenth Day, 276). Modern commentators have wondered why the verse was so difficult to recite if the narrator heard it well enough to count the number of syllables it contained. The narrator may be expressing the difficulty not of simply repeating the verse but of attempting to vocalize this irregular poem according to the standard 5 pause, 7–5 pause, 7–7 syllabic pattern. If *Tosa nikki* is discussing the possibility of adjusting the irregular syllabic count to the proper form, however, how do we account for the seemingly redundant suggestion to read the written poem when the impossibility of vocalization (the failure of the attempted adjustment) is already confirmed? Writing it down and reading it, however, may not seem such a strange thing to do if we consider scansion as a process that is facilitated by visual analysis. The inscription of this irregular poem is suggested, moreover, because a poem's formal structure is thought to be best evaluated and demonstrated in writing. The narrator's belief that the poem could not be read even if it were written down also suggests that the relationship between writing and voice is not mechanically ensured by orthographic rules that assign fixed phonetic values to the graphs (or combination of graphs). Here the voicing of written words must be guided by poetic rather than linguistic rules. The narrator, therefore, is not trying to reproduce an originary voice that the writing represents but to *produce* a poetic discourse from this flawed composition by plotting it in writing. To the extent that this reading mediated by poetics does not attempt to recover a preexisting voice from a text, it suggests a function of writing that is irreducible to speech.

That poetics rather than linguistics mediates the relationship between writing and reading in this scene helps us to better understand the fluid interchangeability between yamato uta and kara uta suggested in *Tosa nikki*. In the text, yamato uta and kara uta blend into each other through the compatibility of their conventions without the process of linguistic translation as we conceive of it today. This is how in Abe no Nakamaro's anecdote the transcription by characters renders yamato uta as a text addressed to the Chinese audience. Heian aristocrats obviously distinguished between yamato uta and kara uta or between Chinese and Japanese words. Yet these differences were not systematically subsumed under what we would consider an overarching division between the Japanese and Chinese languages. Similarly, we should be able to think about the contrast between mana and kana articulated in Heian texts as calligraphic and formal differences without subordinating the pair to the polarity between the Japanese and Chinese languages.

Rethinking the Mana Taboo

The possibility that Heian poetics was not concerned with linguistic differences between Japanese and Chinese, as we conceive of them today, or that kana and mana were calligraphic rather than the linguistic categories has profound implications for understanding women's literary activities in the Heian period. If *mana* is a calligraphic term, its emergence must be linked to the process in which Heian calligraphy was reconfigured in response to the development of kana as a distinct calligraphic style around the late ninth century. And if this is the case the hypothesis that women helped create kana because they could not use mana (i.e., could not use Chinese characters even in vernacular texts) is in doubt. At least, it is difficult to invoke existing historical evidence of women's avoidance of mana to speculate on the gender norms of writing before the rise of kana. There has been very little research into the origin of women's mana taboo. The phenomenon has been customarily accounted for by women's exclusion from the core of the bureaucratic and administrative system at the Heian court, where Chinese was the official medium of written communication. This understanding pushes the beginning of the custom all the way back to the time when the Yamato court established itself as a Chinese-style centralized state in the seventh and eighth centuries. The association of women's avoidance of mana with the formation of kana-style calligraphy in the ninth and tenth centuries, in contrast, is a view that is more consistent with the dates of the textual references to this practice. We should also bear in mind that prior to the mid-Heian period, when kana came into currency, female poets, too, presumably transcribed their poems in modes that would later be categorized as mana writing. And there are also records of well-known female poets of Chinese poetry in the early Heian period.[37]

Rather than assuming that women helped develop kana because they were prohibited from using mana, therefore, we may see the rise of kana as the catalyst for identifying different styles of writing in gendered terms, constituting mana as a style of writing less appropriate for women. This would also mean that the connections between women/femininity and kana, as well as the distance between women and mana, were actively constructed as kana and poems written in this script began achieving significant status and function within Heian court society.[38] In the *Tale of Genji* the main protagonist, Genji, pays a great compliment to kana calligraphy as a discipline that has blossomed even in the age of decline: "This is the dark age of dharma (*mappō*)—everything seems inferior and shallow compared to the past. But only kana has become immeasurably refined. The hands of ancients are faithful to the rules, but they lack the richness, narrowly conforming to particular modes. We do not find writing that is truly sublime until much later."[39] He also praises the calligraphic skills of his beloved Murasaki Lady: "Your hand [calligraphic style] is exquisite in terms of its soft beauty. When one advances in the skill of mana, one's kana tends to become inconsistent."[40] The text seems to valorize the attainment of those who singularly devote themselves to kana calligraphy (i.e., women with advanced calligraphic skill in contrast to men who would practice both mana and kana), hinting at a certain degree of parity between the two modes. It is impossible to ascertain whether Genji's comment reflects the general opinion of mid-Heian court culture. At least, we can assume that by the early eleventh century, when the text was written, kana calligraphy was respectable enough so that Genji, who is portrayed as the paragon of cultural refinement, could express such views.

If we analyze women's mana taboo in relation to the ascent of kana calligraphy and its related sociocultural fields, we cannot simply reduce the gendered differentiation of writing to a symptom of female inferiority in the male-dominated society. At the same time, however, we should caution against swinging to the other extreme and interpreting the emergence of kana as the sign of the autonomy or even dominance of female/feminine culture at the court. The assumption of a neat division between kana-feminine-Japanese and mana-masculine-Chinese in Heian court society has stimulated debates that pit one side against the other—for instance, asking which of the two ultimately represents the essence of Heian aristocratic culture. Such an inquiry, however, precludes the possibility that multiple cultural values and logics may have operated in Heian court society without constituting a sharp dichotomy. The multivalent approach to Heian culture is suggested here not so much to recuperate it as an idealized field of free-floating plurality but as a starting point for exploring its historical specificity in a more nuanced and methodologically self-conscious manner. The status of women and cultural practices/institutions associated with them at the Heian court—such as the nature of the power they exercised as well as the constraints they suffered—may be investigated more productively on such a basis.

The rethinking of the mana taboo in calligraphic rather than linguistic terms also puts in question the assumption that Heian women's avoidance of mana signified their subjection to the native sphere of language and culture, which was clearly separated from that of Chinese and mana writing. In other words, if we abandon the image of Heian court society divided into two autonomous linguistic-cultural closures, we must reevaluate the relationship between Heian court women and Chinese writing. Even if it was not customary for women to receive a systematic education in Chinese letters, as men did (as part of the training required for the service in the state bureaucracy), that did not necessarily translate into a complete lack of contact with Chinese writing or the cultural and social fields associated with it.[41] *The Diary of Murasaki Shikibu* and *The Pillow Book of Seishōnagon* suggest that at least some women possessed sophisticated knowledge of Chinese literature. While both texts seem to approve or at least accept the censure against women who flaunted their knowledge of Chinese letters or overused mana, they also display women's familiarity with Chinese poetry and prose. Furthermore, they tell anecdotes that illustrate how a socially tactful demonstration of such cultivation could earn respect and praise particularly from men.

The Diary of Murasaki Shikibu notes how the emperor, upon reading her writing (possibly *The Tale of Genji*), mused that she must have studied the chronicles of Japanese history (written in Chinese) and marveled at her Chinese learning.[42] The *Pillow Book* recounts an incident in which a male aristocrat sent Seishōnagon a line from a well-known Chinese poem and asked her for the other half of the couplet. She replied with the composition of the second half of a Japanese poem based on the correct answer, creating a stir at the court with her knowledge and wit.[43] At least for female courtiers such as Murasaki Shikibu and Seishōnagon, who were presumably brought in to serve the high-ranking imperial consorts due to their literary talents, the knowledge of Chinese literature appears to have helped enhance their status. What was considered gauche and perhaps unfeminine was not so much their knowledge of Chinese letters or the ability to write mana itself. Rather, women living in a small and competitive court society had to avoid the appearance of showing off and attracting attention to their skills.[44]

Shimura Midori speculates that a broad segment of Heian aristocratic women knew mana and perhaps even read Chinese texts.[45] She draws our attention to references to women reciting Buddhist scripture rendered in Chinese texts or engaging in the popular practice of copying scripture written in Chinese. Furthermore, a number of accounts suggest that a script game, *hentsugi*, which required knowledge of a considerable amount of mana script, was commonly enjoyed by women. Aside from this evidence, Shimura reminds us that Heian women were able to inherit, own, and exchange property, which required direct or indirect dealings with legal documents in Chinese. She lists surviving documents that seem to have been either written or signed by women and suggests that women, too, may have sought to develop basic literacy in Chinese in order to facilitate the management and transaction of their assets.

At the very least, texts such as *The Diary of Murasaki Shikibu* and the *Pillow Book* convey to us how Heian aristocratic women were inevitably situated in the sociocultural space permeated by Chinese writing. Whatever the exact nature of the mana taboo, it did not operate as a strict prohibition; neither could women's relation to Chinese letters be characterized as one of segregation. What women did encounter, it seems, was the pressure to feign some degree of distance and unfamiliarity with that facet of their world. As we have seen, the relationship between women and Chinese poetry that *Tosa nikki* suggests is much more ambivalent than one of simple exclusion. The narrator, who is presumably a woman, seems incapable of writing kara uta. On the other hand, she and other women do know and use some elements of Chinese poetry and its tradition. The text exploits women's relative distance from Chinese letters, in other words, as a condition to be commented on and manipulated rather than a silent, immutable law that operates as a given.

Women and the Purity of National Language

So how do we account for the widespread perception that Heian women (save some exceptional cases) were shut out from the sphere of Chinese language and literature? At least part of an answer to this question may be found in the peculiar role played by women's linguistic practices in the received history of Japanese language and literature. As mentioned earlier, the blossoming of Heian vernacular literature, helped by the invention of kana, has been celebrated as the revival of native culture, announcing the maturation of Japanese language and literature, which had been overwhelmed by the influence of continental culture. It is believed that women, precisely because they were outside the privileged Chinese cultural and literary domain, played a major role in this development.

This narrative has as its background the perceived saturation of Chinese writing among aristocratic men by the early Heian period. For male courtiers, Chinese was the primary medium of writing, and determining exactly what should be considered "native" versus "foreign" in what they wrote is fraught with difficulties. If some of the Chinese prose and poetry composed by Heian courtiers was written with the expectation that they would be "read" as a kundoku discourse, why should they not be counted among Japanese texts?[46] The masculine sphere of writing is full of obvious hybridization—Japanized Chinese texts and sinified Japanese texts—in which the lexicons, word order, and rhetorical forms of the two keep mixing with each other. This is not an environment in which direct and transparent transcription of spoken Japanese can be easily imagined. Orthodox literary history portrays the Japanese language as initially overshadowed by the prestige of Chinese but gradually growing into a sophisticated literary tradition shaped by both continental and indigenous influences. But where can we locate the essence of Japanese language that persists through such transformation and evolution?

Here women and their community, supposedly sequestered from sinific influences, are invoked to prop up the autonomous identity of the Japanese language. The linguistic world of court women is imagined to be monolingual. The mother tongue, the only language they knew, was written in kana, which was the only means of writing they were fully allowed to use. Modern renditions of Heian literary history have turned to women in order to sort out the linguistic mélange; the alleged prohibition against women's reading and writing of Chinese helps ground the foreignness of mana/Chinese and the nativeness of kana/Japanese. Historians and literary scholars imagine the process by which Japanese women achieved literacy in kana in order to posit a native language evolving through time. Women's supposed exclusion from Chinese is transformed into an asset in the history of Japanese language and literature.

At the same time, we need to note that such a construction of history that foregrounds women's linguistic and literary legacies does not object to what it sees as asymmetrical power relations between men and women in Heian society. The focus of its critical attention is placed not on the denial of women's access to socially privileged forms of knowledge but on Heian court society's deviation from its own national identity. Fashioning women as the figure of native-self serves as a tactic for reducing Heian society to the binary of Japanese versus Chinese, positing the latter as a foreign other. The imposition of native-foreign dualism as a frame for understanding Heian culture and society is naturalized by conflating this structure with the gendered alignment of writing styles articulated in Heian texts. The difference between the male and female modes of writing, in turn, is defined as a rigid, mutually exclusive division by overlaying the modern conception of national language on it.

The idealization of women's alleged ignorance of Chinese—in the existing version of Heian literary history—is a typical strategy of cultural politics in modernity. The margin (women and their writings) is exploited in order to reconfigure the center at an alternative site but *not* to question the existence of the exclusionary center and its hierarchical order. The seemingly inclusive gesture of valorizing the marginal reinforces the monolithic and hierarchical construction of Japanese culture and history. Conventional Heian literary history sought to restore and validate not so much women's voices or their lost writing but the national language projected on them. We need to note that the conversion of female/feminine inferiority into superiority from the historical vantage point does not necessarily affirm women's agency and may even invoke misogynistic gender stereotypes. The construction of women as the mouthpiece of the timeless linguistic essence of the nation assigns them a passive rather than an active role. It is, in part, because women and their community prior to the mid-Heian period are "voiceless" (very few substantial traces of their writing have survived) that they offer a convenient site for inscribing an imaginary national past.

That orthodox Heian literary history ultimately constructed a masculine rather than a feminine national subject can be seen in the significance it has traditionally accorded to *Tosa nikki*. Particularly in early kokubungaku scholarship, Ki no Tsurayuki was often treated as a cultural hero because he was perceived to be a man who condescended to speak as a woman for the cause of national literature. Even in the postwar kokubungaku discourse, which toned down the idolization of Tsurayuki, his perceived historical function remained largely unchallenged. He was consistently cast as the first genuinely self-conscious and historical subject of national/kana literary discourse because he *chose* to write (especially the prose narrative) in the mother tongue. This subjectivity is denied to the anonymous Heian women who were supposedly forced into vernacular language and kana writing. Thus it was up to Tsurayuki to give voice to the women whose words remained outside the history. As has been observed in feminist criticism of modern nationalism, women are "typically constructed as symbolic bearers of the nation, but are denied any direct relation to national agency."[47] We have already seen in the analysis of Meiji kokubungaku the process through which women and the feminine are divorced from historical agency under the framework of national literary history. The adoption of a feminine voice by a masculine discursive subject (such as Tsurayuki), imagined as an inaugural event in the history of vernacular prose literature, mirrors the maneuver through which modern scholarship has recuperated Heian women's linguistic practices as the timeless vessel of native language. Tsurayuki's female impersonation as construed by kokubungaku complements the discipline's own gesture of nationalizing Heian kana texts via the feminization of native language and literature.

Despite the association of women with the rise of vernacular literature, not only *Tosa nikki* but the other two representative early kana texts of unknown authorship—*Ise monogatari* and *Taketori monogatari*—are assumed to have been written by men. In other words, the discipline posits masculine agency at the critical juncture when Japanese language emerged on the stage of history as a literate discourse. Once again, overcoming the "lack" embodied by women and the feminine serves as a catalyst for the emergence of the national subject. Heian women writers and their work enter the historical stage only by following the male writers who crossed the gendered division of writing. Heian texts by women are placed between the legacy of their male forefathers' pioneering works and echoes of the unselfconscious and natural discourse of anonymous women whose vanished voices and writings constitute the prehistory of kana literature. As one may imagine from such a pedigree, writing by Heian women is all too often read through essentialized notions of gender attributes and gendered divisions of labor.

This is not to say that such perspectives on Heian women's writing have gone unchallenged. Particularly in recent years, we have seen an increasing number of studies that question existing interpretations of Heian literature by women. More and more scholars are paying attention to the sophisticated and innovative strategies of texts written by Heian women, the texts' self-conscious construction of gender difference, and their representation of women's complicated negotiations with power.[48] Yet even this new crop of scholarship pays little critical attention to the received notion of a gendered division of language in Heian aristocratic society or the alignment of kana, native language, and feminine writing in Heian literary history.[49] In this chapter, I have tried to question the appearance of neutrality in some of these views by pointing out their modern, national frame of reference and its attendant sexist assumptions. I wished thereby to identify the modern gender ideology operating not only in the analysis of Heian writings by women but in some of the basic categories and historical frameworks through which we approach women's literary practices of the period.[50]

CHAPTER FOUR

Politics and Poetics in *The Tale of Genji*

In chapter 1, I examined the ways in which eighteenth-century poetics established some of the major paradigms for the study of Heian literature that continue to resonate in the modern scholarship. In particular, Motoori Norinaga's notion of mono no aware remains one of the best-known terms of pre-nineteenth-century literary criticism. It was through his study of *The Tale of Genji* that the concept of mono no aware was developed, posited as the essence not only of this tale but of poetry in general. The theory and practice of poetry have played central roles in the scholarship on *The Tale of Genji* from earliest stages in the history of its reception. As early as the late Heian period, scenes and poems from the text were frequently alluded to by poets and the *Genji* was a required text for serious students of waka.[1] Norinaga took this link to a new level of theoretical elaboration. His analyses of the text from the point of view of poetics continue to shape the modern understanding not only of the *Genji* but of Heian kana literature as a whole. To this day, the world of Heian literature is often imagined through the popularized understanding of mono no aware—the realm of aesthetic communion in which refined men and women of the Heian court express their deeply felt longing, sadness, and passion through the exchange of elegant and artful poetry. Needless to say, such a perception of the *Genji* both shaped and has been shaped by the feminization of Heian literature.

In the postwar period, some scholars, particularly those affili-ated with the so-called, *rekishi shakaigakuha* (sociohistorical criticism school) began to call into question the powerful influence of mono no aware in the study of the *Genji* and Heian literature. The compari-son between Norinaga's poeticization of the *Genji* and the postwar criticism that challenged the identification of the text with mono no aware highlights the difference in their approaches. It reveals, more-over, their distinct understanding of poetic language, the role it plays in human relations, and the nature of human desire and agency ex-pressed through poetic composition or exchange. This chapter ex-amines the construction of poetry and its function in *The Tale of Genji* in light of these positions. My aim is threefold. First, I ques-tion the relevance of studying the *Genji* through the modern distinc-tions made between what is and what is not poetry—especially the generic division between poetry and prose—by studying the complex interplay between poetic discourse and narration in the text. I also consider a variety of assumptions underlying the conceptualization of literature that insist upon such a distinction. Second, I investigate the complexity of interpersonal relations staged through lovers' poetic exchanges in the text that undermines both the vision of aesthetic community suggested by Norinaga and the ideal of dyadic union be-tween individuals (I and You) envisaged by the modern/romantic notion of lyric poetry upheld in the revisionist approach. Finally, I analyze the manner in which the interplay between poetry and ro-mance in the *Genji* articulates the tension between lovers that under-mines both the poetic and romantic ideals. I argue that the differential positions of lovers/poets based on their gender play a crucial role in the text's construction of love and lovers' poetic dialogue. I suggest that the revisionist criticism sought to displace the poetry-centered approach to *Genji* in order to enable more "political" (in the broad-est sense of the contestation as well as negotiation among differen-tial interests) reading of the *Genji*. Nevertheless, their understanding of literary discourses through strict generic differentiation and their notion of agency centered on a liberal, individualistic model of subject prevented them from recognizing social tension and conflicts articulated through the text's construction of poetry/romance. This also directs our attention to the points at which their perspectives prove inadequate for the discussion of gender relations in the text.

The Poeticization of *The Tale of Genji*

According to Motoori Norinaga, there is no essential difference between poetry and *monogatari* ("tales" in general but especially the *Genji*): "There is nothing in the poetic Way that is not covered in this monogatari [the *Genji*] and there is nothing in this monogatari that is not encompassed by the poetic Way" (*Shibun yōryō*, 4:99).[2] The ultimate unity of poetry and monogatari is assured by their common basis in mono no aware, the central concept in Norinaga's poetics: "Poetry arises from knowing mono no aware and mono no aware is known by reading poetry. The monogatari [the *Genji*], too, is written from knowing mono no aware, and one learns much about mono no aware by reading this monogatari. Thus the true meaning of poetry and monogatari are the same" (4:100). Mono no aware refers to a profound feeling with which one spontaneously responds to a myriad of things and occurrences in the world. To "know mono no aware," which is the aesthetic faculty that Norinaga advocated, refers to one's ability to have such a feeling for certain objects on an appropriate occasion (*Genji monogatari tama no ogushi*, 4:202; henceforth, *Tama no ogushi*). This capacity to experience mono no aware is intimately related to literary production and reception. Norinaga argues that when one is deeply moved, one cannot bear to keep this experience to oneself. Reciting or composing a poem (as well as writing monogatari) is the "natural" outcome of the need to find an outlet for one's emotions. One's pent-up feelings are further relieved when a poem or a monogatari reaches and deeply moves others (*Tama no ogushi*, 4:190).[3]

For Norinaga, waka (or *uta* [song], as he referred to it) not so much represents mono no aware as *enacts* it. As I discussed earlier, this performative rather than referential understanding of poetic discourse is a cornerstone of Norinaga's thought. He explains that the *aware* of things, like a sigh, is a spontaneous response, and waka is the most exemplary discourse of mono no aware because it epitomizes the performative exercise of language. Naoki Sakai writes that "as we have observed in Motoori's conception of mono no aware (meaningfulness of mono), feeling thus concretized was not a product or remnant of some prior psychological occurrence. Song was not a product but a process of production, not an enunciated but an enunciation. Therefore, it was supposed that direct involvement in and immediate adherence to the performative situation should be guaranteed in it."[4] In Norinaga's poetics, therefore, one's experience of an object, a discourse on this experience, and communication of this discourse to others are organically linked in a seamless and dynamic continuum.

That mono no aware is understood as a *process* of signification rather than a static signified distinguishes Norinaga's poetics from simple expressivism. The composition of waka apprehended as a performative act figures the simultaneity of the experience (content) and representation (form) rather than the subordination of one to the other. Monogatari and poetry are indistinguishable, not because they share a certain content or form but because essentially they are both performative processes in this sense.

Norinaga's poetics further departs from expressivism in its endorsement of the highly conventionalized and conservative style of poetic composition practiced by Nijō school.[5] He argues that mono no aware does not take arbitrary shape, since one's feelings, if authentic, would be exteriorized in an appropriate form. A strong emotion seeks its outlet not in ordinary words but in special poetic diction and style (*Isonokami sasamegoto*, 2:108–13, 174). Since one inevitably wishes to communicate such a feeling, he or she will choose beautiful words and employ rhetorical techniques in order to attract and engage others. Thus, mono no aware is expressed and conveyed "naturally" in elegantly formed poetry. This conflation of formalism and expressivism or union between *kokoro* (meaning) and *kotoba* (word) appears to place Norinaga's thought in the lineage of classic waka poetics, which can be traced all the way back to the Kana Preface of *Kokinwakashū*.[6] What is distinct in Norinaga's poetics, however, is his awareness of the profound tension that may obtain between the form and content in human discourse. This is all the more reason why he defines the essence of waka as the coincidence of formal regularity and authentic emotion, privileging poetry as the most ideal exercise of language.

While waka is by definition a perfect harmony of meaning and words, some dissonance may occur between them when the language itself becomes corrupted. Norinaga believed that he lived in an age of woeful linguistic degeneration that had strayed from the original purity of the native language. In other words, he sees the tension between form and content as a perversion of his time. His contemporaries, therefore, could not rely solely on their linguistic and poetic intuition to compose true poetry.[7] Norinaga viewed the Heian aristocratic society in which the foundation of classic waka was laid in stark contrast to his contemporary world—a site where mono no aware functioned perfectly and permeated daily life. In order to experience mono no aware, therefore, Norinaga promotes the study not only of classical mid-Heian poetry but of its "context" as depicted in the *Genji*. The *Genji* plays a crucial role in Norinaga's elaboration of poetics into sociocultural theory because it provides a rich source for envisioning the symbiotic relations between the ideal society bound by communal empathy, on the one hand, and pure, authentic language on the other.

Despite his idealization of the world of Heian aristocrats, Norinaga does not argue that *The Tale of Genji* presents a world without conflict. The characters constantly collide with the constraints of social regulations, but in portraying their emotional struggles the text privileges the power of their feelings. According to Norinaga, all systems of thought are ultimately based on *ninjō* (human sentiments) but didactic doctrines such as Buddhism and Confucianism attempt to censure what they consider to be bad sentiments and promote good ones (*Shibun yōryō*, 4:39). In contrast, genuine poetry and monogatari focus on the feelings themselves, without discriminating between them on the basis of moral standards. Love (forbidden love in particular) has much prominence in the *Genji*, not because the text advocates illicit amorous adventures—as its detractors claim—but because it is interested in the depth of feeling generated under these circumstances. The dilemmas that lovers suffer are not significant in themselves—they are props for staging a situation that displays mono no aware at its height. Furthermore, Norinaga associates depth of feeling with torment and pathos; in his view, sorrow over forbidden and repressed desires is more powerful than joy and happiness and better suited to producing moving poems and monogatari.

Thus, Norinaga attributes to the *Genji* both the expression and a profound understanding of mono no aware. In his commentary of the

Genji, Genji monogatari tama no ogushi, Norinaga presents a lengthy analysis of the "Firefly" (Hotaru) chapter's discussion of monogatari, illustrating the text's self-conscious evocation of mono no aware.[8] He identifies in the *Genji* not only a narrative context for the ideal poetic utterance but a metadiscourse that elucidates the nature of monogatari as a literary form that draws on and generates mono no aware.

Sociohistorical Criticism

Despite *Genji*'s long-standing reputation for poetic sensibility, the poems in the text have not garnered much admiration throughout its history. Motoori Norinaga gives high marks to the text's poems, but this is an exception among the generally lukewarm assessments of other commentators and critics.[9] Masuda Katsumi's essay "Waka to seikatsu" (Waka and daily life), first published in 1954, probes the alleged mediocrity of the poems in the text and casts them in a new light. Although Masuda does not directly refer to Norinaga's study of the text, his central thesis — that poetry in the *Genji* is "unpoetic" — clearly challenges the poeticization of the text advocated by Norinaga. Elsewhere, Masuda identifies the principal feature of postwar scholarship on the *Genji* as the effort to liberate the text from mono no aware.[10] As examples of scholarship that have advanced such a goal, he points to the work of scholars affiliated with sociohistorical criticism, a movement of which Masuda himself was one of the leading proponents. In order to situate "Waka and Daily Life" in the broader critical trend of postwar kokubungaku, I would like to take a moment to outline some of the features and agendas of sociohistorical criticism. This will help us understand the social and political ramifications of the arguments that Masuda makes in the essay, including his insistence on a strict differentiation between poetry and prose, his antagonism toward the conventionality of mid-Heian poetry, and his impatience with lovers' poetic dialogues in the *Genji*.

In chapter 2, I discussed the ways in which Norinaga's notion of mono no aware was appropriated into kokubungaku as a theory of emotional realism while glossing over some of its subversive implications. The postwar challenge to the influence of mono no aware in the study of the *Genji* and Heian literature signaled a revolt against the orthodoxy of kokubungaku. Sociohistorical criticism, which was

promoted by a group of Marxist historians and literary scholars, produced some of the most innovative scholarship on premodern Japanese literature and history during the first phase of the postwar period
—from the mid-1940s to the mid-1950s. In the field of literary studies,
its adherents openly called for reform of the kokubungaku status quo.
They were critical of the discipline, which during the war had passively
and in many cases actively supported the use of literary tradition to
promote nationalist propaganda centered around the cult of the emperor and militarism. Their emphasis on history stemmed not only
from the influence of Marxist historical materialism but from a reaction against the manner in which the wartime emperor ideology and
state censorship had severely hampered serious inquiries into the early
history of Japan. They also expressed alarm at the unfolding policies
of the Japanese state, under the aegis of the Allied Occupation, which
sought to rehabilitate the emperor system as a cultural and symbolic
rather than political institution, complementary to the pro-America,
prodemocracy postwar order. Thus, sociohistorical criticism explored
in premodern texts the traces of history that undermine the official
mythos of modern Japan—the unbroken and tension-free history of
the imperial dynasty—which persisted in the postwar emperor ideology. In particular, they sought to reclaim the genuine history of the
nation as the history of *minzoku* (folk), including accounts of their
social, political, and cultural resistance to oppression (especially by
the state), hence shedding light on the tension and contradictions that
official versions of history had suppressed. In sociohistorical criticism,
the Marxist orientation coexisted with a strong nationalistic impetus,
seeking to reconstitute the national subject of history in opposition to
the official, state institutions. As one might expect, then, it inherited
much of the nationalizing and modernizing conceptual apparatus of
kokubungaku even as it sought to contest the disciplinary orthodoxy.

Through the study of premodern history and society, the sociohistorical critics participated in wide-ranging discussions on democratization during the early postwar period—especially the debate over
how to envision a political subject adequate to the task of resisting
authoritarian rule (or popular complicity with it) and enact genuine
democratic revolution.[11] It was believed that the national past recon-
structed from premodern literary texts offered important insights into
these urgent political questions. Thus, they eschewed the determinis-

tic binary between the base and superstructure that relegates literature to secondary status. In other words, they were skeptical of a historical analysis of literature that reduced literary texts to a mere *hanei* (reflection) of political-economic history.

In this context, Saigō Nobutsuna, a leading premodern literary scholar of sociohistorical criticism proposed to examine literary history through the permutation of genres—the rise and fall of individual genres as well as intersections and tensions among coexisting ones.[12] Such a generic history was deemed autonomous yet indissociably linked to broader sociohistorical transformations, offering a historiographical framework intrinsic to literary studies. The perspective of generic history led scholars such as Saigō and Masuda to view the Heian period in terms of the ascent of *sanbun* (prose narrative). In a seminal article on Heian literary history, "Kyūtei joryū bungaku no mondai," published in 1949, Saigō questions the conventional association of the rise of Heian kana narratives with the cultural splendor of mid-Heian court society, which was controlled by the northern branch of the Fujiwara clan.[13] Instead he links the emergence of the prose genre with writers who were marginalized by the gradual domination of court politics by the Fujiwaras. In particular, Saigō points to the traditional attribution of early kana narratives—including *Taketori Monogatari, Utsuho Monogatari,* and *Ochikubo Monogatari*—to a scholar of Chinese letters, Minamoto no Shitago'o, and speculates that the writers of these tales were in fact men similar to Shitago'o. In other words, they were middle-ranking literati of an aristocratic society (or, as Saigō puts it, the intellectuals of a disintegrating ancient society), whose specialized training centered on Chinese learning had become obsolete with the breakdown of the *ritsuryō* regime (a centralized legal, bureaucratic, and administrative system modeled on the Sui and T'ang dynasties in China). At the same time, by the Heian period the aristocracy had been detached from the archaic sociopolitical and economic organization centered on regionally based clan organization. A majority of the middle- and low-ranking aristocrats could do little but become parasites in the capital, fawning over the powerful aristocratic families that presided over the court. Heian kana tales convey the deep discontent in the aristocratic society wrought by the central contradiction of the Heian period—the ways in which the Fujiwaras' ascent to uncontested supremacy eroded the very sociopolitical and economic order upon which the aristocracy rested. According to Saigō, the literati drew on their intellectual and literary facilities, fostered by the study of Chinese letters, to obliquely air such discontent via kana fiction.[14] In other words, kana narrative was developed by injecting Chinese learning into kana/Japanese forms as a new means of critiquing the existing order.[15]

Saigō points out three major historical factors that contributed to the rise of kana literature by women. First, many Heian female writers, including Murasaki Shikibu and Seishōnagon, were daughters and wives of middle-ranking literati. Their writings therefore drew on perspectives and interests rooted in backgrounds shared with middle-ranking male literati. Second, their literary consciousness was further stimulated by the predicament of women living in the final phase of the breakdown of the ancient (more gender egalitarian) society and the attendant erosion of women's power and status. Last, women and their communities, unlike men, who were saturated with continental culture, kept alive some elements of native folk culture, which enabled their writings. Here we may note that Saigō's folk nationalism subscribes to the ghettoization of Heian women as the vessel of native culture that we saw in more mainstream kokubungaku discourses.

Throughout these discussions, Saigō calls attention to the multiple currents that fed the rise of sophisticated kana literature, which culminated in the *Genji*. Even though he admits that the dominant motif of the *Genji* may be found in the lyrical and emotive sensibility invoked in the theory of mono no aware, he points to the meticulous composition of its narrative universe, which is far more complex than those of earlier poetic narratives such as *Ise monogatari*. Saigō's account of Heian literary history, partly inspired by the work of the historian Ishimoda Shō, became an influential model for his and subsequent generations of scholars, including Masuda. It offered powerful stimuli, especially for those who sought to explore the social and political significance of Heian kana literature against its conventional romanticized image.[16]

The works of Saigō and others in sociohistorical criticism were significant attempts to analyze women's literary production in relation to the social, political, and economic transformations of the mid-Heian period. We still have much to learn from their suggestion that we pay attention to the internal contradictions and tensions of Heian aristocratic society in analyzing kana narratives. At the same time, the way in which Saigō politicizes Heian literary history by singling out "prose" as the genuine vehicle of critical/political consciousness in Heian literature needs to be questioned. The manner in which he describes the development of prose narrative replicates the evolutionary trajectory from poetry/song to prose (novel) laid out in the modernizing accounts of genre upheld by traditional kokubungaku. Moreover, the politicization of Heian texts written by women is identified primarily in relation to their social status and intellectual resources, which were defined by their male kin. While he does mention the conditions more particular to women's experience, these are eclipsed by his emphasis on the "class interest" of the middle-ranking aristocracy as the catalyst of Heian kana literature. At any rate, his notions of the specificity of Heian women's sociocultural conditions, which turn on the romantic vision of gender equality in archaic Japan or women's supposed proximity to native folk culture, are also highly problematic. Despite his critique of the kokubungaku orthodoxy and his attempt to shed light on the oppositional history of the people, he reproduces the established pattern of national history in which women and their practices become historical only when they are subordinated to the broader national/masculine frame. Bearing these issues in mind, we now return to Masuda's essay.

The Poetic and the Prosaic

As mentioned earlier, in "Waka and Daily Life" Masuda takes the extreme position of condemning the poetry in the *Genji* as not just mediocre but outright "unpoetic." Masuda claims that the prevalence of poetry in the everyday lives of Heian aristocrats gave waka a peculiar status of poetic expression that was at the same time essentially "prosaic."[17] Pointing to the conversational function of poetic exchange in the *Genji*, he equates *conversational* with that which is not genuinely poetic. He argues that poetic exchanges in the texts, "are ritualized conversations. In many cases, they do not possess lyricism unique to themselves because they are not outflows of characters' lived emotions but are fragments of rituals that have blended into everyday life."[18] He thus questions the status of waka in the text as the authentic expression of emotion. While for Norinaga the *Genji* is essentially poetic, for

Masuda the text's poetry is ultimately prosaic, adding nothing to the text that is not provided by the prose: "If the poems had expressed internal emotions with the urgency and immediacy of the best poems in *Man'yōshū* or with the sophisticated symbolism of representative poems in *Shinkokinshū*, the role of poetry in the text might have been different. . . . The flat lyricism of mid-Heian waka armed with shallow metaphors was unable to carry an autonomous force within the text."[19] Masuda evaluates the poems in the *Genji* against the general background of the mid-Heian period in which waka, under the influence of *Kokinwakashū* became increasingly codified and conventionalized. As waka secured its status as a popular literary form at the court, Heian aristocrats composed, recited, and exchanged poems in a variety of formal and informal settings. They mastered and internalized stock images and diction, displaying their cultural refinement by means of their familiarity with poetic conventions and traditional literary allusions. With its brief, formalized structure and increasingly strict regulations, waka lent itself to extemporaneous composition as called for on social occasions. Most important in the context of monogatari, which typically string together episodes of amorous adventures, waka played a crucial role in romantic courtship. The Heian tales depict how the exchange of poems served as the primary means of communication between lovers, and skill in composing poetry was considered a crucial attribute of a desirable lover. For a monogatari depicting the lives and romances of Heian aristocrats, therefore, the exchange of waka by their characters was indispensable.

For Masuda, poetry in the *Genji* exemplifies mid-Heian waka, which, in his view, had degenerated into a form of empty social ritual shaped by the formulas of an ossified poetic tradition. He argues that the conventionality of the poems turned them into encoded messages through which the writers conveyed their repressed emotions, which could be mechanically decoded by the addressees as well as the readers.[20] Masuda deems the waka in the text to be lacking in individuality, failing to express the unique attributes of poets/characters.[21] He dismisses them as stagnant literature enslaved by conventionality, a medium of banality and conformism rather than of communal empathic resonance. The poetic practices of Heian aristocrats therefore do not constitute a utopia of collective poetic sensitivity but a lyric wasteland where poetry has slipped into tired cliché. Poetry tamed by the standardized language and worn out by its currency in social exchange cannot serve as a means of communication between passionate lovers defying social censure. According to Masuda, the lovers in the *Genji* turn to waka hoping to break through the constraints of the ordinary world and give expression to their prohibited desire. But the mid-Heian poetic discourse designed to reinforce communal bonding betrays the lovers, falling short of liberating them from societal norms.[22] He defends his argument by pointing out the absence of waka at those critical moments in the plot when the characters, driven by their passion, actually engage in transgressive acts.

It is easy to detect the standard ideological line of sociohistorical criticism (and the early postwar Left) in Masuda's repudiation of the communalism or anti-individual tendencies of mid-Heian waka, codified under the conventions established by the imperial anthology. Furthermore, Masuda seems to brand formalism, conventionalism, and social utility as qualities antithetical to poetry. Roman Jakobson's classic definition of poetic function in language may help us put Masuda's assumptions (which were clearly influenced by the post-Romantic construction of poetry) into a sharper focus. Jakobson identifies six constitutive factors in speech (addresser, addressee, context, code, contact, and message) with six respective functions (emotive, conative, referential, metalingual, phatic, and poetic).[23] According to this scheme, lyric poetry is characterized by the dominant poetic function (focused on the message for its own sake) coupled with the emotive function (focused on the addresser and aimed at a direct expression of the speaker's attitude). For Masuda, the poems in the *Genji* deviate from the definition of pure lyricism by mixing in other functions: referential in their relation to the plot, phatic in their evocation of poetic exchanges as a social custom, conative in their utility as a means of affecting the addressee, and even implicitly metalingual in the sense that they constantly refer to the conventionally determined codes of waka. Yet, Jakobson himself states that a message always fulfills more than a single purpose. Speech acts are classified into the six genres not to mark exclusive distinctions but to indicate the relative difference in the emphasis they place on certain functions over othes.[24] These generic categories, in other words, are constituted in differential relations to each other. Roland Barthes suggests, moreover, that in approaching classical literary discourses we need to imagine radically contiguous relations among discursive modes we tend to differentiate into separate genres: "Classical language is always reducible to a pervasive continuum, it postulates the possibility of dialogue. . . . There is no genre, no written work of classicism which does not suppose a collective consumption, akin to speech, classical literary art is an object which circulates among several persons brought together on a class basis; it is a product conceived for oral transmission, for a consumption regulated by the contingencies of society: it is essentially a spoken language, in spite of its strict codification."[25]

Masuda, who assumes that there exists an absolute, transcendent criterion of poetic language, neglects to identify a context in which the poems in the *Genji* are judged more or less "unpoetic." For instance, the specific manner in which the *Genji* uses waka may be measured by comparing the text with earlier Heian monogatari. In *Taketori monogatari*, poetic exchanges among characters are condensed and versified dialogues that carry information crucial to plot development.[26] In the *Genji*, on the other hand, we find practically no new information overtly presented in waka that makes them indispensable to the storytelling. This very redundancy of poetry to narration itself suggests that poems perform a role distinct from that of prose. That the text underplays the referential function of waka is also suggested by the fact that while the narrator occasionally summarizes the characters' letters and spoken dialogues she never treats waka in such a manner.[27] Waka, in other words, is a discourse that is never paraphrased.

In *Utsuho monogatari* (believed to have been written in the early tenth century), which has a greater proportion of poetry to prose than does the *Genji*, the poetic exchanges closely document the process of courtship and other forms of social intercourse. There we find scenes of formal or informal gathering containing a long series of poems composed by the participants. In the *Genji*, however, even when the text presents poems recited at social events, the narrator usually cites only a few, mentioning the existence of others without actually quoting them.[28] Rather than simply reproducing the ways in which waka circulated in Heian society as a medium of social interaction, the *Genji* presents them in a highly selective manner—they are sparsely inserted primarily in the context of intimate interpersonal interactions with highly charged emotions (particularly among lovers). Whether it is justifiable to say that poems in the *Genji* are "more prosaic" than those in *Man'yōshū* or *Shinkokinshū*, it remains that the texts' use of waka seems to attribute specific functions to it.

The poems in the *Genji*, to the extent that they are all attributed to the characters, are part of characterological discourse. Yet they clearly stand apart from other types of characterological discourses, for one thing by their formal features. The text seems to further emphasize the distinct status of waka by various other means. One passage, taken from the "Sacred Tree" (Sakaki) chapter, depicts the hero, Genji, and his dangerous liaison with Oborozukiyo (she is the sister of his political enemy).

> Dawn seemed to be approaching. Genji suddenly heard a loud voice at an earshot, "Reporting to duty of the guardsman's shift!" Genji listened [thinking], "There must be an officer in charge of the shift hiding in one of the ladies' quarters around here and this fellow was sent to surprise him." He was both amused and irritated. The guardsman kept poking around here and there saying, "The first hour of the tiger!" As she plaintively recited a verse,

> > I see that it is my own heart that makes my sleeves wet with tears, as the herald of night's closing makes me think of your love's ending.

> Oborozukiyo's melancholic look was ravishing. [Genji replied:]

> > Is it your wish that I spend my life in misery without a break? Though the night is closing my sorrow will have no end. (2:97–98; S:195)[29]

The first waka recited by Oborozukiyo is nested within the narration —as utterances by characters usually are. Her poem is tightly woven into the narration at the semantic level as well, serving to illustrate the sadness casting a shadow over her that the narrator describes. Genji's waka, on the other hand, is notable for its clear break from the continuity of the prose. Although supposedly recited, the verse does not accompany such verbal references, and the speaker, Genji, is suggested merely by the context. The special treatment of Genji's waka may be understood through the nature of his role in the scene. Narrative attention is clearly centered on Genji as it both analyzes him and locks into his thoughts and perceptions. The atmosphere of suspense central to the plot is also focused on Genji. This section opens with a reference to the changing political climate following the death of the retired emperor Kiritsubo (Genji's father) and the ascendancy of Genji's political rivals. The scene, therefore, takes place with the understanding that Genji's relationship with Oborozukiyo is becoming more risky than ever. Furthermore, the incident with the guard alludes to the fact that Genji is a captain of the imperial guard, and it is his responsibility to supervise the shift.[30] Thus, even though he quickly realizes that a prank is being targeted not at him but at another prowling lover visiting a lady's quarters, he is annoyed by the voice, which gives him a jolt. Oborozukiyo's waka is framed by narration precisely because of the centrality of Genji in this scene; her recitation of waka is integrated into his impressions of and feelings about her. The lapse in narration between the phrase "Oborozukiyo's melancholic look was ravishing" and Genji's waka suggests the retreat of narrating register. The narrating voice is muted during the unspecified moment of silence before Genji's recitation of his waka because the scene is constructed from his perspective.

We may observe another way in which the text sets up poetry as a crucial counterpoint to narration in a passage from the "Festival of the Cherry Blossoms" (Hana no en) chapter. The scene depicts Empress Fujitsubo's torment over her secret affair with Genji as she watches his exquisite dance at the Festival of the Cherry Blossoms at court (Fujitsubo entered the court of Genji's father, Emperor Kiritsubo, and quickly became his favorite consort, subsequently ascending to the rank of empress).

> Fujitsubo could not help but reflect how painful it is that she is so attracted to Genji.

> "If only I could see this cherry blossom as others see it . . . I would not have even a dewdrop of unease."

> I do not know how we have come to know this poem composed in her mind. (1:425; S:151)

Again the narration breaks at the poem composed by Fujitsubo. Furthermore, the narrator here suddenly assumes a highly limited scope of knowledge vis-à-vis the diegetic world—in the narrational intrusion following the waka, she claims to be ignorant of the circumstance in which the poem was transmitted. The comment, which distances the waka from the narrator, endows the poem with authority as a "real" discourse of the character.

Positing poetry as the most authentic expression of the characters and setting it aside from the prose is an effective yet risky literary device. It exposes the authenticity of fictional characters to severe scrutiny because the text cannot describe the courtly elegance and sensibilities of the characters but must *perform* them through their poetry. The text's awareness of this danger is evident in narrational comments that occasionally accompany the poems, apparently designed to deflect the reader's criticism or skepticism. For instance, the narrator may explain why the poems may not quite live up to the idealized image of the characters and the aesthetic perfection that the scene may seem to call for. Sometimes the narration criticizes a poem in advance, as if to preempt readers' questions as to whether the waka holds up to their expectations of heroes and heroines.

The Poetic Ideal and Fractured Dialogues

The *Genji*'s treatment of the relationship between poetry and prose, foregrounding the distinct properties and conventions of poetic form, further explains the text's importance for Motoori Norinaga. I have already suggested that Norinaga urged his contemporaries to study the *Genji* not only because the text presents a rich account of Heian life permeated by mono no aware, but because it offers a metadiscourse on aesthetic/affective sensitivity. Norinaga's poetics finds a powerful resonance in the *Genji*, where poetry is presented as the most direct and heightened expression of the characters and their feelings. Yet we must note that the means by which the text achieves this effect — putting poetry and prose in a complex relation to each other — is foreign to Norinaga's poetics, where the formal difference between monogatari and uta is dissolved into an indivisible performative effect of mono no aware. It is precisely by not being completely immersed in poetic discourse that *Genji* articulates the aesthetic ideal of waka with the critical awareness that inspired Norinaga.

I contend, moreover, that the text's construction of poetry goes beyond mere reflection and amplification of mid-Heian waka poetics on which Norinaga draws. While investing characters' poetic discourses with the sense of immediacy unattainable in narration, the text demonstrates the manner in which waka may also fall short of the ideal established by the tradition. Masuda's analysis of *Genji*'s poetry is provocative despite its shortcomings because he highlights a certain tension in the text's treatment of poetry. As Masuda points out, it is in the lovers' exchange of waka that the failure of poetic discourse comes most forcefully to the surface.

The following scene takes place between Genji and Fujitsubo, the object of his forbidden passion. The text up to this point has only been hinting at Genji's desire for an unattainable love, without revealing her identity. The text then abruptly turns to a nocturnal liaison between them, informing the readers that this is not the first time they are meeting in secret. The text refrains from giving much detail concerning their night together, simply commenting that it occurred so unexpectedly that it did not seem to be happening in reality. Only when the arrival of dawn draws Genji out of his delirious passion does the text close in on the characters and depict a poetic exchange between them. Frustrated by his inability to pour his mind out to his lover and lamenting the brevity of night in early summer, Genji recites a poem.

> 見てもまたあふよまれなる夢の中にやがてまぎるるわが身ともがな

> Our nights together and dreams coming true are both so rare. . . .
> Let me dissolve into this fading dream.

Fujitsubo is touched with pity as she watches him in tears. She replies,

> 世がたりに人や伝へんたぐひなくうき身を醒めぬ夢になしても

> The idle gossip of others would keep alive my rare predicament even if I were to vanish into an unwaking dream. (1:306; S:98)

Genji's waka in the exchange turns on the wordplay in the phrase *afu yo mare naru*, which means both "rare (*mare*) liaison (*au*) at night (*yo*)" and "rare (*mare*) coincidence (*afu*) in the world (*yo*)," an idiomatic expression that means "a dream becoming reality." Linked to the first *ku* (*mite mo mata*), the phrase reads, "Though I have seen you tonight, our nocturnal meetings are so rare."[31] Linked to the third ku (*yume no uchi ni*), the phrase reads, "in the rare world where a dream comes true." The multiplicity of meanings generated by the wordplay and poetic conventions conflates seeing a dream, seeing a lover, and the fulfillment of a wish (by merging dream and reality). In the first three ku of the poem, therefore, the subject identifies with the world of fiction/dream via a sound link. The poem also alludes to the traditional mythos of love and dream in which lovers separated in reality are said to meet in dreams. Genji's rhetoric rendered in prose would be something like: "To meet you is so rare, like a rare coincidence of one's dream and reality. Thus, this must be a dream and not reality. So I want to fade into this dream and not awaken from it." While the admission that he must disappear into a dream amounts to acknowledging the impossibility of their affair, it is also by virtue of establishing the unrealizability of their liaison in the waking world that Genji situates himself in the world of dream/fantasy, expanding the realm of love therein.

The way in which Fujitsubo responds to the contradictory messages of Genji's address requires careful attention. Her poem works closely with the semantic and rhetorical structure of Genji's waka, adopting the words and images—the wordplay involving yo (world/night) the sense of "rareness," and the perpetual dream. Yet, while Genji's waka is centered on the act of seeing (seeing a lover, seeing a dream), Fujitsubo introduces new elements of speech and communication (gossip and scandal). Appropriating Genji's fictional expression, she shifts the focus from personal longing and fantasy to the social effect of their affair. She undermines Genji's fiction not by disagreeing with it but by extending it, bringing the world of dream and the world of sordid gossip in contact with each other. Fujitsubo neither denies Genji's phantasmic construction of the lovers' world nor fully affirms it, displacing the question his poem poses by providing it with a new context. Her waka suggests that even if the lovers escape into a dream there will be no resolution to their suffering because their freedom will never be total. They will be kept alive and trapped in people's idle gossip, humiliated and degraded even in their absence. The poem suggests a haunting image of lovers who, like ghosts, remain arrested in the world, tormented by the consequences of their passion. While Genji's poem focuses on the dyadic relationship between the lovers, Fujitsubo's response points to their inextricable bondage to society. As in Genji's poem, the rhetoric of Fujitsubo's waka is supported by its reference to poetic conventions. The anxiety about gossip—the intrusion of "others" into the world of lovers—is a principal theme in Heian love poetry.

The allusion to poetic convention in the lovers' exchange, therefore, may serve to both valorize and devalorize the pursuit of desire. Although each works with poetic conventions, Genji deploys the mythology of romantic union central to the waka discourse, while Fujitsubo reminds him that the tradition itself acknowledges the fragility of this union, drawing on the image of gossip as a paradigm of intrusion and obstacles forever plaguing lovers. She thereby refracts Genji's proposal for total identification with the fantasy of love, which amounts to social suicide. The gendered nuances of the difference between Genji's and Fujitsubo's stances and their manipulation of poetic codes are examined later. Here it will suffice to point out how the dynamics of exchange turns not simply on continuity and correspondence but on disruption and displacement of words and meaning. The poetic communications between lovers in the *Genji* may be fractured by a response that resists the address, undermining the effectiveness of waka as a means of constituting the lovers' phantasmic world.

The dynamics of lovers' poetic dialogue puts into question mono no aware as a framework for understanding not only the text's theme but its poetics. In the dialogic structure of exchange, poetic address is simultaneously reflected and refracted by the response—words and images of the address are taken up in the response but with their meaning and perspective shifted in directions that deflect rather than complement the address. The unity of "word" (signifier) and "meaning" (signified) intended by the addresser is rejected by the addressee, who misreads and transforms the message through the interpretation inscribed in her response. The appearance of relatedness between the poems serves as an ironic counterpoint to such disjuncture.

The possibility of poetic exchange being disrupted through the process of communication that the *Genji* suggests sheds a revealing light on Motoori Norinaga's notion of human bonding achieved through poetic affect. As we have seen, the ideal community that he envisioned is held together with pure language, of which poetic discourse is the primary paradigm. Yet the sharing of mono no aware between one person and another is a nondialogic or noninteractive process to the extent that it cannot allow any form of opacity or dissonance to intervene. According to him, through the performative process of mono no aware, the addresser activates in the addressee a shared aesthetic/emotive sensitivity. The particularity of individual utterance (the specific message, context, etc.) is eclipsed by the indivisible affective experience (mono no aware) rooted in human nature. That is to say, the "communication" of mono no aware precludes subtle negotiations that lovers in the *Genji* engage in through their poetic dialogues. Furthermore, if poetic exchanges may fracture over emotional and discursive dissonance, the locus from which the responses and addressses may be equally appreciated as deeply moving would be not that of the lover-poets themselves but that of the "third party," the readers.[32] In other words, the effect of mono no aware applies much better to the readers' response to the text than to the sentiment of the characters involved in the dialogue. Mono no aware in its purest form may be best described as the empathy of a spectator who identifies with the Other without engaging in a relation of exchange or negotiation. Thus, mono no aware calls for a social field that forecloses any attempt to sustain relations among those with divergent interests and positions—in short, a world devoid of politics. In the *Genji*, however, poetic exchanges are where the conflicts between the lovers' desires and perspectives (and, as we will consider later, the differences stemming from the social locations they occupy) find the most heightened articulation.

Here we may also consider the shortcomings of Norinaga's comparison of uta with a sigh, a metaphor that posits poetry as a nonreferential affective gesture/response. As we have seen in the *Genji's* poetic dialogues, no matter how performative a poetic discourse may be, to the extent that it is constituted in language—as a signifier that circulates in society—it may be misquoted, misinterpreted, and miscontextualized. The refractory response reveals the inevitable referentiality of poetry—poetic messages always mean *something* although the poet may not control *what* they mean. Norinaga seeks to make poetry immune to the division between intended meaning and effect or between signifier and signified by subordinating the referentiality of words to the effect of mono no aware.[33] This stance is consistent with his staunch support for the conservative styles of waka composition: the more devoid of meaning the expression is (the specific referentiality neutralized by its conventional diction and forms), the more poetic it is. Norinaga, who believes that authentic poetry and language in general are performative rather than referential, associates the conventionality of Heian poetry with liberation from meaning. But in the *Genji*, when intended meaning of poetic address is re-represented and resignified in the poetic response, the displaced intentionality of the address (the intended effect of the discursive act) awkwardly emerges as that which is neither completely immanent nor completely external to the signifying operation of poetic discourse. The question over the referentiality of poetic language that Norinaga attempts to erase intervenes into the supposedly seamless poetic communication between an addresser and addressee.

By the same token, that the refractory poetic response foregrounds the referential function of the address does not mean that utterances in poetic dialogue can be reduced to their supposed meaning, nor that they are prosaic rather than poetic and could just as easily have been rendered in prose, as Masuda contends. Masuda assumes a fundamentally instrumental definition of linguistic signs — that they are carriers of preexisting meaning. He then draws a strict division between such ordinary language and authentic poetry, which is *more* than a language, transcending the referentiality of prose. In a sense, the definitions of poetic language held by Norinaga and Masuda have a crucial point in common, for both posit poetic discourse as a pure utterance for its own sake, unadulterated by other linguistic functions, particularly the instrumentality associated with ordinary language. Yet, in direct contrast to Norinaga, for Masuda, Heian waka, bound by the strict codes of convention, is merely a banal vehicle of prosaic meaning and social rituals. From Masuda's perspective, waka with encoded meanings is prosaic (prose disguised as a poem) because he assumes that separate linguistic genres (differentiated by their forms) are reducible to each other if they mean the same thing (possessing identical content). But what would distinguish the differential function of language if not the distinct mode of signification, which cannot be reduced to the signified — that is, not only what the word supposedly means but how it makes itself intelligible, how it relates to other signs and configurations of signs? I suggest that in order to examine waka in the *Genji* through such a signifying operation we need to consider the logic behind its use of poetry — how the text assigns poetry an effect distinct from that of prose. Even if poetic language is used to cloak certain messages, as Masuda claims, the critical issue is not the meaning of the disguised message, which the text frequently rephrases in prose, but for what purpose such a mode of signification is chosen.

From this perspective, the lapse between the subjective intent of lovers-poets versus the objective effect of their poems, or the difference between the identity of waka that the text seems to "claim" versus the effect that waka actually achieves in the diegetic context, cannot be dismissed as an artistic failure and an inadequacy of the *Genji's* poetic representation. Rather, we must consider what these schisms themselves suggest, and how they contribute to the effect of the text. Furthermore, Masuda regards the inability of waka in the text to break out of norms as the sign of its failure, since authentic poetry should transcend mundane social constraints. Yet, does it really make sense to assume that poetic language may be free from conventions and regulations of communal linguistic practices? For an utterance to be meaningful, it inevitably relates (even if negatively) to the existing order of intelligibility. The property of authentic poetic language that Masuda finds lacking in the *Genji* is an ideal that is ultimately unrealizable in itself. If poetic language appears distinct and nonordinary, it is only because of differential relations set up against other forms of discourse.

Gerard Genette defines poetic language not in terms of freedom from the predicament of language itself (the arbitrary link between signifier and signified), but as the *figure* of the desire to transcend the perceived limitations and gaps (between sign and meaning or form and content) in language.[34] The divergent assessment of mid-Heian waka by Masuda and Norinaga — divided between banality and spontaneity, excess and dearth of meaning, authenticity and artificiality — is symptomatic of the different ways in which the respective critics have imagined the poetic phantasm: how poetry overcomes the limitations of its Other, ordinary language.[35] For Masuda, ideal poetic language embodies meaningfulness that exceeds that of the everyday utterances, expressing the passion and vision of a poet that defies the prosaic norm of society. For Norinaga, it is not the transcendent significance but the plenitude of performative effect that distinguishes pure poetic discourse from the corrupted language of his time. The complete displacement as well as the extreme excess of meaning that the two attribute to poetic discourse, respectively, contrast poetry with the perceived impurity and ambivalence of ordinary language.

What, then, is the status of the *Genji*'s poetic discourse, situated ambiguously between the fulfillment and failure of the poetic ideal? Why would the text stage the distinct functions of characters' poetic discourses while simultaneously undermining the ideals that confirm their uniqueness? We may recall here Masuda's observation that the poetry in the text fails to function at the very moment at which the lovers break the taboo. But we may also note that such moments are typically left unrepresented by the narration as well. And poetic discourse does take center stage the moment *after* the consummation of transgressive desire. Waka is the medium of choice for lovers parting at dawn—in the intermediary space between night and day, between the dreamlike ephemeral moment together and the waking world in which they must conceal their passion. Poetic language and convention provide lovers with the opportunity for expression and communication in a situation of impasse that inhibits ordinary speech. The address attempts to solve the dilemma of love through fictional and polysemic poetic discourse, displacing their social identities with poetic personae, actual circumstances with the traditional mythos of lovers, and the impossibility of their bond in the world with poetic communion.

A response, however, may frustrate the addresser's intention by refusing to participate fully in the poetic fantasy. It shows that the process of fictionalization (poeticization) of the situation that empowers the address may elicit the ironic response of the other. The poetic license that the address attempts to claim and exploit for its own design is used against it by a response. Precisely because poetry seems to take a greater degree of liberty than does ordinary language in its referential function, the poetic exchange highlights the question of who determines the frame of reference. Poetic dialogues with shared verbal expressions, images, and conventions register the discord between lovers not through the expression of concrete disagreements but through divergent manipulation of poetic rhetoric and forms. For instance, an alternative reality evoked in the address is nullified by the refractory response that proposes another phantasmic possibility, rendering the referential function of the address relative and impotent. What is shared in the dialogue is the space that poetry opens but cannot close—figuring the impossibility of both realizing the lovers' desire in the world and giving up that desire altogether. In the course of the interaction between the address and the response, in other words, the supposed unity and identity of poetic language are broken. By both valorizing and undermining the power of poetic discourse, the text represents the lovers' relation itself as such a dilemma. What Masuda identified as the shortcoming of poetry in the *Genji*—its inability to transcend the prosaic and constitute an autonomous world of love— is itself the fate of lovers, which the dissonance between the address and the response inscribes.

Conventions of Poetic Dialogues

This may be the place to raise a thorny question germane to our discussion not yet addressed: the relationship between poetic dialogues in the *Genji* and the powerful convention associated with the exchange of love poems in the tradition of Japanese poetry. Poetic dialogue between lovers is an ancient tradition in Japanese poetry found in the earliest records of folkloric songs. One of its most consistent norms is the gendering of addresser and addressee as a male suitor and a courted woman, respectively. Accordingly, Genji, to whom the largest number of poems is attributed in the text, is predominantly an addresser rather than an addressee of love poems. In general, female characters initiate fewer poetic exchanges than their male counterparts do.[36] The *Genji*, therefore, seems to conform to the tradition, affirming the assumption that the initiation of poetic dialogue (which suggests taking an active role in romantic courtship) is more appropriate for men than for women. That the responding woman resists, rebuffs, or questions the intention of the poetic address by a male suitor is also an established custom of poetic exchange that can be traced back to the earliest samples of such poems. This schema of gender roles evokes the paradigmatic narrative of romantic courtship in which a pursued woman coyly evades the advances of the male pursuer.

If the exchange of love poems was highly conventionalized, how seriously can we take the failure of communication in *Genji*'s poetic dialogues? In other words, shouldn't the refractory responses of the heroines be understood as an expected feminine gesture of playful flirtation? Isn't the "fracture" merely a conventionalized poetic bantering that pits one's poetic skill and wit against the other's? Here we return to the question of waka's ambivalence between cliché and emotional authenticity—its function as a medium for secret romance between a man and a woman as well as the social game of language in Heian aristocratic society. In a narrative text, however, the contextual information supplied to a poem is incomparably more dense than in other mediums in which waka may be presented.[37] In imperial anthologies of waka, for instance, the circumstances of a poem's composition and circulation are only sporadically provided in typically brief notes. In monogatari, although the anchoring of waka in the narrative context is not total—poems do retain some level of independent signification—the prose can strongly direct the interpretation of poems.[38] For example, the narrative elaboration of the affair between Fujitsubo and Genji reinforces the tone of resistance in her poetic response with a depth and force that cannot be reached by waka alone.

Let us look at the poetic exchange between these two characters during their final liaison that occurs after the death of Emperor Kiritsubo, Genji's father. Again, the text comments on Genji's stealthy appearance in Fujitsubo's quarters as an unexpected and unlikely occurrence, as if it were happening in a dream. This time, however, Fujitsubo firmly resists Genji's overtures, suddenly falling ill rather than submitting to his seduction. Genji also refuses to back off, spending the whole night in vigil beside her and refusing to leave her even at daybreak. The tense interaction between them is further heightened by suspense over the possibility that their affair will be exposed (which would precipitate a catastrophic scandal). A poetic exchange takes place just before Genji finally leaves Fujitsubo without his desire fulfilled, at the second dawn after his arrival.

> "I think I shall die," Genji said, in a burst of passion that frightened Fujitsubo, "since I cannot bear the shame of having you know that I continue to live. But dying in such a manner will create a hindrance for my salvation that will plague me beyond this life.
>
> 逢ふことのかたきを今日にかぎらずはいまいく世をか嘆きつつ経ん
>
> My love for you and the difficulty of seeing you would not end today. So how many more lives would I have to live in sorrow?
>
> My attachment would be an obstacle to your salvation as well." She sighed.

ながき世のうらみを人に残してもかつは心をあだと知ら
なむ

Even if you continue for many lives to bear a grudge against me,
may you one day learn to see your frivolous heart as your enemy.
(2:104; S:197–98)

Again Genji attempts to implicate Fujitsubo in his destructive and
self-absorbed fantasy, linking the impossible fulfillment of desire and
death. Furthermore, the phrase "the difficulty of meeting" (*afu koto no
kataki*) in Genji's poem contains the word *kataki* (難き), which means
"difficult," but it also suggests another *kataki* (敵・仇), which means,
among other things, "enemy" and "the object of one's resentment."
The ominous echo of the second word resonates with the grudge as
well as the threat conveyed in the waka, especially when considered
together with Genji's remark following the poem—that even if he dies
he will remain attached to Fujitsubo and will continue to suffer for
many incarnations, hindering not only his but her salvation. He is
hinting that their fates are linked even if she rejects him, and he will
continue to pursue her not only night after night but life after life,
even at the cost of their spiritual salvation.

Fujitsubo recognizes the hidden menace in Genji's seemingly pa-
thetic entreaty. The longing and lovesickness in Genji's waka are resignified in her poem as an expression of his *urami* (resentment) toward
her, thus reinforcing the second meaning of *kataki*. The rhetorical
force of her poem centers on the wordplay over *ada* (徒), which means
"fickle," "frivolous," or "futile." The expression evokes one of the most
typical patterns of female responses to male overtures—a rebuttal of
his appeal by accusing him of infidelity. But the narrative context indicates that Fujitsubo's sentiment is far from that of a woman coyly
complaining about a lover's fickleness. Though Genji speaks of dying,
it is Fujitsubo who lies in bed stricken, desperately struggling to resist Genji. Furthermore, the word *ada* in her poem echoes another
word, *ata*, which is a synonym of *kataki* (enemy, the object of one's
resentment) and is often rendered in the same characters used for
kataki (仇, 敵), casting Genji's proclamation of undying love as the
vengeance of a slighted lover. She obliquely exposes the hypocrisy and
selfishness in Genji's gesture of concern for their salvation, urging him
to turn his eyes inward and reflect on his own desire as his foe. Fuji-

tsubo sends a sharp exhortation to Genji while deploying the motifs of a conventionalized poetic response.³⁹ Thus, while alluding to the tradition of poetic dialogue as a sportive communal discourse of the Heian aristocracy, the text also provides a context for a much darker and conflictual interpretation of the dialogue. The *Genji* posits multiple layers of meaning in poetic utterances and suggests the ways in which each stratum is to be read. It is not as if waka is *either* a cliché *or* a genuine expression of the characters' feelings. Its effects are generated in reference to both generalized poetic conventions *and* the specificity of the context within the story-world. In short, the text manipulates the multiple ways in which waka functions in Heian society. It exploits the polysemy of poetic discourse not only at the level of individual words or rhetorical figures but at the metadiscursive level — how waka is to be read against a diversity of conventions. Masuda's strict differentiation between poetry and prose as well as Norinaga's reduction of authentic language to poetry fail to grasp the multifaceted operation of poetic discourses in the text.

Mono no Aware and a Ghostly Union

Although I have emphasized the "failure" of poetic dialogues in the *Genji*, it would be misleading to suggest that the text never presents scenes in which poems appear to reach and move others to share the sentiments of the poets. On more than a few occasions, the text elaborately stages moments of poetic resonance between characters with a highly refined sensibility unprecedented in earlier monogatari. If Norinaga's primary concern is to find in poetry the means of restoring authentic sociality (and language), the social effect of waka in the *Genji* is much more fluid. It fluctuates between unity and fracture, opacity and transparency, anonymous conventionality and singularity. The text simultaneously elaborates the affective power of poetry while using poetic exchanges to depict the failure of individuals to share their feelings. We need to probe the logic behind the ways in which the text stages the failure and success of poetic dialogues.

Scenes in which poetic exchanges seem to "work" typically occur when the potential for interpersonal conflict is muted by the powerful experience of loss. For instance, during Genji's voluntary exile to the coast of Suma (as a result of the sexual and political scandal over his affair with Oborozukiyo) we see empathy of this kind between Genji and his attendants, who had left the capital with their master. Genji and his men are all "mourning" their estrangement from home in desolate Suma, which is depicted as a sad but beautiful and otherworldly place. Genji's life there is portrayed as a series of lyrical tableaux in which the prose echoes the poetry in both imagery and form and poems placed at the center of scenes do not fail to move others.[40] Another chapter in which we find the hero's life depicted in a succession of static scenes culminating in poetry is "Wizard" (Maboroshi), the last chapter in which Genji appears. The chapter depicts the aftermath of the death of Murasaki, Genji's most important lover. Left behind by Murasaki, it is as if Genji's own life begins to wind down as well. He exchanges poems with others on the theme of loss and the unrecoverable past. But more often than not his poems are not addressed to a specific interlocutor, merely contrasting the days spent in mourning with emblematic images of the changing seasons. The entire chapter is self-consciously held together by remembrance of the past, the cyclical temporality of the seasons, and poetic imagery that displaces the progressive time of an unfolding narrative.[41]

Even lovers undergoing the most conflict-laden affair may, at a specific juncture, enact a poetic dialogue that achieves a high level of fidelity. An example of such a poetic reconciliation is found in the famous parting between Genji and one of his lovers, Rokujō Lady—the scene which is said to have set a standard for the melancholic farewell between lovers in Heian literature. Genji had succeeded in seducing Rokujō, a proud and refined widow of a deceased crown prince, only to inflict great suffering on her by his subsequently cooling passion. Exhausted from the emotional turmoil over her romance with her flighty young lover, Genji, and assailed by the anxiety that her jealous spirit may have wandered off and possessed Genji's wife, Rokujō decides to break off the affair with him. She is about to leave the capital for Ise Shrine, where her daughter is taking office as high priestess. Genji, whose love for Rokujō has been rekindled by her decision to leave him, visits her at the sanctuary where the mother and the daughter are preparing for the journey. The narrative describes Genji's visit in detail, carefully illustrating the ambiance of the moor at Nonomiya in autumn and the process of the lovers' reconciliation. The awkwardness of their meeting gradually dissolves as they exchange words and poems densely laced with poetic allusions. Exchanging waka that are collages of traditional love poems, they avoid dwelling on their past conflicts and memories of suffering and speak through the fictional realm of love. The characters appear to have managed to resolve their struggle and address each other through the personae of exemplary lover-poets exchanging poems at a dawn parting.

The dawn sky was as if made for the occasion. [He recited:]

> あかつきの別れはいつも露けきをこは世に知らぬ秋の空かな

A dawn farewell is always drenched in dewdrops of tears. But sad is this autumn sky as never before!

The way Genji held her hand, reluctant to leave her, was so gentle and loving. A cold wind was blowing, and crickets seemed to recognize the occasion. Its sound would have moved even a casual listener to tears. Perhaps because their feelings were in such tumult, they could not compose poems with ease. At length, she replied:

> おほかたの秋の別れもかなしきに鳴く音な添へそ野辺の松虫

An autumn farewell needs nothing to deepen its sadness. . . . Enough of your cries, O crickets of the moors! (2:81–82; S:188)[42]

The imagery in Genji's poem moves from the dawn farewell to tears to the unprecedented sadness of the autumn sky. The narration, then, draws back to place the characters within a mise-en-scène that mirrors the emotional state of the lovers. Rokujō recites a verse in which she adopts Genji's imagery of autumn parting and expands it to include the cries of the cricket. The couple's parting is beautiful and sad as they exchange poems that seem to be in accord. The pair of poems marks a sharp contrast with earlier series of poetic dialogue between them, which are highly fractured and conflictual. Here the poems are tightly linked, with the words and emotions of the two characters intimately intertwined with each other and the external environment in which they are situated.[43]

Yet, we need to attend to the equivocal nature of this poetic communion. The scene is destined to be the finale of the couple's love affair, and the lovers' dialogue here is deeply shadowed by their awareness of the pending separation. The fidelity of their dialogue is attained through mutual commiseration over the "end" and "loss" of their romance. The text reserves the closure of the poetic dialogue precisely for the moment when their relationship is doomed. The lover-poets in the *Genji* are not freed from dilemma and dissonance unless their love is already virtually dead. We find in the *Genji*, therefore, a depiction of what appears to be a harmony of feelings that Norinaga invoked through his notion of mono no aware. Yet in the text's narrative, the aesthetic effect of this communion is often offset by the awareness that it constitutes a ghostly union of the dead or dying. Earlier I associated mono no aware with the response of a spectator—that is to say, the empathy of the one who has no stake in the story-world. The characters in the text must also renounce their agencies and desires in their world in order to share their affective/aesthetic experience with others. The lover's poetic exchange in the *Genji* is paradoxical—its failure marks life while its success marks death.[44] This is because the text constructs amorous desire itself as a paradox of union and separation—drawing people together while at the same time marking the irreconcilable difference between them. This difference explains the volleying of poetic utterances that deflect and transform the meaning of the others' words. As argued earlier, the internal tension of love means that the seemingly futile dynamics of poetic exchange that keeps deferring the closure of communication is not an aberration but an exemplary dialogue between lovers whose relationship is still in the process of unfolding.

Female Discontent

Both Masuda's and Norinaga's views on the function of poetry in the *Genji* are limited by their failure to grasp the complex texture of tension that constitutes the romantic relations in the text. What Masuda perceived as the gap in poetic communication that suggests the failure of the poetic ideal also serves as the text's commentary on the impossibility of perfect romantic union. Lovers in the text are trapped in an impasse between erotic/romantic desire and the prescriptive forces of the social and spiritual orders. They have nowhere to escape, being at odds with the laws of "this world" as well as the "other world" (i.e., the realm of spiritual salvation).[45] Masuda assumes that authentic poetic expression should overcome the lovers' dilemma, affirming transgressive passion, if not in reality then at least in the imagination, through poetic language and its transcendent power. It is in the outpouring of defiant passion that he locates the authenticity of poetic language, poetic subjectivity, and the dyadic bonding between the poetic subject and its addressee. Norinaga, on the other hand, envisions the sublimation of this conflict through the ghostly union of pathos, aestheticizing the very impossibility of the fulfillment of desire. According to him, suffering over unattainable love expressed through poetry enables not the connection between the romantic dyad but generalized sociality, transfiguring personal woes into a communal reverberation of sympathy.

It is difficult to find anything akin to Masuda's notion of poetic/romantic transcendence that militates against social forces in the discourse on love and poetry in the *Genji* as well as in other Heian monogatari. Masuda himself acknowledges that the defiance of taboo is not a theme indigenous to waka tradition.[46] While the *Genji* presents lovers' suffering as powerful and genuine, it also concedes the triviality of amorous sentiment with respect to the dominant temporal and spiritual values of the society. Lovers themselves repeatedly acknowledge the futility and inconsequentiality of romantic passion and poems expressing their longing and torment. This absence of legitimacy in their desires and sufferings accounts for the fact that the overriding tone of the text is melancholic rather than tragic. The ethical basis for aestheticizing an individual's revolt against external forces that Masuda appears to yearn for is clearly absent.[47]

As we have seen, lovers' poetic responses consistently recast their relations in *social* rather than transcendent terms by invoking poetic conventions in specific ways. In this sense, Norinaga's aesthetics of pathos seems more pertinent to the text—a sociality formed through mutual commiseration over their bondage to the given condition of the world.[48] It should be recalled here that Norinaga does not impute any transcendental value in love itself—love is merely fodder for the powerful feelings (especially the torment over frustrated desire) that provide the basis for such communality. What Norinaga does not seem to take into account, however, is the text's simultaneous gesture of undermining the bonding wrought by romantic pathos. As we have seen in love affairs that are still "alive," the lovers' dialogues resist reaching a state of commiseration—but not by rebelling against social mores, as Masuda may have hoped. Instead, poetic dialogues foreground the chasm that opens *between* the lovers themselves, preventing their shared deviation from sociospiritual strictures to form a closed circuit of sympathy.

Neither Masuda's picture of lovers as a heroic dyad facing social taboos together nor Norinaga's image of their harmony in aestheticized impotence accounts for such tension arising within lovers' poetic exchanges, overdetermining the impossibility of romance. The *Genji* suggests that even if both parties in a love affair may not escape the social forces that repress their desire and squelch their hope for romantic fulfillment they do not necessarily experience this condition in an identical fashion. For one thing, the lovers' strength of passion and their attitudes toward their relations are rarely in perfect alignment. But the text's construction of love goes far beyond the melodrama of lopsided passion insofar as it involves socially determined differences between the lovers as the source of their division.

The social order that may be held at bay by poetic fantasy (at least for a time) returns by another path—not as forces external to the lovers but as aspects of their own social positionalities that complicate their desire for each other. It is on this ground that gender difference comes into play as a critical factor in the text's construction of love and lovers' dialogues. The fact that refractive responses in poetic dialogues are typically issued by female characters not only conforms to poetic conventions but suggests that for heroines the impossibility of romantic fulfillment has a specific contour distinct from that of men. The agency of a heroine is doubly suppressed, both by social censure of her amorous affairs and by the prescription of gender roles that oblige her to be passive and reactive in relation to her male lover. While heroes may resent the imposition of societal norms and rules on amorous desire, they often participate in the reinforcement of gender norms that confer upon them power and privileges over their female lovers (e.g., they have greater latitude to act and speak according to their desires). The text presents its primary protagonist, Genji, as a highly idealized romantic hero, but it does not fail to shed critical light on the imposition of his selfish will on his lovers. And the eloquence with which Genji controls the representation of himself, his lovers, and their relations, is repeatedly ironized in the text by the understated rejoinders of the heroines (often in their poetic responses).

In the series of exchanges between Genji and Fujitsubo examined earlier, her poems—by refusing to passively mirror the hero's addresses—expose narcissism, selfishness, and even menace in his poetic overtures. While Genji's waka focuses on the suffering of separation from the beloved, Fujitsubo's responses point to their love affair itself as the source of torment that cannot be resolved even if they escape into a phantasmic world. Genji's addresses inscribe his disengagement from the rest of society while Fujitsubo's responses express her disengagement from him and his fantasy. Poetic exchanges serve as one of the most significant means through which the heroine's specific fears and desires are inscribed in distinction to those of their lovers. The polysemy and diversity of the interpretive convention of poetry are manipulated in heroines' poems not simply to sustain the fictional sanctuary of romance but to negotiate a delicate balance between speaking their minds (in opposition to those of their lovers) and risking the loss of their desirability as women (by appearing to be too aggressive and strident). Fujitsubo, for instance, rebuffs Genji's self-serving discourse while adopting, at least on the surface, the accepted voice and language of the coy and flirtatious female lover-poet.

We have discussed the manner in which a response in a lovers' exchange of waka may refract the poetic ideal invoked in the address—undermining the power of poetry to move the addressee and create an alternative reality for lovers. Recognition of the dilemma that a heroines faces suggests that the fracturing effect of her poetry is closely related to the built-in ambivalence of female discursive agency. Her response not only rebuffs the phantasmic overture of the hero but it is also divided within—it does not speak in a singular voice or articulate a singular desire. The poems by the heroine do, at least in part, take on the expected female poetic persona that her lover's poetic address invokes. In this very process, however, she also registers the sentiments and perspectives that exceed those that have been called for by the address—pathos, melancholy, and discontent that arise not with but *against* the poetic address. Lovers' poetic discourses in the *Genji* are dialogic, presenting multiple voices and perspectives that work with and against each other in more than one way.

In a famous passage from the "Evening Mist" (Yūgiri) chapter in the text, Murasaki Lady airs her dismay over the predicament of being a woman.

> Such a pathetic, constricted life women are made to live! How can we enjoy prosperity in life or dispel the tedium of the ephemeral world when we must hide within ourselves our understanding of things that are deeply moving (mono no aware) or occasions that are elegantly amusing. Since women are deemed ignorant and insignificant creatures, even our parents are denied much satisfaction from the labor of raising us. How regretful it is that we must keep locked up in ourselves the understanding of both good and bad, like the mute prince in sad parables that priests tell. I also wonder how I can remain much longer in such a precarious state. (4:442; S:699)

Norinaga interprets this passage as expressing general bitterness about a life in which one cannot act on and articulate one's true sentiments. He points to it as indisputable proof that mono no aware is the ultimate theme of the *Genji*.[49] He hears the author's own voice through that of the heroine, suggesting that Murasaki Shikibu refused to keep her powerful emotions to herself, producing the text that exemplifies mono no aware. Norinaga, however, fails to consider the possibility that when women find ways to express their feelings in spite of the forces that restrain them, their discourses may not feed the communal harmony of mono no aware. In the *Genji*, the fracture in lovers' poetic dialogues typically erupts over the female pathos inflected by despair that cannot be shared with the lover.

If the discussion in this chapter has identified something akin to gender politics in the *Genji*'s construction of romance and poetic discourse, then we also need to account for the difference between these "politics" and the rebellion against the external social forces that springs forth from one's interiority, which Masuda envisioned.[50] We need to recall that the female poetic response is mediated *through* the poetic conventions and gender norms inscribed therein. It is through the manipulation of the sociality of poetic discourse that heroines resist becoming subsumed under the poetic/romantic fantasy of their lovers. Thus, it is not enough to merely transfer the subject of contestation from "lovers" to heroines — constituting them as the true subject of the political and oppositional reading of the text. Female pathos is no more transcendent of ethical-spiritual values than the melancholic flights of fancy of male lovers. If we are to discern in the *Genji* political or at least critical perspectives on the organization of gender in Heian aristocratic society, we need to fix our attention not so much on the intensity of the repudiation of the social order by an individual subject as on the sharp precision with which the text marks the specificity of the oppressive conditions that female characters face. The *Genji* offers a highly intricate and multilayered portrayal of interpersonal conflicts—especially in what is expected to be among the most powerful forms of affective bonding—without constituting the agents who think and speak as autonomous, heroic, and psychological subjects. The tensions and negotiations between lovers that the poetic dialogues articulate, in other words, cannot be understood through the modern binary between individualism and collectivism or resistance and conformism.

These are some of the issues contributing to the difficulty of reading texts such as the *Genji* today. On one hand, it is eminently readable and seemingly responsive to our modern expectation of the social as a paradoxical field of human union and isolation and desire as the condition of hope and despair. On the other hand, it continues to elude our modernizing hermeneutics and challenges our assumptions on issues such as identity, affect, and the relations between self and Other. In this chapter, I have tried to account for such effects of the text by reading it against the modernist assumptions of Masuda as well as Norinaga's perspective, which anticipates antimodernism. Rather than pursuing these issues further here, I return to them in the last chapter and the epilogue, where I discuss the issue of subject formation in Heian narrative discourse.

CHAPTER FIVE

Tokieda's Imperial Subject and the
Textual Turn in Heian Literary Studies

The rise of the textual and formal study of Heian narratives and its de-velopment into one of the dominant methodologies in the field exem-plifies significant transformations seen in the discipline since the late 1960s. This chapter analyzes a major theoretical source of the textual turn in Heian literary studies—Tokieda Motoki's theory of Japanese language. I question whether Tokieda's theory actually provides what Heian scholars have sought in it and, if not, what that can tell us about textual/linguistic approach as it is practiced in the field. In the first part of the chapter, I examine how and why it is believed that Tokieda, by offering a theory of language and subjectivity based on the specific characteristics of Japanese, enables us to read Heian narratives out-side modern Western literary conventions. In the second part of the chapter, I locate the impasse of Tokieda's theory (and of the efficacy invested in it by Heian scholarship), both in its dependence on the Japan versus West binary and in its failure to address the sociality and historicity of discourse.

Outside Heian literary studies and to some extent within them as well, the general perception is that the linguistic and textual approach to literary criticism is an obsolete academic trend, supplanted by a host of new theoretical currents. What is less certain is whether this transition was mediated by sustained critical investigations into the shortcomings of past methodologies. In this and the next chapter, I consider the limitations as well as the potential of studying Heian literary discourses through close attention to their formal characteristics. For one thing, we have hardly resolved the problem highlighted by the formalist study of Heian literature: the immense theoretical complexity of reading texts from a distant time against our own interpretive horizon. At the same time we need to consider the hazards of taming this challenge by reducing it to the predictable binary differences between modern and premodern or Japan and the West. I believe, furthermore, that the effort to avoid such dualism calls for the exploration of textual forms that simultaneously open us to historical and sociopolitical inquiries.

The Formalist Trend in Heian Literary Studies

Some of the most innovative and methodologically sophisticated scholarship on Heian literature in the last couple of decades has argued for the incompatibility between Heian kana narratives and the critical conventions shaped through the study of modern Western novels. For instance, Richard Okada's *Figure of Resistance*, published in 1991, was a significant intervention in the field. The study vigorously interrogated the applicability of canonical terms of Western literary studies as a means of understanding Heian texts. Around the same time, two of the leading scholars of Heian literature in Japan, Mitani Kuniaki and Takahashi Tōru, published a series of essays that focused on distinct properties of narrative forms in texts such as *The Tale of Genji*. Mitani writes, "*Genji monogatari* appears before us as a text that estranges and relativizes not only modern literature but modernity itself."[1]

These studies, which asserted the formal specificity of Heian narratives, emerged out of a broader trend in the discipline since the 1970s largely led by scholars who received their training at universities during the turbulent era of the late 1960s.[2] They openly raised questions about the methodological orthodoxy of the discipline — in particular, the positivistic stances through which literary studies in Japan were conducted. They were critical of the ways in which mainstream academic studies of literature tended to explicate literary texts through external determinants such as the life of the author, the social conditions under which the text was produced, or the bibliographic history of textual transmissions and variances. Calling into question the transparency of the objects of analysis, they sought to stimulate more fundamental inquiries into the literary texts themselves.[3] The shift from a discussion of the author to a study of the textual narrator and narratorial voice epitomized the theoretical and methodological changes that occurred through this process. Rather than assuming the objective presence of an author as the origin and the unifying principle of a literary work, attention was paid to the ways in which narrative discourse constructs the subject of narration.[4] The specific ways in which Heian narratives constitute discursive subjects (particularly in contradistinction to the subject formation in modern novelistic discourse) became one of the focal points of revisionist scholarship.[5]

We can identify at least two distinct theoretical currents that influenced this post-1970s development in Heian literary studies. One, of course, is the formal analysis of literature developed in Europe and North America broadly under the influence of structuralist linguistics. The methodologies of formalism, narratology, semiotics, and so on helped transfer the focus of literary studies from the content to the form, resignifying the form not as the external shell of the internal content but the very condition of signification. Literary texts were reread as complex systems of conventions that cannot be reduced to individual consciousness or intention. The notion of individual authors — self-conscious subjects expressing their thoughts and experiences through their literary creations — was itself reconceptualized as an effect of cultural codes and signifying practices.

The interrelated displacement of the transparency of language as a representational mechanism and the individual authorial subject as the source of the unity and autonomy of a literary work challenged the mimetic theory of literature central to the mainstream European novelistic and critical conventions. The realist representational mode was denaturalized as an apparatus that camouflages its artifice by virtue of its compatibility with the dominant ideology of modernity. The eclipse of a personified narrator in favor of seemingly less intrusive third-person narration in realist novels, for instance, was understood not as the removal of a layer of mediation — progress toward a more realistic representation of the world and a more authentic expression of the authorial voice and vision—but as the emergence of a new form of mediation.

This critical stance also fostered interest in literary and other cultural production that does not conform to realist paradigms or the standard belletristic notion of literature. Materials previously excluded from literary and cultural analyses such as texts from popular culture or nonliterary social documents, were increasingly recognized to be worthy of serious critical attention. Roland Barthes's *Empire of Signs*, for instance, found in an eclectic assortment of Japanese culture and arts a "text" that refracts the subjectivism and anthropocentricism of the modernity and the West. These developments in literary theories inspired young generations of Heian literary scholars to approach Japanese premodern texts that deviate from modern conventions in a new light, encouraging them to challenge the status quo in their discipline (including the reverential treatment of these texts as national literary canon).[6]

Alongside the waves of literary theories that entered Japan from abroad, there was another significant theoretical ingredient in the debate over narration and narrative subject in Heian studies: Tokieda Motoki's theory of Japanese language. Tokieda is widely known in Japan as an influential grammarian and a central figure in the field of "national language studies" (kokugogaku) from the prewar to postwar periods. Kokugogaku emerged in Japan in the late nineteenth century along with the rise of kokubungaku, evolving into a modern academic discipline as language and literature came to play increasingly critical roles in the construction of national identity. The theory and methods of European linguistics, furthermore, helped define the study of language as an independent academic discipline separate from the study of literature—a distinction that was absent in pre-Meiji kokugaku. As it was the case with kokubungaku's relationship with Tokugawa scholarship, however, the powerful influence of European academic disciplines did not mean that kokugogaku made a clean break with the kokugaku tradition. While some scholars of Japanese language sought to build the discipline exclusively on the foundation of gengogaku (modern linguistics), others reacted against the perceived subordination of kokugogaku under a framework imported from the West. The latter defined kokugogaku in contradistinction to modern linguistics, in part through their continued engagement with the texts of the past rather than confining their research to the study of contemporary spoken language.[7]

Tokieda is reputed to be the most sophisticated antimodernist in the debate over the study of Japanese language, taking a self-consciously contestatory stance against the wholesale adoption of modern Western theory and methodology. Instead, he attempted to develop a comprehensive theory of language through the examination of the specific qualities of Japanese. Not only did he closely examine the grammatical forms found in classical literary texts but he skillfully incorporated kokugaku views on language into his theory. Defining Japanese in opposition to Western languages and Western theories of language, Tokieda drew on a kokugaku project that defined the native language and literature in contradistinction to Chinese and the study of Chinese classics. Furthermore, he linked the kokugaku's vision of Japanese as a language that privileges affect, corporeality, and immediacy with modern concerns over questions of subjectivity and language. Tokieda saw language as a process activated by the subjective function of a speaker communicating in a particular context, and he argued that the Japanese language was uniquely suited to making the fundamental nature of language explicit.

Originally, the influence of Tokieda's theory on postwar literary scholarship was more or less confined to the linguistic wing of kokubungaku in which scholars typically examined the grammatical structures of premodern literary texts. In the 1950s and 1960s, however, Tokieda's work began drawing advocates from different directions. Critics such as Miura Tsutomu and Yoshimoto Takaaki saw in it a means of rejecting the positivistic and instrumentalist view of language, including the Stalinist theory of language that was widely accepted in Marxist academic circles in Japan.[8] Furthermore, they found in Tokieda's work, hints for connecting the theory of language with the theory of expression — a new framework for linking the study of language with the analysis of art and literature.[9] The radical intellectual climate of the late 1960s, which criticized not only the conservative Right but the orthodoxy of the postwar Left, which held sway over mainstream academia, stimulated a new interest in Tokieda's theory (in large part via the work of Yoshimoto, who was an intellectual icon of the period).[10] By the 1980s, Tokieda's theory was frequently referred to in literary scholarship that approached Japanese narrative through the specific characteristics of Japanese language, especially its allegedly discourse-oriented nature.

If the new current of Euro-American literary theories encouraged the scholars of Japanese literature to question realist assumptions, Tokieda's work was often used as a basis for claiming a model of language, literary representation, and linguistic/literary subjectivity specific to Japanese language and literature. This combination of a narratological approach, on one hand, and the assertion of the distinct properties of Japanese language and narrative forms, on the other, characterizes an important trend in Japanese literary studies since the 1970s involving many leading scholars.[11] The study of Heian kana narrative, particularly the analysis of a narratologically complex text such as *The Tale of Genji*, was greatly energized, and it became one of the focal points of the trend, cutting across the division between modern and premodern segments of the field.

The Narrator in Heian Kana Texts

Before I move to the analysis of Tokieda's work, let me provide some illustrations of the problems involved in discussing the discursive subject in Heian kana narrative that the textual approach addressed. I use as an example a text generally considered to be one of the earliest existing kana narratives: *Taketori monogatari* (*The Tale of the Bamboo Cutter*), a tale revolving around a celestial maiden banished to the earth and the misadventures of her mortal suitors.[12] Contemporary critics generally regard *Taketori* to be narrated by a functional and transparent narrator with an omniscient point of view who freely merges with the thoughts and perspectives of the characters.[13] At the same time, though a narrator is never explicitly identified, narratorial intrusions scattered throughout the text hint at some sort of storytelling agent. *Taketori* ends with a phrase: "Thus, the story has been passed down."

There have been a number of influential studies on the *Taketori* narration that focus on the text's use of the *jodōshi* (auxiliary verb) *keri*.[14] Scholars have pointed out that while *keri* (and *jodōshi* in general) is rarely used in pre-Heian narratives, in *Taketori* it is frequently used in a seemingly deliberate manner.[15] The function of *keri* in the Heian period has been variously described: as a marker of tense (storytelling past), aspect (continuation of the past and present condition/action), or modality (hearsay). A theory widely supported among literary scholars is the one proposed by Takeoka Masao. Takeoka argued that *keri* in Heian prose signifies not a particular tense but an epistemological stance that a speaker takes when he or she represents a world or scene other than that in which he or she is presently located.[16] *Keri*, therefore, was thought to be an exemplary expression in Heian tales that typically related a fictional world removed from that of the real author and reader.

One may expect, then, that the narration in *Taketori* would take this jodōshi throughout the entire text. In *Taketori* and other Heian kana narratives, however, this is not the case. The phrases punctuated by *keri* in the text are concentrated at transitional sections — at the introduction and conclusion of the text as well as the beginnings and endings of its subsections. Except for these specific instances, most passages in *Taketori* end with verbal stems without jodōshi (which scholars often classify as the present tense). According to Takeoka, this dual structure indicates the movement of narrative perspective. Once the narration guides the reader into the fictional world by means of phrases using *keri*, it can shift to the present tense or a perspective located in the time/space of the world narrated.[17]

Takeoka's analysis of *keri* suggests that the narrational perspective of *Taketori* does not constitute a consistent point of reference from which the narrative reconstruction of events is organized. The grammatical properties of Heian Japanese, such as the absence of an explicit system of personal pronouns and verbal tenses, the lack of distinction between direct and indirect discourses, and frequent ellipses of the grammatical subject further contribute to the perceived ambiguity of narrating perspective. Indeed, in reading *Taketori* it is often impossible to tell whether the narrator is speaking from the perspective situated in the story-world (either as an impersonal observer or through the viewpoint and the voice of a character) or in the context of narration in which the narrator addresses the audience. As a result, *Taketori*'s narrational voice is explicitly discursive (in the narrow sense of implying a speaker and a listener) without being anchored to a consistent spatio-temporal and thematic coordinate of a singular speaking subject. We may note that in modern novels even a third-person narrator whose intervention into the diegesis seems minimal inscribes his or her fixed stance vis-à-vis the events narrated, typically adopting a consistently retrospective point of view.[18]

By contrast, the narrator of *Taketori* is a medium without a stable positionality. The palpability of his voice is counterpoised by his disembodied, phantom-like quality, and not just because he is not explicitly identified and personified. Rather, the narratorial subject seems elusive because the text fails to establish a coherent basis for distinguishing and relating the registers of enunciation (the context of narration) and enunciated (the context of the events narrated). This ambiguity suggests that despite its discursivity, *Taketori* narration does not invoke something like an *instance of discourse*, the instance in which language is actualized in speech by a speaker as distinguished from the temporality of events and situations referred to by the discourse.[19]

Language Process Theory

If *Taketori* does not constitute the narrator in ways expected by the linguistic model used in mainstream narratology, should we see this as a sign of inadequacy or a shortcoming on the part of Heian narrative literature? It has been suggested that Tokieda's theory of language can help us understand the Heian narrative form through its particular logic, which defies the assumptions of modern Western linguistic and narratological theories.

Tokieda pitted himself against what he saw as a positivistic stance of Saussurean linguistics or more precisely the facile manner in which Saussure was appropriated and applied by linguistics in Japan.[20] In his *Principles of National Language Studies* (*Kokugogaku genron*), in which he elaborated his *gengo katei setsu* (language process theory), language is apprehended dynamically rather than as a static system activated through an individual's concrete usage and engagement in speaking, listening, reading, and writing. He thereby attempted to theorize the agency of the *shutai* (discursive subject) which he felt had been excluded from conventional linguistics.[21]

Tokieda argued that every concrete utterance consists of dual elements, *shi* and *ji*, morphological-grammatical categories that support the objective (referential) and subjective (communicative) registers of language, respectively. Tokieda's discussion of the topic was inspired in part by the kokugaku study of language. Tokieda related his notion of shi and ji to discussions of so-called *te-ni-wo-ha* (a word derived from the principal particles used in Japanese — *te, ni, wo, ha*) by a number of kokugaku scholars. The term originally referred to the diacritical marks that supplemented kundoku readings of kanbun texts, signifying grammatical parts in Japanese with no equivalents in Chinese. The term *te-ni-wo-ha* (or *te-ni-ha*) was adopted in waka poetics, particularly of the Nijō school, where it was generally associated with particles and jodōshi.[22]

It was through the work of Motoori Norinaga and his followers that te-ni-wo-ha was transformed from an arcane topic in waka poetics to a more general concept for discussing Japanese language.[23] In the fourteenth-century poetic treatise "Teniha taigaishō,"[24] te-ni-wo-ha was contrasted with shi or "kotoba" (nominals and other independent morphemes). Norinaga, however, identified te-ni-wo-ha with the syntactic principle of language in general (or how words are aligned syntagmatically) and shi with the semantic value of isolated words. The privilege of te-ni-wo-ha for Norinaga lay in the fact that it was the part of native discourse that had to be added to Chinese texts in kundoku readings. It, thereby, played a significant role in Norinaga's construction of pure native language in contrast to what he saw as the corrupt linguistic practices of his contemporaries, who had been contaminated by Chinese influences. He challenged the conventional literary hermeneutics (nurtured in the tradition of studying literary Chinese), which searched for the correct interpretation of key words while paying less attention to the syntactic and rhetorical composition of a text. Kanno Kakumyō comments that Norinaga astutely recognized a fundamental limitation of the kundoku tradition in Japan, which read texts as concatenations of words or meanings of the words (insensitive not only to the text's phonetic values but to its subtle syntactic nuances).[25] Norinaga turned on its head the hierarchy of what modern linguistics may classify as syntax versus semantic. Instead of viewing te-ni-wo-ha as a mere supplement to meaningful words, he identified it as the foundation in which the force of language resides.[26] The true essence of poetic discourse, for instance, was to be found not in the meaning of words themselves but in the ways they are put together. Te-ni-wo-ha, likened by Norinaga to a cord that strings gems together, was posited as the basis of the affective force of poetry.

Tokieda developed his own theory of shi and ji as a clarification and theoretical elaboration of the distinction between shi and te-ni-wo-ha made by the kokugaku study of language. He refers to shi as a *gainen go* (conceptual word), bringing under this category not only nominals but verbals and adjectivals that represent both abstract and concrete objects. Ji, on the other hand, is referred to as a *kannen go* (ideational word) that marks the "nonobjectified" function of the speaker. Various types of particles and jodōshi are classified as ji—for example, jodōshi marking the speaker's attitude toward the stated topic of the sentence (exclamation, speculation, negation, etc.) or toward the addresser (e.g., various levels of honorific).

The speaker's thoughts and feelings, once objectified as "anger," "joy," "suspicion," and so on, would be represented by shi. The speaker's happiness may be expressed as *watashi wa ureshii* (I am happy). The same word, *ureshii* (to be happy), however, can be used to express the happiness of another person, as in *kare wa ureshii* (He is happy). In contrast, ji, such as the modal jodōshi of conjecture, *mu*, can only refer to the attitude of the speaker, thus the jodōshi *mu* in the phrases *kare ika<u>mu</u>* (He will probably go) as well as *ware ika<u>mu</u>* (I will probably go) refers to the speculative mood of the speaker. Ji is a privileged medium of subjective function because it is deictically related to the speaker rather than the *sozai* (theme).[27]

Tokieda thinks that shi and ji are the basic syntactical components of a complete utterance in Japanese. He explains that in contrast to the subject-copula-predicate structure of Western languages, likened to a pair of scales, in Japanese shi and ji constitute an *irekogata kōzō* (box-in-box structure). Shi, which refers to the object of utterance is contained or framed by ji. Ji, in turn, marks the function of the speaker (shi encompasses the equivalents of both "subject" and "predicate" in Japanese). Tokieda argues that an utterance in Japanese should be analyzed not as a concatenation of individual words connected to one another but as nested modules that are explicitly or implicitly made out of shi contained in ji.[28] Shi contained in ji may be nested in increasingly larger frames that keep reinflecting the utterance with new nuances, forming multiple layers of embedded structure, with the outermost frame including all elements that came before it. The sentence *Tonari <u>no</u> hana <u>ga</u> sai<u>ta</u>* (The flower next door bloomed) can be analyzed as: "next door" (*Tonari* + genitive particle

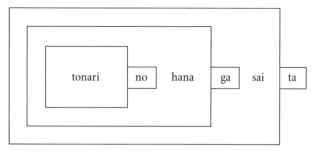

FIGURE 1.

no) — "flower" (*hana* + nominative particle *ga*) — *sai* "bloomed" (*sai* + jodōshi of past-tense-aspect *ta*) (fig. 1). While in English grammar a genitive marker is affixed to a noun and is understood to be functioning *between* the two nominals it connects, the particle *no* in Japanese is a separate morpheme that, according to Tokieda, frames *tonari* (neighbor), constituting a phrase *tonari no* (neighbor's). This phrase is embedded in the subsequent phrase *hana ga* (flower), where the particle *ga* serves as a frame. The final *ta* (very approximately the past tense) establishes the communicative level of the entire complex preceding it. By containing and framing shi, ji unifies and completes a phase or an utterance, performing the pragmatic and communicative function of relating addresser, message, and addressee.

Thus, according to Tokieda, ji inscribes the speaker by marking his or her attitude toward the thematic content of the utterance and toward the addressee. The first-person pronoun "I" (e.g., *watashi* or *ware*) does not represent the discursive subject, shutai — it does not express shutai's function. To the extent that it is an *objectification* of the speaker, "I" is a shi, no different from the third-person pronouns such as *kare* and *kanoj* (he and she). This also means that shutai is strictly distinguished from any form of *shugo* (grammatical subject). Tokieda argues, furthermore, that shugo in Japanese never achieves the syntactic importance that the grammatical subject commands in Western languages — the privileging of the grammatical subject as the referential center of persons and tenses does not apply to shugo. According to Tokieda, a Japanese sentence does not require an explicit shugo since the subject is already implicit in the predicate: verbals and adjectivals in Japanese do not represent abstract concepts of action and condition as such but action and condition as experienced by someone.

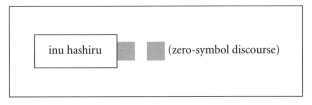

FIGURE 2.

The shutai function, therefore, does not depend on the presence of a grammatical subject. Ultimately, however, the shutai function does not even rest on the presence or absence of ji as a class of morphemes. Analyzing a common construction in a modern Japanese sentence that ends with a verbal stem without any jodōshi attached to it, Tokieda argues that the shutai function in such a case is expressed by a *rei kigō* (zero-symbol). In the sentence *Inu hashiru* (A dog runs), although there is no specific ji morpheme, the entire phrase is framed by the implicit assertive attitude of shutai making the statement as outlined in figure 2. Note that, although ji is absent, the zero-symbol has a definite place — at the end of the utterance. Tokieda seems to suggest that regardless of whether *ji* is explicitly present the structure of box-in-box is always there.[29]

If the completion of an utterance is constituted not by the relation among words and their grammatical functions but by a frame that can be implicit, then practically any word can, in itself, be an utterance as long as it is mobilized by shutai's intentionality in a given context of communication. A word *kaji* (fire) in itself is a single word in the lexicon. But if someone, upon seeing a burning house, exclaimed "Kaji!" it turns into a complete utterance.[30] The issue, again, is not that this exclamation can be expanded to its "proper" syntactic form with requisite grammatical parts (e.g., *Kaji da*, "There is a fire") but that it can convey what Tokieda calls the "complete thought of shutai." The distinction between a mere word (an entry in a dictionary) and an utterance, then, is not determined by grammatical rules but by pragmatic conditions, a theme verbalized through shutai's intention in a concrete context of communication.

Thus, Tokieda refuses to analyze a sentence defined by grammatical regulation. His object of study is not a sentence but an utterance, a function of shutai, which is for him the only meaningful way in which language can be deployed. In his view, Japanese discourse is always *shutaiteki* (marking the function of discursive subject). The zero-symbol utterance is no less subjective than an utterance with explicit ji. Tokieda, furthermore, points out that, although all languages are subjective, in Japanese in which there is a distinct class of words (ji) that serve as discursive markers, this fundamental nature of language is made more explicit.

Tokieda's discussion of ji suggests that he locates the essential characteristic of discourse in its self-reflexivity. In other words, discourse not only refers to an object out in the world but inscribes its enactment by a speaker addressing an interlocutor. Thus, even if the subject of an utterance (shutai) and the subject of a statement (shugo) appear to be identical (i.e., in so-called first-person discourse), the two must be differentiated. Through his attention to the self-referentiality and performativity of discourse, Tokieda objected to the representational and instrumental understanding of language. The subject, in turn, is identified with discursive agency, marked by signifiers (ji) that are both mobile (indexical) and empty of objective referents. Thus, Tokieda's definitions of shutai departed from the naive notion of a self-conscious subject in that it is not defined in terms of conventional attributes such as personal experience, memory, or the inner sense of self.

Reading Heian Texts through Tokieda

Although Tokieda did not discuss narrative forms as such, his theory offers a number of tantalizing implications for the study of Heian kana narrative. The disembodied narrator of *Taketori monogatari* ceases to be a puzzle once we view the text in light of Japanese grammar as discussed by Tokieda. As a discourse of shutai, there would be no inconsistency between the palpability of *Taketori* narration's voice and its lack of stable positionality. Subjectivity in Japanese discourse is not inscribed by tense and pronominal systems functioning as the central point of reference that relates and differentiates the context of narration and the context of events narrated. Rather, shutai is marked dynamically by ji that inflects the utterance with communicative gestures, subjective impressions, and attitudes. We may also recall a feature of *Taketori* narration mentioned earlier: passages ending with *keri* frame the rest of the narration without jodōshi marking. This narratorial organization of *Taketori* itself seems to echo the box-in-box structure and relations of ji containing shi as discussed by Tokieda.

Using Tokieda's work, we may now reformulate the initial questions raised concerning the *Taketori* narration's alleged inconsistencies—its inability to maintain a neutral third-person point of view and its failure to establish a consistent distinction between the context of narration and the context of the events narrated. Modern written narratives are typically organized around the point of view of narration, which constitutes a single trajectory both linking and separating the narrating subject and the object narrated in a seemingly consistent manner. Premodern Japanese narrative, based on the box-in-box structure, allows a much greater degree of multiplicity and fluidity of spatial, temporal, modal, and other orientations of narratorial perspective. Shifting points of view are held together or contained by the constant redrawing of communicative context, for instance, by the framing passages addressed to the audience. Furthermore, there is no fundamental division between the passages with emphatically discursive ji marking and those without it if, as Tokieda argues, a discourse cannot help but mark the speaker of the given utterance. The ambiguity between the subjective and objective, between narratorial and characterological discourses, and between the point of view located in the time of narration and the time of events narrated is not transgressive in Japanese narrative since shutai does not constitute transcendent unity but effects ever-dynamic recontextualization.

Tokieda's work thus offers considerable theoretical and explanatory resources for challenging the use of Eurocentric models of language and narrative forms in the study of Heian texts. Here, however, I should confess my own ruse. I have hypothesized that Tokieda's theory can explain the problems posed by Heian narration, but the kind of scholarship I referred to in setting up that problem is itself broadly influenced by Tokieda grammar. Takeoka's discussions of *keri* in *Taketori*, for instance, are clearly inspired by Tokieda's notion of shi, ji, and shutai. In other words, it was precisely by presupposing Tokieda's theory that he studied the specific grammatical elements in Heian narrative and identified the dynamic movement of narratorial perspective. We cannot consider *Taketori*'s refraction of the modern norms of narrative discourse and subject formation as a neutral problem somehow suggested by the text itself. Before we marvel at the ways in which language process theory sheds light on the unique characteristics of Heian narrative economy, we need to pause over the fact that the construction of the "autonomy" of Japanese language and language studies was one of Tokieda's major intellectual agendas. Tokieda's theory of Japanese language may help us read Heian narrative against the grain of modern novelistic paradigms, but that does not mean that it provides an unbiased and immanent basis for reading these texts. In the next section, I consider Tokieda's work in relation to some of the disciplinary, geopolitical, and theoretical contexts in which they were developed, analyzing its polemical confrontation and its complicity with conceptual apparatuses of modernity that it sought to refute.

The Impasse of Antimodernism

Karatani Kōjin has called for the historicization of the "language process theory"—to recognize how Tokieda viewed Japanese from an ideologically and historically inflected position.[31] He links Tokieda's project with the intellectual milieu of Japan at the advent of the Pacific War (*Kokugogaku genron* was published in 1941). This was the period in which the definition of Japanese cultural identity was sought with a new urgency, provoking a concerted critique of the modernization and Westernization of Japan. Karatani suggests that Tokieda's rejection of uncritical adherence to Western models of linguistics responded to such antimodernistic and nationalist intellectual currents at the time, epitomized by the notorious *kindai no chōkoku* (Overcoming of the Modern) symposium.[32]

That Tokieda's theory has repeatedly resurfaced in cultural debates, particularly since the 1960s, may be attributed in part to the continued relevance of its critique of modernity and Eurocentrism in the postwar history of Japan and the world. Tokieda objected to the simplistic binary between particular and general, which destined the Japanese language (and the study of it) to become a mere specimen vis-à-vis the language in general defined by the modern, Western order of knowledge. For him, language is not transparently available to us as a positive entry—either in its universality or its particularity (e.g. Japanese language). Instead, it must be explored and defined through rigorous critical investigation. Thus, he saw no sense in simply positing Japanese as a particular species of language subordinated under the larger genus of "language." Correspondingly, he rejected the standard division of labor between kokugogaku and general linguistics, insisting that on one hand the examination of the specific nature of Japanese must also involve broader philosophical exploration into the essential nature of language and on the other hand that there is no way to theorize the nature of language aside from studying individual languages in their specificity.[33]

We should bear in mind that Tokieda took care not to make a hasty claim for the universality of Japanese. In his view, an understanding of the true nature of Japanese, which will also reveal the universal truth about all languages, is not available as a "given" but functions as the unrealized goal that continually shapes and reshapes the discipline. This is also why he rejected defining Japanese through existing, objectified entities such as ethnicity and the state (e.g., that Japanese is a language spoken within Japan or by Japanese people). While he insisted on studying Japanese in its specificity—refusing uncritical claims to universality made by modern linguistics—he also resisted facile racism and xenophobia in his approach. In this sense, Tokieda's antimodernist stance made him eschew naive linguistic nationalism. Kamei Hideo suggests that Tokieda's approach to language as an individual speech act arose in response to a blatantly reductive identification of language with the state.[34] It was not Tokieda but some of the advocates of modern linguistics who ended up trumpeting the uniqueness and superiority of Japanese as the embodiment of national spirit, precisely because they accepted the framework of the discipline (including the legacies of evolutionary linguistics) anchored by the ideology of the modern nation-state system.

Nevertheless, Tokieda's notion of the Japanese language as a subjective and experiential process open to any individual or community that uses it (transcending the boundaries of race, culture, ethnicity, and so on) was an idea rife with problematic implications in view of Japanese colonialism. This was especially so given his assessment that the specific characteristics of Japanese make it particularly suited to revealing the essential nature of language as a whole. Tokieda, after all, did argue that the coincidence between particular and universal in Japanese has to be postulated as the starting point of pursuing kokugogaku.[35] Kamei, who defends Tokieda from the charge of vulgar nationalism, also points out that the linguist advocated more refined and internalized means of spreading Japanese language in the colonial context (rather than externalized imposition by brute force). In an article written in 1942, Tokieda, who held a post at Keijō Imperial University (a colonial outpost of the imperial university in Korea), pointed out that the statist view of language based on ethnic nationalism could not validate the dissemination of Japanese in its colonies. In other words, such a perspective could not adequately address a situation in which the Japanese state sought to establish Japanese as the common language within its multiethnic empire. Instead, Tokieda repeatedly insisted on the language policy in Korea, which promoted the *enjoyment* of Japanese, and the reinforcement of Japanese education among Korean women so that their children would grow up speaking it as their "mother tongue."[36]

Japanese language construed as an open-ended horizon that ultimately merges with universality and the kokugogaku defined by its mission of uncovering the essence and beauty of the language, therefore, were in accordance with the expansionist logic of Japanese imperialism and its agenda of producing imperial subjects out of colonial populations. This compatibility with the project of Japanese imperialism highlights the universalistic scope and ambitions that subtended Tokieda's theory. Perceiving the self-contradiction that the simple modernization of language studies ran into (passively assimilating to modern linguistics), he theorized the discipline in ways that more fully and actively embodied the paradoxical identity formation of modernity. In other words, he defined kokugogaku as a truly modern subject, locating its identity in the transcendence of the tension between modernity and tradition or of particularity and generality. While Tokieda was no doubt more theoretically self-conscious than most of his academic foes, his attempt to "overcome" modern paradigms did not go much beyond the effort to claim the subject-position for kokugogaku and Japanese as constituted by the discipline. In other words, it was arrested in the effort to invert the Eurocentric mapping of knowledge, rather than raising more fundamental questions against the fallacy of universalism.

These limitations of Tokieda's disciplinary critique are echoed in his linguistic analyses as well. Tokieda, as we have seen, not only made claims about the particularity of Japanese language but he also questioned the validity of existing paradigms of linguistics as a context in which this specificity can be grasped. His determination to challenge Saussure and his incorporation of pre-Meiji kokugaku scholarship notwithstanding, we need to question whether Tokieda effectively established a theoretical stance independent of the assumptions of modern linguistics that he repudiated. For instance, he argued that the referential subject is not really elided in Japanese utterances even in the absence of explicit shugo (grammatical subject) because the predicate in itself implies the subject of an action/condition. In other words, the subject (what is conceived as the subject of the statement according to the Western model he objects to) is not completely denied but is rediscovered as the subject implicit in the predicate. Thus, while rejecting the notion that the Japanese language elides the grammatical subject as being Eurocentric, Tokieda appropriated this absence (of explicit subject) and turned it into a basis for his own claim that the subject and the predicate (or the agent and the action) are inextricably united in Japanese.

The referential subject implicit in the predicate parallels shutai as the subject of utterance that cannot be abstracted from the dynamic context of discourse. Shutai that is inscribed without being objectified is an entity that transcends the supposedly misguided binary of subjective versus objective assumed in modern linguistics. Here it is worth noting that subjective function in Japanese, both at referential and discursive levels, is thought to be implicit (i.e., without a fixed, objectified presence).[37] Tokieda himself, however, would have objected to such characterization of his theory—that is, shutai is not merely implicit because a specific category of words, ji, marks its intentions and attitudes. On a closer look, however, there are serious questions as to whether this all-important characterization of ji is sustainable.

Apart from the definition of ji as a class of morphemes with a variety of specific functions (such as those of jodōshi), ji also inscribes the box-in-box structure in which the referentiality of an utterance is always contextualized by a discursive and pragmatic frame. The function of ji in this sense may not be even called syntactic because we are not really talking about the relation within a given linguistic unit (the way words and phrases are put together) but the metalevel relation between the referential content and the pragmatic frame of enunciation. Ji as the marker of shutai's function, therefore, is said to make explicit the contingency of meaning to the signifying context, and, as the notion of zero-symbol discourse suggests, ji is ever-present in discourse in this sense. Given an appropriate context, any single morpheme (whether it be a nominal or a jodōshi) can be located in a box-in-box structure. At the same time, ji, once it is encased in another subjective frame, is equivalent to shi by virtue of being "contained." With respect to the box-in-box structure, therefore, the precise difference between shi and ji morphemes appears to be irrelevant. This puts in doubt the privilege of ji morphemes as specifically shutaiteki signifiers. Nothing prevents us from postulating an invisible zero-symbol framing an utterance ending with an explicit ji. If this is the case, the box-in-box structure is *always* marked by an implicit zero-symbol, unrelated to any concrete signifier. Tokieda, then, could not account for his definition of ji that conflates the pragmatic function of morphomes such as jodōshi (the specific inflections that they supply) and the function of the zero-symbol in the box-in-box structure.

Tokieda's negation of the "nominally based subject" of the Western model thus served as the backdrop against which he fashioned the unity between subject and predicate, agent and action, or subjective and objective that Japanese language allegedly demonstrates. In other words, the subject of utterance that exteriorizes itself without ever being objectified is staged by projecting the specter of "subject" onto the Japanese language. Freed of any concrete signifier, shutai haunts the language as a foundational assumption, ghostly but omnipresent. Through the hypostatization of shutai as a pure subject, his theory of Japanese language — its emphasis on discursivity and its unique economy of inscribing the subject — was caught in its binary relation to and dependence on the modern linguistic model he sought to overcome.

The Ghostly Subject of Heian Narratives

I have discussed the problems in Tokieda's theory that arose over the Japan versus West dichotomy, which deeply informed his thoughts. Now I would like to consider Tokieda's theory of shutai from a slightly different angle by examining the ways in which it was applied in the study of Heian narratives. A number of leading contemporary scholars of Heian literature have postulated an implicit, flexible, and nonobjectifiable subject of discourse in Heian narratives that draws on

Tokieda's work.[38] Fujii Sadakazu directly quotes from Tokieda's theory of zero-symbol discourse to argue that Heian narrative is in neither the first, second, or third but the *muninshō* (zero-person), the implicit and formless subjectivity that underlies all discourses.[39] It is worth noting that Fujii's concept of zero-*person* does not completely renounce the framework of *person*. Instead, by being coupled with the signifier of negation, *zero*, the zero-person figures the freedom from the binary between the first and third persons, the transcendence of the person from within.

Takahashi Tōru identifies in *The Tale of Genji* a chimerical subject, a ghostly narrator (*mononoke no yōna katarite*) that straddles absence and presence. He points out that the narratorial voices in the *Genji* at times materialize in the shadowy figures of *nyōbo* (ladies-in-waiting) while at other times they appear to be thoroughly immaterial, entering into a character's thoughts or describing scenes that they could not have witnessed. He thus likens the narrators of the *Genji* to ghostly spirits who occasionally possess the characters in the tale.[40] He suggests a parallel between the spectral narrator and the roles that ladies-in-waiting played in Heian court society—a constant and yet scarcely recognized presence in the lives of the high aristocracy they served. In Takahashi's work, the ghostly subject of discourse is privileged not so much for eluding the binary of the first and third persons but for subverting the power relations in the story-world centered on the highborn characters. Precisely by being marginal in the story-world, the narrators/ladies-in-waiting throw revealing critical lights on the main characters and their fates. In other words, the negativity vis-à-vis the story-world endows them with a critical agency. As intriguing as Takahashi's analysis is, one cannot help but notice the unresolved tension between the concrete social identity and the chimerical immateriality ascribed to the narratorial voice. The figure of the possessing spirit becomes a trope that allows Takahashi to circumvent this problem rather than wrestling with it straight on.

Mitani Kuniaki's discussion of narratorial voice in the *Genji* offers an analysis that is more theoretically consistent than Takahashi's view. Like Takahashi, Mitani links the narratorial voices of *The Tale of Genji* with the social status and function of ladies-in-waiting—abject stagehands in the dramas of Heian aristocratic society often rendered invisible in the eyes of masters and mistresses.[41] For Mitani, however, the

Genji's narratorial discourse achieves its unity through a wholly de-personalized and purely functional discursive subject, *washa*, which is distinguished from the ideologically and socially inflected narratorial voice. Mitani argues that, although the voices of the half-identified narrators (ladies-in-waiting) at times frame the discourses of the explicitly personified characters, we need to recognize the presence of the even more impersonal and immaterial frame of washa. Mitani schematizes *Genji*'s narration through Tokieda's box-in-box structure: characterological discourses are framed by semipersonified narratorial discourses, which in turn are framed by the discourses of purely functional washa, the outer limit of narrative textuality.[42] Like Fujii's notion of zero-person discourse, Mitani's washa is inspired by Tokieda's notion of zero-symbol. In the light of Tokieda's zero-symbol, we may understand Mitani's washa as an *implied narrator*, which need not be positively inscribed in the text. It is a theoretical construct that establishes a depersonalized and nonmimetic discursive agency that frames the text as a whole.

Mitani's theory of washa, which was first proposed in essays published in the late 1970s, posed a significant challenge to the conventional conflation of the discursive subject with an author outside the text or personified narrator(s) situated in the story-world. Mitani is one of the most theoretically astute critics among his generation of Heian literary scholars, drawing not only on structuralist narratology but also on theorists such as Derrida and Foucault who have critiqued structuralists. Contesting the standard understanding of Heian tales that perceived them to be the outgrowth of oral storytelling and vernacular poetic practices, he has called for the establishment of a distinct interpretive perspective for understanding them as written texts.[43]

He argues that, unlike oral storytelling and the recitation or singing of poems and songs, Heian tales as written discourses do not presuppose the presence of the addresser and addressee. Instead, they are self-consciously marked by detachment from the actual context of discursive production as well as reception. Through this disembeddedness, furthermore, they created an autonomous fictional world that estranges and critiques existing assumptions about reality. In studying the narratorial structure of Heian tales, he focuses on what he refers to as the dispersion and fragmentation of subject that results from the process of writing—the drawing and redrawing of the division be-tween the subject of utterance and the subject of statement (between the speaker *I* and the spoken "I").[44] Washa figures the absent discursive subject *I* that keeps eluding fixed representation within a text. Heian tales are privileged by Mitani precisely for foregrounding the divided subject that is typically hidden in everyday speech as well as in oral literature.[45]

Mitani's analysis of narrative form hinges on the differentiation be-tween literacy and orality as well as that between Heian narration and modern novelistic discourse. The concept of washa implicates writ-ten narrative as both a negation *and* the superseding of orality. Heian tales as written texts served as a counterpoint to the mythical pleni-tude (the unity between signifier and signified) attributed to oral and performative literature. At the same time, unlike the fabricated neu-trality of the omniscient third-person narrator of the modern novel, the concept of washa suggests that Heian tales retained certain forces and structure of first-person voice. They remain true to the authentic subjectivity and self-referentiality of discourse while undermining the phantasm of presence associated with oral/poetic forms of first-person discourses. Thus, Mitani carefully distinguishes the function of washa from the kind of stationary and transcendent perspective attributed to the omniscient third-person narrator of the modern novel. The washa, in texts such as *The Tale of Genji*, does not reduce the multiplicity of competing perspectives, meanings, and voices under a totalizing gaze. Instead it *frames* them (as in the box-in-box structure) with their di-versity intact.

The sophistication of the critical position that Mitani carves out in his study of Heian narrative has to be acknowledged (e.g., complicat-ing the modern/premodern juxtaposition with the orality/literacy di-chotomy located within premodern literary history). His arguments, however, may be questioned on a number of points. For one, if written texts undermine the naturalistic assumptions concerning the identity between the speaker *I* and the spoken "I," why should we retain a con-cept such as washa, which installs some form of subjective presence (albeit depersonalized and purely functional)? Is washa necessary be-cause if we do not postulate the existence of first-person subject, we *necessarily* fall into the fallacy of transcendent third-person narration? Mitani fails to consider the possibility that the distinction between the first and third person itself may be a construct that warrants scrutiny (I discuss this issue further in the next chapter).

Furthermore, Mitani justifies his notion of washa by arguing that the first-person discursive subject is *demanded* by the fact that a narrative discourse such as the *Genji*, with its multiple perspectives, retains its integrity as a text. Once we move from the commonsense positivity of "book" to a theoretical category such as "text," however, it is far from obvious why the textual unity of *Genji* must be presupposed as a premise that cannot be questioned. The argument that the washa must be deduced from the textual integrity is tautological—as was the case with the relation between the complete utterance and the shutai function in Tokieda's theory—unless there is an explanation as to why and how the unity of the text must be assumed in the first place.

To be fair to Mitani, it should be mentioned that the integrity of text for him is not a static closure that inheres in a text but a flexible boundary that is reestablished through varied reading practices.[46] Correspondingly, the washa (and the box-in-box structure that it sustains) is not only an apparatus of narration but also of reading, the frame through which readers grasp the text.[47] Nevertheless, we need to consider whether Mitani's theory of washa, influenced by Tokieda, is adequate to the task of theorizing the interrelation between narrating and reading, the subjective and objective or text and context, without stagnating in the prioritization of one over the other. The term washa inevitably draws our attention to narration, subject, and text, and these are certainly the concepts to which Mitani's theoretical writings keep returning. Mitani's schematization of three discursive levels—particular voices attributed to the characters in the story-world, the personified narrators (i.e., ladies-in-waiting), and then washa—reveals the hierarchical order that favors a progressively abstract discursive subject with superior scope of textual integration. This hierarchy is set up not only by privileging the structural force of framing but also by equating the distance from the embodied presence in the story-world with "critical" insights. The washa, in other words, not only brings together but also distances and critiques the discourses it contains.[48]

We need to consider the ramifications of postulating an entity such as washa—characterized by the absence of specific attributes and by its distance from the concrete story-world—as a more authentic and reflexive subject that holds the text together. What seems underdeveloped in Mitani's discussion is the theoretical return path from the stratosphere of structural washa to the distinct voices that constitute the text, a methodology that allows us to approach them in their very specificity. Mitani offers a disclaimer that washa, in a sense, is a reader as well as a textual narrator, who must continually engage with those fragmentary elements of the text. The box-in-box structure through which washa is defined, however, traces the movement away from rather than toward the desegregated particularities of textual discourses that bring characters as well as events to life. It does little, in other words, to prevent construing our process of reading in terms of a uniform trajectory tending toward the discovery of the structural integrity of the text. In questioning this tendency in Mitani's work, however, I do not mean to call for simply returning to close reading of concrete and discrete aspects of the text. Considering the issues of textual form and structure is crucial not only for what it teaches us about the text in question. Just as important, it also stimulates our reflection over our own modality of reading—theoretical mediations unavoidably involved in our interpretive processes. The question, then, is how to develop the impetus as well as the methodology for approaching texts in their concrete materiality without disavowing the indispensable role of such a critical self-consciousness. In the next section, I return to Tokieda's work and investigate further its inadequacy in the light of this project. This discussion can help us explore alternative strategies for studying Heian narratives, which I consider in the next chapter.

The Sociality of Language

In the field of Japanese linguistics today, Tokieda's language process theory has been discredited for manipulating purely theoretical constructs, such as shutai and zero-symbol, that cannot be accounted for empirically. Explaining everything and nothing, they are deemed irrelevant in the effort to develop an understanding of the ways in which Japanese language actually works. What I regard as problematic in Tokieda's work, however, is not the degree of its abstraction or its alleged lack of empirical accountability. Rather, I contend that we cannot fully come to terms with the reactionary tendency of Tokieda's thought unless we recognize that his negation of the nominalized subject and his refusal to define language as an objective system fall short of addressing the *negativity* of the discursive subject. His adherence to the binary form of difference, such as Japan-West, particular-universal, and modern-premodern, which I discussed earlier, is symptomatic of his preservation of the reified notion of subject and the coherent discursive order that it underwrote. In the following pages, I illustrate what I mean by the negativity of the discursive subject through a critique of Tokieda's theory. This discussion moves our analysis from issues of language and subjectivity to that of the sociality of language.

Tokieda claimed that language is nothing but a mute material (i.e., meaningless) unless it is mobilized by shutai. Dislodging meaning as an immanent property of language, Tokieda defined the signified as that which is generated by shutai's intentionality vis-à-vis the world of which and to which it speaks. Shutai's intentions frame and reframe the objects referred to, providing a context that anchors the meaning. Ji, according to Tokieda, is the class of morpheme that marks this shutai's function. It not only conveys the specific attitudes and stances of shutai but also inscribes the structural relation between the speaker's intentionality and the referential content in such a way that the latter completes and contains the former (a box-in-box structure). As I have suggested, however, if we can always postulate an implicit zero-symbol as the outermost frame of discourse, then the dual role of ji as a signifier of a specific subjective inflection *and* the box-in-box structure in general may be put to question.

Without ji linking the two functions ascribed to the discursive subject, there is nothing to guarantee the identity between shutai as the subject of concrete intentionality and shutai as the subject of the zero-symbol, or the structural integrity of an utterance. This points to a fundamental flaw in Tokieda's theory of shutai as an undivided entity. The dual function of ji presupposes a self-contained context of discourse (what Tokieda refers to as *bamen*), in which intentional and enunciatory agencies of shutai operate simultaneously.[49] If shutai's intentionality gives rise to a discourse, however, the subject of intention would have to *precede* the subject of enunciation. This temporal gap suggests that the intentional content and the enunciatory context cannot form a neat closure of box-in-box structure, illustrated by Tokieda as a series of closed rings nested inside one another.

Tokieda disavowed the implication of his own theory that unless shutai is somehow divided within, its signifying process will be without meaning, as he said the language is before it is mobilized by shutai's intentionality. Discourse, in other words, cannot be meaningful (i.e., convey shutai's intentionality) if shutai consistently escapes objective determination as a dynamic agency of framing and reframing.[50] Tokieda disavowed this dilemma by constituting shutai as an impossible subject that thinks and posits the limit of its thought (the completion/framing of utterance) at the same time. This denial of the division between the intentional and enunciatory agencies of the discursive subject, furthermore, amounts to a denial of its sociality. The definition of language as a communicative act does not necessarily mean that Tokieda grasped it as a fundamentally social practice. While he emphasized the interlocutive context in which language is used, shutai's agency, which is completely self-sufficient, is also completely monologic, always moving from the subject to the Other in a single direction.

This feature of Tokieda's perspective may be further highlighted by the works of M. M. Bakhtin. While Bakhtin, like Tokieda, rejected the grammatically defined unity of the "sentence," he also staunchly refused to reduce the utterance to an act of an individual subject.[51] His argument for the impossibility of defining an utterance through the singular agency of a subject serves as a basis for his notion of the "dialogic." Tokieda located the unity of utterance in a complete thought of shutai. For Bakhtin, the completion of an utterance is not determined by the original intention of a speaker but by the intrusion of the Other, who breaks the monotony of a particular utterance.[52] The unity of utterance is located precisely in the break between the self and the Other, between the agency of the subject and its limit. What holds an utterance together, then, is the dialogic encounter with the Other that marks the vanishing point of the subject. The displacement of one discursive frame (organized around a subject) by another completes an utterance, which cannot determine its own closure.

Bakhtin's theory ultimately challenges the concept of the closure of an utterance in a more radical sense. The utterance is constituted in the chain of displacement in which the final utterance is impossible, as an utterance that is not displaced by another is not yet complete. As long as there is no "last word" in this chain, the completion of any utterance is always provisional.[53] We need not look at the ultimate end-point of a signifying chain to consider the implications of applying this perspective to the study of a concrete text. Bakhtin's argument seems commonsensical enough when we think of it in terms of "natural dialogue," relying on the organic authority of voice as the basis for distinguishing one subject from another. But the analysis of written texts reminds us that the question — who exactly is speaking? — may not have a simple, self-evident answer.[54] In the textual field, the shift among speaking subjects does not occur as one fully formed and unitary subject (and its discourse) displacing another. Rather, the vanishing point of the subject produces the displaced subject retroactively, and the displacing subject (the Other) itself will be constituted through the process of its own displacement to occur in the future.

Thus, we need to caution against the popularized interpretation of *dialogic* that hypostatizes the Other subject or the intersubjective space of communication as a total context against which an utterance is determined and made positive. The break/completion of a given utterance cannot be reduced to a break from and to the reified utterance of an Other. If the context (without which an utterance cannot be meaningful) is produced retroactively, there is always some disjunction between discourse and its context. The theory of the dialogic addresses not only the break between the discourse of self versus Other but also this constitutive fissure and the temporal loop in the discursive operation. Thus, even if discourse cannot represent its origin/subject as such, it may take part in *effecting* its own origin. The retroactive production, however, undercuts the ontological priority of the origin (e.g., shutai and its intentionality as the ground of discourse). This is the theoretical basis on which the concept of dialogic undermines an independent, autonomous instance of discourse that can be abstracted as a single unit of signification that functions on its own. Instead, every utterance, by virtue of its incompleteness, participates in the social space of discourse that is itself never a closed field.

Psychoanalytic theory of Jacques Lacan offers helpful insights into the problem of the subject understood through the retroactive operation of signification. Lacan suggests that the subject relates to itself by the act of announcing or enunciating itself and then grasping it as it returns from the future (Other) via alienation: "the subject becomes at each stage what he was before and announces himself—he will have been—only in the future perfect tense. . . . in this "rear view" (*rétroviseé*), all that the subject can be certain of is the anticipated image coming to meet him that he catches of himself in his mirror."[55] I discussed earlier the fact that Tokieda rejected the representational and instrumental understanding of language by identifying the subjective truth of language in the self-reflexivity and performativity of discourse. What Lacan argues is that the reflexivity of discourse—that it points back to its (subjective) origin as the basis of its meaningfulness—does not mean that this referring achieves perfect closure.

Wittgenstein, in his famous refutation of a private language—the impossibility of language to function as anything but a social practice—illustrates how the self-reflexivity of discourse misfires. He questions whether the subject of utterance can ever be represented in itself, without being aligned with an "objective" reference. While indexical signifiers such as "I" (or jodōshi) appear to point to the speaker, they do not point to any specific socially defined agent, unable to close the gap between self-referentiality and objective referentiality: "When I say 'I am in pain,' I do not point to a person who is in pain, since in a certain sense I have no idea *who* is. . . . I did not say that such-and-such a person was in pain, but 'I am.' . . . Now in saying this I don't name any person. Just as I don't name anyone when I *groan* with pain. Though someone else sees who is in pain from the groaning."[56] In a sentence such as "I have pain," in which the signifier "I" is customarily understood to be denoting the subject of utterance, Wittgenstein argues that the pronoun has no referential value. "I" doesn't point to any object in the world—to a particular body or a socially defined agent. The reflexity of "I" is a tautological gesture that points not to an object but to its own pointing.[57] A similar critique may be made about Tokieda's notion of ji. For ji or a demonstrative pronoun to be meaningful, two distinct points must be established: the indexical reference and the anchoring point that locates this indexical reference in the world, distinguishing it from the others. While the signification of the former depends on the latter, the positing of the latter requires a perspective away from it that contextualizes and maps it against the other possible positions. The reflexivity of the utterance, in other words, will simply float unless it is attached to some objective determination that self-reference cannot establish by itself—like a needle without a face on a compass.

A self-reflexive signifier such as "I" marks everyone and no one unless it is aligned with a specific object in the world. Wittgenstein reminds us that an utterance such as "I, Ludwig Wittgenstein, hereby state" makes sense in the first place because neither the "I" nor "Ludwig Wittgenstein" means the same thing or performs the same function. At the same time, however, the metaphorical, partial suture of "I" and "Ludwig Wittgenstein" (of self-referentiality and objective referentiality) is integral to the specific operation of first-person discourse. In first-person discourse, the speaking subject must be presumed—partially fixed onto some kind of objective identity—even though "I" is not identical to "Ludwig Wittgenstein."

We have seen that for Wittgenstein self-reference without an objective referent is empty. Lacan insists that his void *is* the subject of the signifier that drives a wedge between the signifier and the signified, marking the impossibility that the two can correspond to each other perfectly. In other words, the Lacanian subject is not a signified that any signifier may represent but the impossibility of full signification (the perfect alignment between signifier and signified) that gets relayed from one instance of signification to another.[58] Note that the critical issue at stake is not so much the assertion of *difference* between the signifier "I" and the actual speaker *I*. One can imagine the subject signified and the signifying subject to be different but tightly aligned with each other through a concept such as ji. Rather, Lacan is pointing to a more radical disconnection erupting over the discursive self-reference that refracts a neat correspondence between signifier and signified. This is the crucial difference between Lacan and Tokieda and the issue often overlooked by those who try to incorporate Tokieda's work into contemporary critical theory, including the critics in Heian literary studies.

Self-reflexive and indexical terms such as "I" may *designate* the subject of utterance, but they do not *signify* it. Tokieda misrecognized this negativity of subject, imagining a ji that captures it perfectly by tracking its movement—not designating but *gesticulating* the subject. Yet, a ji that supposedly mimes the subject also fails to respond to the question of identity: "Who is speaking?" In this sense, first-person discourse is no more faithful to the self-referentiality of discourse than the third person but not because all discourses articulate shutai, as Tokieda believed. Rather, it is because they all fall short of doing so.

The vacuous subject of self-reflexivity foregrounds the lack lodged in the circuit of linguistic representation, always on the verge of failure, not saying what it sets out to say, and saying what it is not supposed to say. The critical point of this observation is not the indeterminacy of meaning (the total arbitrariness of the signifier) but the fact that this failure is the indispensable condition for language to function as language, that is, as a social practice.[59] The individual appropriation of language is possible not because its objective dimension is secondary to the subjective, as Tokieda theorized. Rather, it is because the imperfect and partial juncture between objective (pointing to the other) and subjective (pointing to self) that occurs in discursive practices prevents the discursive field from being unified neither by the organizing force of a transcendent center, nor by a flexible frame as Tokieda theorized. This enabling failure helps us conceive the irreducible sociality of discourse without having to posit its metaphysical priority to an individual agent. It is neither that the subject is simply an effect of a preexisting linguistic structure nor that it is primordial or transcendent to the social practice of articulation. The symbolic network functions as that which is "always already there" — the indispensable context of an individual enactment of language — but without an ontological priority. Thus, the impossibility of the self-same subject cross-checks with the impossibility of the social field of language defined as a self-consistent and autonomous whole. One of the reasons why the issue of language and linguistic practices has been so central to contemporary debates on subjectivity, I believe, is because it offers a model for exploring the complex relation between subjectivity and sociality. A critical itinerary suggested from these discussions, therefore, is the one that takes us from recognition of the negativity of subject facilitated by linguistic analysis to an investigation into what this may imply for our understanding and experience of the everyday practices and materiality of our social world. This line of inquiry is expanded in the next chapter and the epilogue. There I discuss more specifically how we may proceed from an examination of the interrelated contingencies of the linguistic field and subjectivity to the analysis of individual identity and social formation.

Our ongoing analysis alerts us to the unexamined premises embedded in a question such as "Is there a subject (or an alternative economy of subject) in Japanese?" The inquiry presupposes the subject as a positivity that may be absent in one context but exist in another. It thereby invites simplistic East-West cultural comparisons armed with hosts of other familiar binaries such as communalistic tendencies in Japan as the counterpoint to the individualism of the West. Through an examination of Tokieda's work, I have tried to suggest that there is no alternative model of language and subjectivity in other cultures or historical epochs that can be marshalled to patch together the division of discursive subject (or the fissure between objective and subjective in the operation of language) that has riddled modern debates on the topic. The binary between the modern Western subject and the specifically Japanese economy of subject, with the implicit inversion of their hierarchical relation, fails to address this fundamental impasse.[60]

At the beginning of the chapter, I referred to an issue raised by the post-1970s textual analyses of Heian narrative that continues to be relevant today: how to read these texts through and against our modern interpretive frames. Heian kana narratives, of course, presuppose very different conventions from those assumed by modern novels. Inquiries into linguistic and formal features of literary discourses are crucial means for exploring the complex contours of this difference and the alternative logics that may be operating in them. Yet we need to caution against a hasty leap from the acknowledgment of differences to the dichotomy between the modern West and the Heian as two distinct and totalizable linguistic or cultural systems. What gets lost in such reductive analysis is the contingent and provisional status of concepts such as "Heian texts" or "Heian discourses"—in other words, the historicity of the frame itself. As I have tried to demonstrate in this chapter, the validity of the critique against Eurocentrism in Tokieda's work does not mean that his theory offers a neutral and unbiased basis for discussing premodern Japanese language or literature.

My objection to Tokieda's theory, however, is not solely concerned with the particularistic approach to Japanese language and texts that it has sometimes supported. The affinity for particularism in Tokieda's thought needs to be critiqued in relation to his idealism: the assumption that one can somehow explicate the signifying process by postulating a nonalienated subject such as shutai as its ground. Regardless of the validity of his rejection of the objectifying approach to language, we need to be alert to the shortcomings in his concept of shutai. Although Tokieda's language process theory sought to extricate itself from the authority of the modern Western order of knowledge, it remained bound to the paradoxical interdependence between first-person subjectivity and third-person objectivity that is at the center of modern philosophical debates on the subject.[61] The withdrawal into the radical antiobjectifying perspective of shutai disavows the very ground on which this theoretical impasse arose, that is, the field of history not as an objective (independent and primordial to the subjective) but a *social* space that refracts the schema of identity and relations presupposed by the self-contained and autonomous notion of subjectivity. The continued viability of the formalist methodologies depends on whether we can deploy them without the expectation that linguistic structure (and for that matter any formal configuration of symbolic practices) displaces the need to attend to the problematics of historicization. This is one of the central issues that the textual approach to Heian literature must work through if it is to address the methodological exhaustion expressed by some members of the new generation of scholars in the field.[62]

Let me close this chapter with another attempt at historicizing the problems I find in Tokieda's theory and the deployment of it in the post-1970s textual turn in literary studies—why I regard them as an incomplete attempt to critique the modernizing impulse of kokubungaku and the masculinist national subject that it constitutes. I would like to return to Tokieda's stance on colonial language policies during the war. My objective is not to "contextualize" Tokieda in relation to the history of Japanese imperialism—for instance, by discussing the causal relations between Tokieda's theory and Japanese colonialism (to what extent his thoughts were inspired by Japanese imperialism or whether his work had a direct effect on colonial language policies). I simply wish to point out that Tokieda's ideas were in dialogue with specific problems that emerged out of Japanese colonialism and that seeing his theory in this light reveals significant political ramifications and unexpected inflections in his approach to language.

During the war Tokieda did not mince his words in advocating the virtues of making the colonial population abandon the Korean language and adopt Japanese as its native tongue. Whatever disagreements Tokieda may have had with reactionary linguistic nationalists over the design of colonial language education, it was apparently not over the goal: to establish Japanese as the uncontested imperial language of Asia. Yasuda Toshiaki wonders if Tokieda could have launched a more fundamental rejoinder against colonial language policies if he was genuinely invested in the standpoint of discursive subject that his theory espoused—that is, if he recognized the violation of the subjectivity of Koreans.[63] In my view, however, Tokieda's stance on the matter was consistent with his theoretical formulations. He claimed that Koreans would benefit in the deepest sense by avoiding the hazards involved in bilingualism and renouncing a Korean language that had been adulterated and confused by the oppressive influence of Chinese and by more recent "contact" with Japanese.[64] Thus, we find here a justification of linguistic cleansing from an emphatically nonjudgmental (nonobjectifying) stance toward language and subjectivity. It is not that the Korean language was inherently flawed or inferior to Japanese. Nor was it that some grand scheme of historical destiny dictated that the Korean language had to be subordinated to imperial Japanese. Rather, given the degeneration of Korean caused by arbitrary external conditions, its elimination would enable Koreans to function better as linguistic subjects at peace in their unified and less circumscribed linguistic world. Tokieda apparently assumed that from the genuinely shutaiteki perspective of an imperial subject, one who is already thinking in and living with Japanese as his or her mother tongue, the historical and political circumstances under which this occurred would be of secondary concern.

As I have suggested, Tokieda's theoretical strategy against the modern historicist/objective notion of language and subjectivity left unexplored the possibility of developing an alternative mode of historicization. Set against the colonial language policy, we see the chilling implications of shutai and its hermetic authenticity construed in a historical and social vacuum. We may also recall the role Tokieda assigned to Korean mothers as the mediators of the proper and joyous linguistic subject of Japanese empire. The burden of history falls on the maternal figure split between her own mother tongue (Korean) and the mother tongue (Japanese) that she is to impart to her child. The happy unity and fullness that Tokieda ascribed to the imperial linguistic subject, therefore, would stand on the shoulders of the self-divided maternal. Where would we locate the enjoyment of this maternal subject, who is at once identified with the abject bilingualism of the colonial linguistic condition and with her role of eradicating it? Her entrapment in the despised hybridity of colonial language would be further reinforced through her designated task of raising her child in the linguistic image of the colonizer. Considerations that situate the formation of subject in a sociohistorical field, however, are foreclosed in Tokieda's perspective. The role played by the maternal in the production of the imperial linguistic subject harkens back to the gendered dialectic of the national subject that we have already examined. The feminine is once again invoked as the negativity that provides the catalyst for transcendence—from the dividedness of the colonial subject to the integrity of the imperial subject. Even if shutai, by definition, has no gender, primordial to and transcendent of the asymmetrical divide that gender marks, it nevertheless reproduces the masculinist principle that underwrites the national subject. While he sharply denounced the static and objectifying conceptualization of identity presupposed in the modernist view of the linguistic subject, Tokieda preserved the national subject in a modified framework that responded to the challenges faced by the imperial state. The self-referential, autonomous, and dynamic functions of shutai complemented the logic of the imperial subject, which is defined by self-generative, self-legitimating, and expansionist tendencies and freed from the normative standards of fixed territoriality, ethnicity, language, culture, and so on.

In comparison to shutai, even the dialectical subject that Fujioka envisioned falls short of accommodating the demands of empire. It may have offered a sufficient narrative for producing a national subject out of native Japanese to be mobilized in the imperial project of the state, but it had much more limited utility for plotting the production of imperial subjects out of colonized populations. Fujioka posited a national subject who arises out of the dialectical confrontation between the singularity of native essence and the discrete, potentially disruptive forces of alterity (femininity, Asian cultural influences, etc.). The wholeness and originary status of native essence is reaffirmed by the figure of the national subject, who absorbs and reconfigures the diverse elements constituting his or her past into the historical process of national synthesis. The identity of Japan/masculinity as the subject (privileged over racial or gendered Other) was sanctioned by its agency of relating the past to the present in a transformative as well as integrative manner.

The native essence to be repressed/conserved in Tokieda's schema is not defined in terms of linguistic-cultural particularity such as Korean or Japanese. Rather, it is identified with the primordial, undisturbed wholeness of the linguistic experience of shutai. For the colonized population, then, such an unsullied experience of language is to be recovered through radical detachment from the colonial linguistic condition (including ties to Korean as a degraded native tongue) by becoming the shutai of imperial language. The alleged corruption identified in colonial language serves as an alibi for ascribing the wholeness to imperial Japanese. Tokieda's identification of colonial bilingualism with corruption and alienation contradicts his own imperative of approaching language from the standpoint of shutai. From the properly subjective viewpoint of shutai, which defies the objectification of language as a system, the intermixing or cousage of imperial and native languages need not be apprehended as a *bilingual* or linguistically fragmented experience. If there are greater degrees of tension and antagonism involved in such linguistic practices, they would have to be attributed not to the bilingualism in itself but to pragmatic conditions—circumstances in which colonial populations are forced to construe their linguistic practices in terms of the binary and hierarchical differentiation between the imperial language, with its integrity intact, and the debased native tongue. Furthermore, it is inconceivable that linguistic mixing in the colonial context could be a purely one-sided affair. Rather, it would inevitably affect the language of the colonizer as well. The wholeness attributed to the imperial language, therefore, is an extralinguistic and geopolitical construct; what secures the unity of the imperial language despite its hybridization are the military, political, and economic forces of the empire.

The familiar valorization of "native language" is reproduced in Tokieda's vision of the linguistic empire via the structural equivalence posited between the originary purity of language prior to the linguistic miscegenation on one hand, and the wholeness of imperial linguistic experience guaranteed by the geopolitical and military power of the Japanese empire on the other. At least in theory, then, the constitution of the subject in Tokieda's linguistic empire depends less on sociocultural processes than it would in Fujioka's literary nation.[65] Tokieda's prescription of colonial language policy implicates not the evolution from particular to universal (from man to Man) through history but a much more abrupt and noncontextual transformation of the potentially alienated colonial Other into the imperial subject. This truncation of sociocultural and historical forms of mediation helps us see how the logic of shutai may support a highly expedient means of legitimating the state's exercise of power over its (colonial) subjects. In Tokieda's nondogmatic analysis, it does not take much more than the facticity of Japanese colonial occupation to justify the policies designed to violently absorb the colonized population into imperial linguistic unity.

In this sense, shutai reproduces the classic duality of the modern subject divided between potency and impotence. Shutai is an absolute subject of language that expresses itself without limits, constituting its linguistic universe without being subjected to externalized rules and regulations.[66] Yet this total freedom in language is enabled by its complete submission to extrinsic social and historical forces that secure the phantasm of undisturbed linguistic interiority. Shutai, denied the ability to acknowledge, much less contest, this condition of its alleged freedom, is the subject of linguistic empire in the double sense of subjectification and subjection. For a subject to break out of this bind, it must not only reject its native and particularistic origin (reified identity of native tongue and its purity) but also renounce the possibility of experiential and dynamic unity that a notion such as shutai invokes. Only then can it be an agent that may critique the very frame enthroning it as a paradoxical master of its linguistic universe.

Despite the appearance of being apolitical and even antinationalist, therefore, Tokieda's discussion of shutai offers a narrative of imperial subject formation. As I have argued, he ended up recuperating the national subject and its mechanism of producing/subordinating the abject Other by insisting on the integrity of shutai and the coherent discursive order that it reigns over. A genuine critique of the national subject and the attendant gender ideology, then, would have to contest not only modern (dialectical) historicism but also the brand of antihistoricism for which Tokieda argued.

CHAPTER SIX

Gender and Heian Narrative Form

Perhaps more than any other existing works of Heian kana narrative, *Kagerō nikki* is a text read through the persona of its supposed author, the woman known to posterity as the Mother of Michitsuna. The text has been anointed as the masterpiece of so-called *heian joryū nikki bungaku* (Heian female diary literature) by modern kokubungaku and is known as a frank confession of female suffering. The diary/memoir, which spans the twenty years between 954 and 974 A.D., relates the gradual deterioration of the heroine's marriage, plagued by the husband's involvement with numerous mistresses and wives. One of the seminal studies of the text by Ikeda Kikan, published in 1927, claims that the text is a "blood-drippingly raw human document . . . [and that] the suffering depicted in *Kagerō nikki* is surely the eternal suffering of 'women.'"[1]

Modern commentators have described *Kagerō nikki* as emotional, rambling, and infantile. For instance, Watanabe Minoru, while acknowledging the emotional expressivity of the text, faults its lack of storytelling skill. In this respect, he considers the text to be regressive in the development of kana narrative, exhibiting less objective clarity compared to earlier narrative texts such as *Tosa nikki* and *Taketori monogatari* (texts generally attributed to male authors). He points to *Kagerō*'s use of deictic expressions with ambiguous references as an example of its self-absorbed inarticulateness, treating readers as if they were already familiar with the events and milieu that the text describes.[2]

Such assessments of the *Kagerō nikki* not only belie the gender stereotypes that slip into the biographical readings of the text but display the unexamined application of modern linguistic and narratological concepts in the study of Heian texts. In the following, I challenge the identification of the text with a singular, narcissistic, and subjective voice of the author by examining its narrative form. I question the applicability of the category "first-person narration" and a whole array of expectations that it invites for a study of *Kagerō nikki*. Instead, I argue that the construction of the heroine as the primary affective, perspectival, and discursive agent in the text is achieved through its narrative apparatus, which refracts some of the basic assumptions concerning first-person narration and the modern notion of subjectivity that it presupposes. This discussion will also put into question the validity of using Tokieda's language process theory as an aid in understanding the narratorial voice of the text. Reading *Kagerō nikki* not as a first-person narrative can have a variety of significant ramifications for our understanding of it. I suggest that the rethinking of the text's narrative form draws our attention to the complex strategies through which the heroine articulates her perspective and her story both in relation to and against the existing discourses on women and female destiny.

The Heroine as an Other

Kagerō nikki opens with the following prologue.

These times have passed, and there was *one* [*hito*] who drifted uncertainly through them, scarcely knowing where she was. It was perhaps natural that such should be her fate. She was less handsome than most, and not remarkably gifted. Yet, as the days went by in monotonous succession, she had occasion to look at the old romances, and found them masses of the rankest fabrication. Perhaps, she said to herself, even the story of her own dreary life, set down in a journal, might be of interest; and it might also answer a question: had that life been one befitting a well-born lady? But they must all be recounted, events of long ago, events of but yesterday. She was by no means certain that she could bring them to order.[3]

The above passage is from the English translation of *Kagerō nikki* by Edward Seidensticker. Seidensticker renders the passage in the third-person voice. This is because the word *hito*, translated as "one" in English, appears to mark the narrator's objectifying stance toward the heroine.[4] Except for this initial instance, however, there is no explicit reference to her as hito in the rest of the prologue. The English translation interpolates grammatical subjects absent in the original text, inserting third-person pronouns throughout the section. The translation has us assume that the "one" introduced at the beginning of this passage serves as the subject of the entire prologue. On the basis of Heian syntax, however, after the first phrase containing *one*, the section could be translated into English as a first- *or* third-person voice; there is no grammatical or stylistic regulation that posits *one* as the antecedent for implicit subject of the rest of the prologue. The translation of these passages into modern Japanese in *Nihon koten bungaku zenshū* indeed avoids making the "person" explicit, rendering it in a prose that could be read as either the first- or third-person discourse.[5]

In the rest of the text, however, we often find the heroine referred to as *ware*, a word that is generally equated with the first-person pronoun in English and modern Japanese.[6] This lexical marker and the text's reputation as an emotionally charged confession by a woman have supported the widespread assumption that *Kagerō*'s narration is primarily in the first-person voice.[7] Yet the references to the heroine as hito are not limited to the prologue but are found scattered throughout the text. Furthermore, particularly in the last of the three books (or scrolls) in the existing versions of the text, we find the narration frequently relating the heroine's experience through modal expressions of speculation and uncertainty. Modern commentaries conclude that *Kagerō*'s narration, which is in the first-person voice, switches into the third person from time to time, oscillating between identification with and objectification of the heroine.

Let us look more closely at what standard commentaries have labeled the explicit first- and third-person discourses in *Kagerō*'s narration and the assumption that they reflect the narrator's subjective and objective stances toward the heroine, respectively. Among the four instances in which the heroine is referred to as hito, three examples clearly put her in a contrastive relation to another character. The following passage describes the parting between the heroine and her father, who is leaving his home in the capital to assume post as a provincial governor.

いまはとて、みな出で立つ日になりて、ゆく人もせきあへぬまであり、とまる人はたまいていふかたなく悲しきに...

Finally, the day set for [his] departure came. The one who is departing (*yuku hito*) could hardly hold back [his] tears. As for the one who will be left behind (*tomaru hito*), no words can express [her] sorrow. (Tenth Month of Tenryaku 8; 133; S: 36)[8]

It should be noted that the pronouns in brackets, which confirm and clarify the referent of the oblique hito, are only implicit in the original.

The reference here to the heroine as hito juxtaposes the father and the daughter in a parallel construction. The narration, which up to this point seems to speak from the heroine's perspective, pulls away from her to bring the father and daughter together in a single frame, representing their state of mind in relation to each other. Although the accent ultimately falls on the daughter, whose depth of sorrow is said to exceed that of the departing father, we may note that the "objectification" of the heroine does not put a singular focus on her; rather, it links her to another character. The contrastive or comparative nuance that the reference to the heroine as hito produces may be present even when she is not explicitly pitted against another character.

天下の物ふさにあり。山の末と思ふやうなる人のために、はるかにあるに、ことなるにも、身の憂きことはまづおぼえけり。

Lavish gifts were brought all the way from the capital to the one [hito] who is considering making this deep mountain [her] home. Feeling unfit to receive such gifts, [I] could not help but be reminded of the sad state of [my] affairs at the present. (Sixth Month of Tenroku 2; 271; S: 105)

Gender and Heian Narrative Form 185

The passage describes the heroine's reaction to elegant gifts delivered from the capital during her stay at a mountain temple retreat where she has sought refuge from her unhappy marriage. There is a clear contrast drawn between the heroine in voluntary exile in a rustic dwelling and the glamorous life (and people) in the capital where the lavish gifts originated.

Commentaries usually interpret the third-person references to the heroine as expressions of the author/narrator's *self*-objectification and *self*-detachment. If, as I have suggested, the narration refers to the heroine as hito in order to draw a contrast between her and others or her condition and those of others, then the "objectification" marks not so much the relationship between the narrator and the heroine as that between the heroine and the others in the story. Compared to these examples, the reference to the heroine as hito at the beginning of the prologue stands out as an exceptional instance in which the term refers to the heroine in isolation, without situating her in some form of social relation. The assumption that *Kagerō*'s narration occasionally switches back to the third-person register established at the opening needs to be modified in view of this difference between the function of hito in the prologue and in the rest of the text. In the prologue, the reference to the heroine as hito appears to draw our attention to the relationship between the subject of utterance (narrator) and the subject of statement (heroine) because the heroine is the only figure in focus. I examine the peculiarity of the prologue's reference to the heroine as hito later in this chapter. Here it suffices to note that in the rest of the text, in contrast, casting the heroine as hito serves to map out the relations between her and the other characters.

The Heroine as Self

We may now turn to the text's use of the word *ware*, commonly understood to be the first-person pronoun. According to the commentaries, ware both makes explicit and confirms the fact that the narration is in the first-person voice. As it is this norm that the objectifying reference to the heroine is said to transgress, the examination of the text's deployment of ware should help elucidate the purported instability of person in the text. An index of terms used in the text, *Kagerō nikki sōsakuin*, lists thirty-eight instances of ware used in narration that refer specifically to the heroine.[9]

We notice that the passages that use this term frequently foreground the heroine's disjunction, isolation, and discordance with other characters. It is also often paired with particles—for example, *ware ha* (*I but not others*) and *ware nomi* (*I alone*)—and used in phrases expressing a contrastive relation of dissimilarity between the heroine and other(s). The following example occurs in a scene in which the heroine has just sent a poem to her increasingly absent husband on a rainy evening, reminding him of the days when pouring rain did not deter him from visiting her.

> と書きて、いまぞいくらむとおもふほどに、南面の、格子も上げぬ外に、人の気おぼゆ。人はえ知らず、われのみぞあやしとおぼゆるに、妻戸おし開けて、ふとはひ入りたり。

> At about the time that the messenger should have reached [him] [husband] with [my] message, [I] sensed someone at the south side of the house, where the shutters had been lowered. The others (*hito ha*) did not notice; [I] alone (*ware nomi*) felt that something was astir. Suddenly, [he] came in, pushing open the side door. (Twelfth Month of Tenroku 2; 299; S: 119)

The expression "I alone" (*ware nomi*), contrasted with "others" (*hito*) underscores the heightened sensitivity of the heroine, who is perpetually waiting for the husband.

We also find ware used in passages where heroine and others are to be put in a *structurally* parallel position, but the emotive force of the scene draws attention to her, inscribing her sense of dissonance with others. In the next passage, ware is joined to hito in order to depict the mutual animosity erupting between the heroine and her husband.

> 心のどかに暮らす日、はかなきこと言ひ言ひのはてに、われも人も悪しう言ひなりて、うち怨じて出づるになりぬ。

> [We] were spending a day together peacefully, but a series of trivial exchanges led to both "I" (*ware mo*) and "he" (*hito mo*) hurling angry words at each other, and [he] ended up storming out of the house in a rage. (Eighth Month of Kōhō 3; 183; S: 60)

The passages with repeated use of *ware* typically involve emotional crises that force the heroine into isolation from or tension with others. Here is the text's description of the heroine among her family and relatives, who have gathered to mourn the death of her mother.

わざとのことなども、みなおのがとりどりすれば、われはただ
つれづれとながめをのみして. . . これかれぞ殿上などもせね
ば、穢らひもひとつにしなしためれば、おのがじしひきつほね
などしつつあめる中に、われのみぞ紛るることなくて

People were preparing the memorial ceremony and offerings on their own (*onoga toridori*), but *I* (*ware*) could only sit and gaze out absent-mindedly. . . . As no one [in the family] had to attend the court, we stayed together at home during the period of purification. *Everyone* seemed to be occupying *themselves* (*ono ga jishi*) with the preparation of their living quarters, moving around the screens and curtains for partition; *I alone* (*ware nomi*) remained apart from all the commotion, unable to take my mind off the grief. (Fall of Kōhō 1; 169; S: 53–54)

The contrast between ware and other people in the household, repeated twice in a short interval, sharply distinguishes the heroine from others in the context of mourning. The passages suggest that the others, who manage to attend to funeral preparations or mind their own business, are not as deeply affected by the loss, leaving the heroine to despair in isolation.

As it was with the case of hito, the narration's reference to the heroine as ware occurs when she is positioned in relation to the other(s).[10] The explicit (rather than implicit) references to the heroine through the use of terms such as *ware* and *hito* locate her in interpersonal contexts, highlighting relations within the story more than relations between the narrator (the subject of utterance) and the heroine (the subject of the statement). The difference between these two modes of references (ware versus hito) lies in the fact that referring to the heroine as hito implies a perspective originating outside of her, while positing her as ware invokes a perspective originating from her. We may question, however, whether the latter perspective as it is presented in the text is "subjective" in the sense assumed in the concept of "first person"—that is, invoking the speaking/narrating agent who is, strictly speaking, outside the context established by what is spoken/narrated.

Fukazawa Tōru suggests an alternative view to the widespread understanding of the function of ware and hito in the text. According to Fukazawa, the two terms perform an identical function in *Kagerō nikki* as signifiers of self-objectification. Ware, when it frequently appears in the text, points not to the speaking Mother of Michitsuna but to the self of the past who is being objectified by her in the instant of narration.[11] Fukazawa's discussion draws on Tokieda Motoki's theory of Japanese grammar. He contends that while words such as *ware* and *hito* serve to objectify the past self the narrator's own opinions and attitudes (at the moment of narration) are expressed by what Tokieda referred to as ji. As we saw in the last chapter, Tokieda argued that in Japanese first-person pronouns do not directly express the speaking subject (shutai).[12] Although Tokieda did recognize the special deictic function of the pronouns that sets them apart from other nominals (insofar as they are related to the speaker), he insisted that speakers could not be inscribed by them. Thus, Fukazawa writes: "The speaking 'Mother of Michitsuna' violently distances and objectifies her past 'self' as *hito* or *ware*. Then she judges, evaluates, gives meaning to, and relentlessly captures that 'self' by means of ji at the end of the sentence."[13] The question not clearly addressed by Tokieda's discussion, however, is exactly how these two types of deixis—pronouns and ji—relate to each other. In Fukazawa's analysis of *Kagerō*, while both ware and ji refer to the Mother of Michitsuna they point to her at different temporal points: her past self as opposed to her present (in which she narrates her past).

The narration of *Kagerō nikki* suggests, however, the possibility of a more radical break between the indexical orientations of ji and nominal deixis in a single continuum of discourse. The following passage describes a scene from yet another pilgrimage that the heroine's unhappiness drives her to make. The desolate path to a mountain temple reinforces her melancholic reflections on the wretched state of her life. After spending the evening praying at the temple, her entourage prepares to embark on the trip home.

夜明けぬと聞くほどに、雨降り出でぬ。いとわりなしと思ひつつ、法師の坊にいたりて、「いかがすべき」などいふほどに、

ことと明けはてて、「蓑、笠や」と人は騒ぐ。われはのどかに
てながむれば、前なる谷より、雲しづしづと上るに、いともの
悲しうて、

　思ひきや天つ空なるあまぐもを袖してわくる山踏まむとは

とぞおぼえけらし。

Close to the dawn, rain began to fall. Dismayed by the change in
the weather, [we] debated over [our] plans in the priests' quarters.
Meanwhile, the morning had arrived and the others (*hito ha*) were
bustling around fetching rain cloaks and umbrellas. *I* (*ware ha*) idly
gazed at a cloud rising in the valley. [I] felt so sad.

> Who could have known that I would come to this? Treading
> deep into the mountain, parting the gray clouds with my sleeves.

Such *seemed to have been [my] thoughts.* (Second Month of Ten'en
2; 355; S: 148)

Again, ware is used with an explicitly contrastive nuance against *hito*,
staging an opposition typical in the text—the inactive and isolated
self alienated from active "others." In the original, the phrase does not
break but continues on to the poem the heroine recites. Note that the
end of the phrase "[I] seemed to have thought" (*oboekerashi*) is inflected by a jodōshi compound, *kerashi* (*keri* plus a modal suffix of
conjecture, *rashi*). While the nominal, ware, posits the heroine as the
self (contrasted with the others in the scene), the jodōshi of speculation, *rashi*, inserts some distance between the perspective of the narrator and that of the thematic topic (heroine). In other words, while
the reflexivity of ware points back to the heroine as the origin of perspective, the reflexivity of ji, *kerashi*, points elsewhere. The two types
of deictic references in a single phrase therefore appear to invoke different anchoring points.

　Standard commentaries routinely explain the modality of uncertainty and conjecture frequently used in *Kagerō*'s narration as the nar-
rator/heroine's lapse of memory about her past. The text, from the
very beginning, refers to itself as a recollection of the past from a temporal and cognitive remove. Nevertheless, we need to pay more attention to the deployment of the distance inserted between the narrator

and the heroine. For instance, although the narration suddenly lapses into the modality of uncertainty at the end of the passage cited above, just a few lines earlier it describes the external landscape and the heroine's state of mind with great clarity and immediacy. If we do not presuppose a "natural" identity between the narrator and the heroine, we may recognize more clearly the differentiation of the two perspectives. Furthermore, modal suffixes of uncertainty and conjecture are most frequently found in the final section of the text. If we suppose that the text is a memoir recalling past events after some passage of time, then the context of events should move closer to the context of narration as the text unfolds. Yet the epistemological and psychological dissonance between the narrator and the heroine appears to increase rather than decrease in the later sections of the text. The naturalistic view that explains the narration's distance from its thematic topic (the heroine and her experience) in terms of mnemonic difficulty fails to account for this.

Before pursuing further the question of exactly when and how the text inscribes cognitive distance between the heroine and the narrator, we may address a more basic question: whether the standard notion of deixis serves as a useful category for analyzing *Kagerō nikki*. The splitting of the phrase along the dual anchoring points described above goes against the basic definition of *deixis* as an "orientational" device that places a statement in relation to the *speaker* and his or her viewpoint. In English, when the first-person pronoun is introduced in an utterance the speaker is identified with "I" and the orientation of deixis must be organized accordingly.[14]

The absence of a consistent alignment of the deixis with the positionality of the speaker is observed in other deictic expressions as well; we find frequent use of nominal deixis that does not seem to presuppose the narrator as its point of reference. The expression "*wa ga*," which is usually translated as the first-person possessive pronoun "my," for instance, is used in the narration to refer to the heroine in most cases, but we find instances in which it clearly does not.[15] Referring to the wife of Governor-General Minamoto Takaaki, who has returned to her residence after suffering repeated tragedies in her life (the exile of her husband and the destruction of his mansion by fire), the text states, "The governor-general's wife moved to *her own* (*wa ga*) mansion at Momozono" (北の方、わが御殿の桃園なるに渡りて) (Sixth Month of Anna 2; 212; S: 75).

The text's use of deictic expressions of temporality also exhibits the ambiguity of referential context. *Kagerō nikki* repeatedly describes the humiliation inflicted on the heroine by her increasingly distant husband, who passes her house on his way to visit other wives and lovers. A particularly poignant episode is found in book two a few days after the husband has failed to make the customary New Year's visit to her home for the first time since their marriage. Despite her disappointment and anger at this affront, further intensified by the rumor of his involvement in yet another amorous affair, a few days later she prepares to greet him at the sound of his entourage approaching her gate. Yet again he passes by without paying his respects. The text states, "Imagine [if you will] the even greater humiliation [that I experienced] *today*" (今日まして思ふ心おしはからなむ; First Month of Tenroku 2; 250; S: 94). The passage is inflected by the desiderative particle *namu*, which appears to be directed to the reader. The temporal deixis *kefu* (today), however, takes the "here and now" of the story as its anchor. Since narratorial intrusions are relatively infrequent in the text, the phrase would have foregrounded the narrating register. At the same time, the specification of "today" connects this particular incident to what occurred in the plot a few days earlier, underscoring the heroine's humiliation. The temporal point of view here is multiple and mobile regardless of whether we understand this utterance as spoken from the point of view of the heroine at the time of the event (thus deviating from the purported premise of the text that it presents a recollection of past events) or from that of the narrator with the inconsistent use of temporal deixis.[16]

Heian Narratives and Linear Perspectivism

The conclusion we may draw from this discussion, then, is that nominal deixis (including pronouns) in *Kagerō* narration functions not so much to index the speaking subject and the context of narration. Instead, it marks the relations between the "self and other" or "now and another time" *within* the story. The deictic anchoring point, furthermore, is not absolutely tethered to a single source but can float among various instances and agents in the story-world. The heroine and her actions are of course the most frequent node of reflexivity not only because she is referred to as *ware* but because other characters are often identified in relational terms that take the heroine as the point of reference. Her father, for instance, is referred to as *wa ga tanomoshiki hito* (the one on whom I rely). The heroine's privilege, however, is relative and cumulative—she is not the absolute point of reference. Furthermore, specific uses of *ji* in narration may fracture the centrality of the heroine and her actions by positing a point of view distinct from that of the heroine. What I am suggesting, then, is that *Kagerō nikki* is not written in the first-person voice.

Even though the protagonist is referred to using a reflexive term such as *ware* (a word that is understood today as a first-person pronoun), the word functions more as self than "I." Although it connotes reflexivity and invokes a point of view originating from an agent referred to as such, this perspective is not linked to some transcendent position in which the story-world is united. Its reflexivity is based on relations within the story-world; the heroine is the primary point of focus vis-à-vis other characters. This also suggests that the reference to a character using the term *ware* does not necessarily mean that the narrating voice will consistently adopt the position of that particular character.

Although in *Kagerō*'s narration *ware* is only used to refer to the heroine, in standard classical Japanese dictionaries *ware* is glossed as (1) the subject pronoun "I," (2) the second-person reference "you," and (3) the third-person reflexive pronoun "oneself." In another kana Heian diary, *Sarashina nikki* (written a few decades after *Kagerō* and attributed to a niece of the Mother of Michitsuna), we find *ware* used to refer to the heroine and her father in a single phrase.

> 母は、尼になりて、おなじ家の内なれど、方ことに住みはなれ
> てあり。父はただ、われをおとなになしすゑて、われは世にも
> 出で交じらわず。

Mother became a nun and although she stayed in our house she moved to a wing separate from our living quarters. My father immediately set *me* (*ware*) up as the mistress of the household, while he *himself* (*ware*) withdrew from the world.[17]

The first *ware* refers to the heroine and the second refers to the father. Other so-called first-person pronouns found in Heian kana texts, such as *onore*, also behave in this way.[18]

How should we understand the linguistic conventions apparently devoid of "I" or a narrative structure that seems to preclude the positionality of "I"? In order to answer these questions, we need to consider the concept of the "first-person" and narrative subjectivity assumed in the dominant discursive conventions of modernity. In modern European languages—with their obligatory subject "I" and subject/predicate agreement—the first-person discourse constructs a distinct relationship between the subject of speech (*I* the speaker) and the subject spoken about (the signifier "I" inscribed in the discourse). While the speaker is situated outside the field of representation (it is the referrer and not a referent), the signifier "I" and other grammatical regulations such as the tense system serve as consistent indices of a speaker. The speaker and the signifier "I" or their respective spatio-temporal contexts may not be exactly identical, but the two are strictly aligned (e.g., I may speak of my experience as an infant in the first-person voice although I have no direct recollection of it). The first-person voice in modern narratives manipulates this structure for its effect.

The mirroring correspondence between the speaking subject and the subject spoken and the use of this relation in literary representation may be illustrated through a comparison with the linear perspective system in painting. In linear perspectivism, the space is organized around a centric ray connecting two points—the viewpoint (the position of the originary locus of the artist and subsequently of the viewers) and the vanishing point (the apex of the pyramidal recessional space around which the image is organized). This centralized representational field organized around a single trajectory, which both links and separates the referrer (subject) and referent (object), is the dominant paradigm of modern realist representation. It is important to note that the representational field constituted around this axis is at once subjective (determined by the position of the viewer) and objective (governed by an impersonal, mathematical law). In one of the most influential studies on linear perspectivism, *Perspective as Symbolic Form*, Erwin Panofsky defined modern perspectivism through its paradoxical conjunction of the subjective and objective: "The history of perspective may be understood with equal justice as a triumph of the distancing and objectifying sense of the real, and as a triumph of the distance-denying human struggle for control; it is as much a consolidation and systematization of the external world, as an extension of the domain of the self."[19]

The imbrication of subjective and objective that Panofsky refers to can be found in the representational field of literary discourse as well. Whether the referrer/origin of the narration is inscribed (first person) or erased (third person), the central trajectory linking the referrer and referent itself is presupposed as the basic spatial, temporal, and other structural organization of dominant modern narrative convention. The third person that epitomizes the voice of classic nineteenth-century European novels embodies at once impersonality and subjectivism because, on one hand, it generates the impression of autonomy and the presence of the object by disavowing the function of the referrer, while on the other hand the perspective always implicates the voyeur/creator at its origin. The narrator may not be identified and fleshed out, but it is expected to occupy a more or less fixed or consistent stance vis-à-vis the object of representation. This is why, classic third-person narration adopts the past tense as its normative mode.[20]

The first-person narration in classic novels is most commonly presented as a recollection, allowing the speaker in the "present" to objectify himself or herself in the past until, typically, the convergence of narrating time and the narrated time is reached at the end of the text. Thus, the narrated subject and the subject of narration are aligned but never completely "one"—it is critical to maintain a fluctuating distance between them as the narration unfolds. We rarely find a first-person narration in the present tense (e.g., "play-by-play" discourse of sportscasting) sustained over a long period in conventional novels. First- and third-person voices, therefore, are not in strict opposition, as the subjective versus objective dichotomy associated with these modes suggests. Rather, they both presuppose a common representational structure centered on the clear alignment between the subject (referrer) and the object (referent).

It goes without saying that a modern representational regime such as linear perspectivism is not a transparent representation of "natural" space. Rather, as many have pointed out, it is a semiotic field based on the assumption of homogeneous, measurable space unified under a highly artificial monocular and stationary vision. Furthermore, the viewpoint as well as the vanishing point around which the perspectival space is organized cannot be represented in the picture—the view-point is always outside the frame, and the vanishing point, as the term suggests, is the closure that ultimately evades representation. They are ideal and structural loci that the centered and mathematically ordered visual space calls for. Linear perspectivism, in other words, is a norm (ideology) that regulates practices without having a fixed referent in reality.

Likewise, we must caution against naturalizing the structure of first-person narration. For one thing, we need to question the obvious-ness of "I" as the marker of a speaker. As was discussed in the last chapter, the signifier "I," which purportedly marks the subject of dis-course, does not really point to a particular person. The referentiality of "I" is purely formal and structural; it is a tautological signifier that points to its own pointing. "I" functions by virtue of the fact that it can refer to any agent of utterance, but this generality means that strictly speaking it cannot refer to any specific person in the world. We suture this formal signifier "I" to the writer or a narrator of the text we are reading about, not because of the meaning inherent in this word but because we have internalized the conventions that I have been discuss-ing. It is by reading the text against this structure that we construct the subject of narration as the conjunction of the formal pointer "I" and a person with concrete social attributes provided and elaborated in the text (with a name, gender, personal history, and so on). What we call first-person narration, in other words, is not a discourse that trans-parently represents the coincidence of the subject of speech and the subject spoken about but an attempt to signify and manipulate such an ideal coincidence. Thus, first-person narration, like linear perspectiv-ism, has to be understood as a historically contingent and ideological formation.

The "Self" and "I"

The notion of *person* is inappropriate for analyzing *Kagerō nikki*, therefore, not because its narration wavers between the first and the third person. Rather, it makes little sense to ask whether *Kagerō nikki* is written in the first-person voice or not if the text does not presuppose the specific conventions of representation on which the concept of person is founded. My contention, therefore, is that the structure of the first person — the strict correspondence between the subject of utterance and the subject of statement — is alien to *Kagerō*'s narrative apparatus. Although *Kagerō*'s narration does at times seem to speak as the heroine, this impression is borne not by the formal structure of the first person but by the emotional and vocative coloration of the discourse. The following passage describes the beautiful scenery the heroine sees during her pilgrimage as if the vista is unfolding right before her eyes.

> それより立ちて、いきもていけば、なでふことなき道も山深き ここちすれば、いとあはれに水の声す。例の杉も空さして立ち わたり、木の葉はいろいろに見えたり。水は石がちなる中より わきかへりゆく。夕日のさしたるさまなどを見るに、涙もとま らず。

> Continuing on the way, although there [was] nothing special about the path, [I felt] like [I] was deep in the mountain and sound of river [touched my] heart. The trees [stood] against the sky, and [I saw] the leaves in myriad hues of autumn. The river [churned] against its rocky bed. [I] couldn't stop tears from flowing as [I watched] the afternoon sun casting a slanting ray on this vista. (Ninth Month of Anna 1; 197; S: 67)

Note that the grammatical subjects and the past tense of the verbs (in brackets) are added in the English translation. The description of the scene framed by the act of "seeing," or an emotional response to it, suggests the presence of an agent through whose eyes and feelings the landscape is perceived. Fukazawa Tōru, who, as mentioned earlier, reads *ware* as the signifier of the narrator's self-objectification, cites the above passage as an instance in which the narrator identifies and merges with the experience of the past "self," reliving it nostalgically as if in a dream.[21] Positing the Mother of Michitsuna as the speaker of the narration, he assumes that the narrator and the heroine are identical, albeit separated by the passage of time. So the highlighting of perceptual impression that gives subjective tone to the discourse is understood as the narrator's "reliving" of her past experience.

Nowhere in the text, however, is such relationship between the narrator and the heroine explicitly indicated if we question the status of ware as the sign of the speaker's *self*-reference or *self*-objectification. In other words, the fact that the use of ware establishes the heroine as the relative center of the story-world and an anchoring point of reflexivity does not mean that she is identical to the subject of the narrating. The Other against which self/ware achieves its meaning is not "you," the audience of narration, but the other characters in the story. Unlike the dominant mode of modern narratives, in which the tenses and persons project and retroject the locus of closure and origin in a centered organization, in *Kagerō*'s narration there is no grammatical signifier on the textual surface that consistently positions the narrator in relation to the unfolding events in the story. Once we stop presupposing the structure of person, we may question whether the *Kagerō*'s narration is actually more subjective or first person than those in other Heian narrative texts in which the narrator seems transparent and functional—e.g., such as *Taketori monogatari*, which is commonly assumed to be in the third-person voice. In *Taketori*, too, the narration takes on vocative and emotional tones, at times rendering it indistinguishable from the characters' utterances and points of view. So in both *Kagerō* and *Taketori* metalevel comments attributed to the narrator (e.g., modality or judgments marked by ji) float without being aligned to a specific temporal and spatial coordinate.

The representational field presupposed by *Kagerō nikki* does not constitute the mirroring relations between the subjects of statement and that of utterance, foreclosing the subject as "I" (whether as the personified narrator with an identity in the story-world or as an anonymous and abstract authorial voice that unifies the story-world from outside the frame). Thus, I argue that the distinction between *Kagerō* and earlier narratives such as *Taketori* does not lie in the identity of the narrator and the principal character in the story (the label "first-person narration" is as erroneous for *Kagerō* as "third-person narration" is for *Taketori*). Rather, *Kagerō* differs from *Taketori* in the ways it posits the focal character, who emphatically occupies the position of "self." In the same vein, its narrative form also differs from that of *Tosa nikki*—an earlier kana text, which is generally assumed to be narrated in the first-person voice. In *Kagerō* the heroine is the primary locus from which the others are perceived and the locus to which the reflexive references return. This is the self implicit in the prologue's notion of "writing a diary on one's own life." What I am trying to elucidate is the critical difference between this self and "I" and the broader implications that this distinction may have for our understanding of *Kagerō* and Heian kana narrative in general.

The absence of "I" (as the ideal coincidence of the formal pointer and socially contextualized self) in *Kagerō*'s narration finds its ocular metaphor in book three.

さて、ついたち三日のほどに、午時ばかりに見えたり。老いて恥づかしうなりにたるに、いと苦しけれど、いかがはせむ。とばかりありて、「方塞がりたり」とて、わが染めたるともいはじ、にほふばかりの桜襲の綾、文はこぼれぬばかりして、固文の表袴つやつやとして、はるかに追ひちらして帰るを聞きつつ、あな苦し、いみじうもうちとけたりつるかな、など思ひて、なりをうち見れば、いたうしほなえたり、鏡をうち見れば、いと憎げにはあり。

He appeared at about noon on the third day of the month. [I] felt tormented by the shame of [my] unseemly old age, but what could [I] do? After a while, he remembered that the direction of [my] house was forbidden [due to the geomancy] and prepared to leave. He was dressed in clothing [I] had dyed myself (*waga sometaru*): a white robe with a deep purple lining lavishly woven in an intricate pattern. His trousers were made of a glossy material with subdued patterns. [I] do not wish to sound self-congratulatory, but the attire was most elegant. As [I] heard his outrunners clearing the way in the distance, [I] regretted how unprepared [I] was for his visit. [I] took a look at [my own] clothing and saw that it was rumpled and worn. [I] took a look at [myself] in the mirror and found [my] face loathsome. (Second Month of Tennen 2; 341–42; S: 141–42)

The scene is organized around complex relations between self and other. The heroine is overwhelmed by the sight of her husband magnificently dressed in the robe that she herself had dyed (the narration inscribes this with the nominal deictic *waga*). His abrupt departure forces her to direct her perspective back to herself. We may note that the turning inward of the gaze is mediated by the overt gestures of looking at her clothes and her face reflected in the mirror. Rather than identifying her clothes and physical appearance as her *own*, she distances herself from them (mediated by an outward act) in order to hold them in her gaze. It is as if objective attributes such as her appearance are not in the possession of the heroine as the agent of seeing. We may note that this absence of "possessive" relations between the self and its attribute suggests a profound difference between the notion of subjectivity presupposed in modern narratives and the self constituted in *Kagerō*. We may recall, for instance, that John Locke famously defined the integrity and identity of an individual subject through the relation of possession: "every man has a property in his own *person*: this no body has any right to but himself."[22] For the "I," the unity/possession of its attributes is a "given," guaranteed by the principle of identity (or God-given right) that need not be anchored in concrete acts and events. The self, on the other hand, is concrete, defined by social relations, so, its attributes must be ascertained through a concrete, socially situated act of reflexivity. Put in another way, the "I" of modern narrative discourse figures the formal unity of modern Man; while it is itself abstract and vacuous, it serves to forge the coherence among concrete, multiple, and contextual selves.

The division between the heroine as the seer and the seen (her own image) is analogous to the noncoincidence between the narrator (subject of utterance) and the heroine (subject of statement) in the text. In the following passage, found at the end of book two, the text depicts the critical worsening of the heroine's marital relationship. A reflective passage frames the section.

> 忌のところになむ、夜ごとに、と告ぐる人あれば、心やすらか
> であり経るに、月日はさながら、鬼やらひ来ぬるとあれば、あ
> さましあさましと思ひ果つるもいみじきに、人は、童、大人と
> もいはず、「儺やらふ儺やらふ」と騒ぎののしるを、われのみ
> のどかにて見聞けば、ことしも、ここちよげならむところのか
> ぎりせまほしげなるわざにぞ見えける。雪なむいみじう降ると
> いふなり。年のをはりには、何事につけても、思ひ残さざりけ
> むかし。

Time passed as [I] spent days tormented by the report that he [the husband] was visiting that loathsome place [the residence of the other woman] every night. [I] was mortified by the realization that the year had already come to its close. Others (*hito ha*), both young and old, were raising a ruckus celebrating New Year's Eve, shouting

200   Gender and National Literature

and chasing the demons away, while I alone (*ware nomi*), quietly watched the commotion. It occurred to [me] that such festivity only befits a household with happiness worth protecting. [I] heard people say that the snow was falling heavily outside. By the year's end, [I] *seemed to have* tasted every possible kind of bitter brooding. (Twelfth Month of Tenroku 2; 300; S: 120, emphasis added)

The passage revolves around the heroine's consciousness of her own misery and isolation from the rest of the world, again with the typical contrast between the active others and the passive, melancholic self. The narration draws our attention to the heroine's self-reflection (ware established in contradistinction to the others) and then distances her at the end, with the (past) speculative *kemu*. While the heroine's self-consciousness is most powerfully underscored in such a moment of contrast with the other, this self-reflection quickly turns into the distancing of self that divides the perspective. This powerful instance of self-mediation is framed by the narratorial perspective, which ends up moving away from the heroine, inflecting the self-reflection with the viewpoint of the other. The hyperreflexive "looking at myself looking" that sutures modern subjectivity to itself is evidently alien to this representational field. The reflexive gaze instead splits the seer and the seen, generating an alternative register of discourse. *Kagerō*'s narration evokes the self in relation to the others, but it does not articulate the self in itself.

How to conceptualize language and subjectivity in a manner that does not conflate the narrating subject and the subject narrated (i.e., between *I* the speaker and "I" the linguistic subject) was a central problematic of Tokieda's theory that in turn helped inspire notions such as zero-person discourse and washa, in Heian scholarship. As I argued in the last chapter, however, their discussions do not offer an adequate explanation as to why we have to assume that the narrating voice posits a discursive subject as its origin. The assertion that the coherence of the utterance/text demands a subjective presence such as washa or shutai remains tautological, relying on the presumed unity of text/utterance. The moments when *Kagerō nikki* seems to objectify the heroine, holding her in remove, have been often equated with the text's foregrounding of the narratorial agent (drawing the readers' attention to the fact that she is speaking about her past from the context of narration). Could it be possible instead to understand such instances as "excesses," something that cannot be articulated from the perspective of self as constituted in the text? Do we have to presume that the "estranged voice" of narration necessarily *belongs* to a subject?

A frequently made association between Heian narratives and orality suggests another line of argument for assuming that the narrating voice in these texts implicates the presence of a narrating subject. In other words, if Heian narrative discourse is modeled after storytelling practices and was customarily read aloud, doesn't this presuppose a scene of narration (with a narrator/reader and an audience)? We need to be cautious about the erasure of distinction between the forms of everyday speech and narrative discourse implied by this question. In *Kagerō*, we find subtle formal differences between narratological versus characterological modes of discourse (quoted words of the characters in the story-world). For instance, in what appears to be the quotation of a character's speech, we find the use of ware, which deviates from the pattern I have identified. The passage below depicts the heroine becoming ill due to sorrow and exhaustion after the death of her mother. Fearing that she may also die before her husband reaches the mountain temple where she had nursed her mother, she communicates her will to her young son.

> 幼き子を引き寄せて、わづかにいふやうは、「われ、はかなく
> て死ぬなめり。かしこにきこえむやうは、『おのがうへをば、
> いかにもいかにもな知りたまひそ。この御後のことを、人々の
> ものせられむ上にも、とぶらひものしたまへ』ときこえよ」と
> て、「いかにせむ」とばかりいひて、ものもいはれずなりぬ。

Drawing the young child close to [me], [I] barely spoke these words: "*I* (*ware*) may waste away and die soon. Please tell over there [i.e., her husband], '[he: husband] shouldn't trouble [himself] on my account (*ono ga uhe*). Just please be sure to do more than what is customary to mourn for my mother.' But what are we to do?" After this, [I] couldn't utter another word. (Fall of Kōhō I; 165–66; S: 52)

In the phrase, "[I] may waste away and die soon," (*ware, hakana-kute shinurunameri*), ware does not carry any obvious contrastive/comparative nuance, and its reflexivity appears to point straight back to the speaker, who is performing the function equivalent to that of the first-person pronoun in a conventional sense. The use of ware in the heroine's speech situated in the story-world, therefore, does not seem to follow the pattern with which ware appears in other parts of the text.

Of course, given the fact that the distinction between narratological and characterological discourses is not clearly marked in Heian kana texts, one must be cautious about treating any passage as a direct quotation. The scene above, however, clearly foregrounds not just the content but the performative aspect of the heroine's utterance. The central drama unfolding is that of the heroine imparting what she believes to be her final words to her son. Holding him, the heroine desperately tries to make him accept the unbearable possibility that ware, the beloved mother before him, may be dying, and he, despite his tender age, must perform the duty of conveying her dying wishes to her husband. Her utterance, furthermore, is framed, both at the beginning and at the end, by references to her *act* of speaking. Thus, the text seems to emphatically attribute the voice uttering ware to the heroine. If ware refers to the *speaking* heroine in this passage, why should the term not refer to the discursive agent (narrator) in narration? In order to respond to this question, we need to consider it in the light of the text's narrative economy.

The peculiar usage of ware in *Kagerō*'s narration, which cannot be equated with the first-person "I," suggests the disjunction between the registers of narration and events narrated in the text. In other words, the levels of enunciation and enunciated do not form a coherent relation (of correspondence or identity) as expected in modern narrative conventions. The ware in the passage cited above does not transgress this narrative economy because the heroine's utterance is explicitly situated in the story-world—in the interlocutive context of dialogue between her and her son. Its self-referentiality does not transcend the context of events narrated and create a vertiginous closure of "speaking about myself speaking." The structural disjuncture between the story-world and narration that I identify in the text can be observed in earlier narrative texts such as *Taketori monogatari*. However, it is formally more salient in *Kagerō nikki* precisely because it establishes the primary point of view within the story-world (the heroine) as the self.

In order to see how this structure relates to the broader organization of the text, let us return to the closing passage from book two. The slipping away of the perspective from the self—away from the heroine's contemplation of her relation with the others—prevents not only the closure of self-reflection (looking at myself looking) but also the structural closure of the text. The increased use of both ware and speculative jodōshi in later sections of the text has been considered paradoxical, emphasizing both subjective and objective stances of the narration. There is, however, no contradiction in the simultaneous increase in the number of passages with ware, on one hand, and those with speculative jodōshi on the other. The stronger the emphasis on the heroine as the self—inscribing *her* point of view—the more estranged the narrating voice becomes, as if it were returning to its point of departure: the explicit separation of the heroine and the narrating voice at the beginning of the prologue. The link between the structural composition of the text and the deployment of deictics, such as ware and various types of speculative jodōshi, warns us against limiting the study of perspective to syntactical or morphological issues. In the final section of this chapter, I consider the relationship between the text's thematic organization and the formal construction of the heroine as a self.

Gendered Self

Among the Heian kana narratives extant today, the complex narrative apparatus of *Kagerō nikki*—that is, constituting the primary character of the story-world as a self from whose point of view the others are perceived and to whom the reflexive gaze returns—is unprecedented. We can never be sure whether and to what extent this was an innovation of *Kagerō*, given the limited samples of kana texts that have survived from the period. Some thematic elements of *Kagerō*, however, offer clues to the factors that may have contributed to the deployment, if not the invention, of this narrative form. As I suggested at the beginning of this chapter, not reading *Kagerō* as a first-person narrative can have a variety of important ramifications for our understanding of this text. For one thing, this view demands that we rethink the ways in which we address questions of gender in studying the text, moving us away from the naturalized association between this text and femininity or the female point of view that the autobiographical reading of the text has encouraged. The questioning of the simple equation between the heroine and the narrator helps us focus our attention on the sophisticated ways in which social norms and expectations regarding gender and gender relations function as central frameworks through and against which the heroine, her perspective, and her act of writing about her life are constituted in the text.

The construction of self in *Kagerō nikki* is grounded in the text's mapping of the heroine in the socius—while "I" is structurally transcendent to the empirical identity, the self cannot be abstracted from specific social predications. This is not to say, however, that the self is reducible to a preexisting social context. The self is articulated through the tension between the existing assumptions about women and women's lives and the heroine's experience inscribed through her point of view. The problem of gender emerges as a critical issue in the present analysis of *Kagerō* not because the text is infused with the femininity of the author. Rather, the thematically and formally complex structure of the text constitutes the heroine with specific social positionality—in particular, her gender and social status. The analysis of the text's narrative form, therefore, calls for consideration of the social inflection of self.

Let us once again take a close look at the prologue, this time through my translation.

かくありし時過ぎて、世の中にいとものはかなく、とにもかく にもつかで、世に経る人ありけり。かたちとても人にも似ず、 心魂もあるにもあらで、かうものの要にもあらであるも、こと わりと思ひつつ、ただ臥し起き明かし暮らすままに、世の中に おほかる古物語のはしなどを見れば、世におほかるそらごとだ にあり、人にもあらぬ身の上まで書き日記して、めづらしきさ まにもありなむ、天下の人の品高きやと問はむためしにもせよ かし、とおぼゆるも、過ぎにし年月ごろのこともおぼつかなか りければ、さてもありぬべきことなむおほかりける。

Thus, time has passed. There was one who drifted through life helplessly. [She] was resigned to a life of little consequence—given [her] poorer than average looks and the lack of talent and wisdom. As [she] let the days and nights slip by, [she] had occasion to glance at popular old tales and found them full of banal fabrications. [She] figured that even the dreary story of [her] life set down in writing might appear strange and amusing, and it could answer questions concerning the life of [being married to] people of the highest ranks. But the memories of bygone years are no longer clear, and much of what has been written may not be very accurate.

In the first-person narration of modern narratives, the prologue — presumably situated in the context of narrating — would have been the most obvious place to establish the identity between the narrator and the heroine. *Kagerō*'s representational economy, however, does not constitute such a seamless unity between the subject of utterance and the subject of statement. Thus, the narration does not posit its identity with the heroine whose *mi no uhe* (circumstances of life) the text is about to present; instead, the heroine is introduced as hito. As I have pointed out, the prologue is unique in its reference to the heroine as hito that does not involve explicit or implicit comparisons with other characters. The passage therefore foregrounds the disjunction between the narration and the story narrated, highlighting the estranged voice. The prologue as a whole operates as an outer frame of the text that is in some ways discontinuous to it. The distancing stance toward the heroine, furthermore, may also be understood through the sociality of self. If the self is always inscribed in relation to others, at the beginning of the text, before this context is established, she cannot be represented as such.

After the heroine is introduced, the prologue turns its attention to her reflections concerning herself and her life; her evaluation of old tales, which she condemns as fabrications; and her motives for writing a *nikki*. It ends with an evaluation of the nikki itself as not being factually reliable. The narrating perspective is both fluid and multiple throughout this section. While the narrational voice introduces the heroine from a remove, as it depicts her appearance, mental resources, and the state of her life the distance between the discourse of the heroine and that of the narration becomes blurred. The narration refers to her thoughts and actions from a point of view that could be attributed to herself. Finally, the narration presents the heroine/writer's sense of uncertainty about her recollections of the past. The temporality of discourse hovers among the times prior to writing, at the beginning of the writing, and after the writing has commenced, depicting the heroine and the scene of writing from different perspectives. The seemingly duplicitous status of the narrating voice, which both speaks with and speaks of the heroine, is paralleled by the prologue, which simultaneously is and is not the nikki to which it refers.

I have been referring to the hito in the prologue as a "heroine" and have used feminine pronouns, although in the original there is no explicit grammatical indication of her gender. Despite the fact that the information that would indicate her gender is still limited at the opening of the text, the prologue does imply that she is a woman, for one thing, through the mention of the old tales (*furu monogatari*), a generic term for popular kana tales in the Heian period. As kana tales were expected to be read by women and children, the "one" who had lived (her) life meaninglessly, reading these tales to ease the tedium, would presumably be a woman. The text's reference to furu monogari not only implies the gender of hito but it suggests the nature of the nikki that she writes. When the narrator/heroine criticizes old tales as fabrications and sets her diary/memoir against them, she implies a certain "truthfulness" in her own writing. This contrast establishes not only the difference between the nikki and the old tales but a commonality between them that serves as the basis of the comparison.

Although available samples of old tales from the Heian period are scarce, the existing texts lead us to surmise that they were largely tales of supernatural events and romantic adventure catering to a female audience. In the late tenth-century collection of Buddhist tales *Sanbōe kotoba*, edited for a devout imperial princess, we find a harsh critique of the tales, warning (female) readers against the harmful effects of such frothy romances.[23] There are also telling passages in *Kagerō nikki* itself that support this description of the tales. Although the prologue points out the disparity between the tales and the heroine's nikki, the text also at times likens "real life" events to the scenes in monogatari. Waxing sentimentally over the dramatic reunion arranged by the heroine between her husband and his estranged daughter, the text states that it was just like something out of the tales.[24] Nevertheless, the gap between romantic tales and the heroine's own experience is an issue raised both explicitly and implicitly throughout the text. The contrast raises multiple sets of expectations about the text—for example, what it is and what it is not. In other words, by pitting itself against old tales the text anticipates its thematic focus to be on a female character, her romantic/marital experience, and female life in general. Both *Sanbōe* and *Kagerō* take critical stances against monogatari, but while the former censures it as frivolous and sinful the latter takes issue with it for its flawed depiction of female destiny.

Aside from allegedly providing an unusually truthful account of one's life, the nikki is presented in the prologue as a response to the question over the (life of) people of the highest status. The passage "and it could answer questions concerning the life of [being married to] people of the highest ranks" has been variously interpreted. Since it is deemed unlikely that the heroine, who is from a middle-ranking aristocratic family, would claim herself to be of the "highest ranks," it is generally read as a reference to the husband and his clan or to the heroine, who is *married* to a man of high rank. Whichever may be the case, the prologue further defines not only the identity of the heroine/writer but that of the audience to whom the text is addressed. They are readers familiar with the old tales who are also curious about the lives of the highest-ranking aristocrats of society. This self-reflexive construction of the heroine, text, and reader highlights the text's consciousness of itself as being in dialogue with existing representations of the ways people of a specific gender and social status experience their lives. The prologue defines itself in reference to various forms of discourse—that of the old tales, a journal of one's life, and others inquiring about the life of high-ranking aristocrats—and brings into question how a woman and a woman's life can be represented. The representational agency of a woman who writes about her life is a crucial intervention to the way women's lives are *already* told.

Throughout *Kagerō nikki*, conventional views on a woman's life and her happiness are juxtaposed against the heroine's own perspective based on her experience, drawing a sharp contrast between them. In the series of passages between the Fifth to Eleventh Months of Kōhō 4, the text relates how Kaneie, the heroine's husband, rapidly ascends through the official ranks.

> 悲しびはおほかたのことにて、御よろこびといふことのみき
> こゆ。あひこへなどして、すこし人ここちすれど、わたくしの
> 心はなほおなじごとあれど、ひきかへたるやうに騒がしくなど
> あり。

[We] should have been mourning [for the deceased emperor], but people kept sending [us] congratulations, and as [I] received all the well-wishers [I] was accorded a measure of validation. But [my own] private sentiment remained unchanged; it was only that [my] life was suddenly besieged by crowds and activity. (Fifth Month of Kōhō 4; 187–88; S: 62)

The new appointments announced at the change of reign included Kaneie's big promotion. While the heroine's social standing is acknowledged by the visits of well-wishers, who congratulate her on her husband's success, her "private sentiment" (*watakushi no kokoro*) remains disgruntled. Note here the use of the word *watakushi*, which means "private" as opposed to the "public" (or "official")—a distinction that was introduced alongside the principles and institution of ritsuryō, which upheld the public order centered on the imperial court.[25] Again the reflexivity of the self is inscribed not in itself but in relation to the other. That is to say, the text speaks not of "my sentiment" but of "private sentiment." I have already pointed out that while "I" subordinates its empirical characteristics as that which it possesses, the self is related to various properties and attributes through concrete, socially contextualized forms of mediation. *Private* in the context of *Kagerō* and Heian kana texts refers not to an autonomous realm of human experience ultimately centered on the interiority of a subject but a social domain peripheral to (but not necessarily outside of) the official sphere centered on the imperial court. This distinction is particularly resonant for the heroine's depiction of her life, given the success that her husband enjoys as a court bureaucrat.

The passage just quoted, which quilts together mourning and celebration, the official glory bestowed on Kaneie and the isolating gloom that plagues the heroine, is followed by short sections containing poetic exchanges between the heroine and her acquaintances—one with the deceased emperor's consort and the other with a woman who became a nun when her husband suddenly left his family and took tonsure. After the text underscores the deep sorrow that the heroine feels about the fate of these women, the text returns to Kaneie, reporting his further promotions.

かかる世に、中将にや三位にやなど、よろこびをしきりたる人は、「ところどころなる、いとさはりしげければ、悪しき

を、近うさりぬべきところいできたり」とて、渡して、乗物な
きほどに、はひ渡るほどなれば、人は思ふやうなりと思ふべか
めり。

While some were undergoing this lament, the other [Kaneie] celebrated a string of promotions to assistant chief of the Palace Guards,
to the Third Rank, and so on. Explaining that [his] busy schedule
made it more difficult to visit [me], [he] moved [me] to a place near
[him]. The new house was close enough [for him] to come without
the bother of a carriage. Others must have thought that [my] life
was fulfilled. (Eleventh Month of Kōhō 4; 189; S: 63)

The text describes the heroine's feelings as more in tune with the
women who had suffered the loss of their husbands and must endure
the decline of their fortunes than with her husband, who is blessed
with unstoppable success in his bureaucratic career. Her ambivalence
is not expressed directly but is hinted at in her comments about how
others would apprehend her as being content with her situation. The
objectification of the heroine from the point of view of others puts into
relief the disparity between the perception of the self and the Other
over the conditions of her life. The irony of this statement is marked
not only by the earlier reference to her disaffected sentiment amid the
bustle of celebration (of her husband's promotions) but by other instances of her reflection over the dissonance between her supposed
prosperity and her emotional torment repeated throughout the text.
The text typically inscribes the heroine's solitary suffering against the
background of official ceremonies and festivals where Kaneie basks in
triumph as the rising star in the court hierarchy, buoyed by public attention. While others expect her to identify with and rejoice over her
husband's thriving career, the heroine expresses distance from Kaneie
and the expectations of the others that she should be satisfied with
her life. The husband's success and the heroine's happiness are set in
inverse relation to each other in part because his busy career provides
excuses for his increasingly infrequent visits. Also the passage of time
brings Kaneie continual growth in stature while she languishes as a
neglected wife and her physical decline as a woman further clouds her
prospects for marital happiness.

This sequence also exemplifies the subtle way in which the schism
between the heroine and the husband (as well as the others who expect

her to wholly identify with the husband) serves as a backdrop against which it depicts social connections and interactions that the heroine herself cultivates. Although I have so far focused on the text's constitution of the self through isolation and discord, I should also note that the text describes the heroine's agency in forging interpersonal relations and networks of her own, consonant with her sensibility and views on life. For instance, her composition of poetry often serves as a means for creating and maintaining these interpersonal ties. The heroine's interest in fostering these discursive relations with others also reminds us that the prologue sets up the text itself in the dialogic context of communication with others. The heroine is motivated to write not only by her dissatisfaction with the old tales but by her desire to respond to others' questions.

The project of representing a woman's life story that differs from the existing discourse is expressed from a different angle in yet another instance of textual self-reference. At the end of a section describing the banishment of Minamoto no Taka'akira, which shocked aristocratic society, we find the following comment.

身の上をのみする日記には入るまじきことなれども、悲しと思ひ入りしもたれならねば、記しおくなり。

Although this is a journal in which [I] should set down only the personal matters of one's life, the sorrow of the banishment was something [I] felt deeply within [me]. So [I] believe [I] will be permitted to put it into writing here. (Third Month of Anna 3; 207; S: 73)

The text acknowledges the political scandal surrounding Minamoto no Taka'akira to be a topic outside its expected parameters. We may note that here, as in the prologue, the term *mi no uhe* is used to predicate the nikki. *Mi* is a word with an extremely broad range of meaning including body, self, and social status. In Heian texts, it is often used as a reflexive noun equivalent to *myself, oneself, himself*, and *yourself*. *Mi no uhe* refers to the conditions and circumstances of one's life, specifically those pertaining to personal rather than public and official matters. Again the heroine's discourse invokes some form of public versus private distinction, associating itself with the latter.

The passage further specifies the nature of the "nikki on one's life" by insinuating the presence of other kinds of nikki, which would include accounts of public events—journals of male courtiers written in kanbun that record official affairs at the court. For a woman's nikki on one's life, public affairs are apparently considered an inappropriate topic to breach. At the same time, the text takes exception by commenting on the so-called *Anna no hen* (Anna Disturbance), the catastrophe that had beset Minamoto no Taka'akira, who was charged with treason against the emperor and exiled from the capital. Even as it separates itself from public events, the text demonstrates how it may encroach on the public topic. What compels the heroine to address the political affair is the force of her powerful sympathetic reaction to the downfall of a celebrated aristocratic family. Once again, the feeling licenses the heroine to connect and identify with those who experience a tragic eclipse of their status and fortune. The ironic effect of the passage is sharpened by the fact that the Anna Disturbance occurred against the background of the rivalry between Taka'akira's faction and that of the heroine's husband's clan, the northern branch of the Fujiwara family. Whether or not the text was written with knowledge of the machinations behind the incident (i.e., whether her lament for Taka'akira cloaks oblique hostility toward her husband and her clan), its explicit sympathy for the "losers" in court society suggests her aloofness toward the victors, exemplified by Kaneie and his family.[26]

In general, it is the heroine's feeling of unhappiness and frustration that provides the basis on which she pits her writing against the received notion of female destiny and the conditions of female happiness. Affect, then, plays a structural role in the heroine's self-articulation. It supports the personal accounts of her life and the contrasts between her words and perspectives as opposed to more conventional expectations. The authority of affect that gives credence to the heroine's discourse, however, is not that of subjective authenticity—the truthfulness of feelings that spring from one's interiority. Rather, the power of feeling lies in its function of mapping the heroine's social alliances and position in ways not entirely dictated by the prescribed forms of gender relations and interrelated norms of social hierarchy in mid-Heian aristocratic society. It is a force that can refract dominant social codes, not because it is outside of or transcends the social (e.g., private interiority in the modern sense) but because it can stimulate an alternative configuration of social relations. The repeated references to the heroine's sense of unhappiness, solitude, and vulnerability in the text, therefore, cannot be reduced to pure and disorderly bursts of sentiments.

The prologue posits as the origin of the nikki the heroine's wish to write about her life. It is her discursive act, mobilized by this resolve, that underwrites the text's claim to difference from banal and fraudulent old tales. The truthfulness of the nikki she writes is based not on a static standard of accuracy — the prologue states that her recollection of the past is less than reliable. The authenticity that it claims is relative: her story is true in comparison with widespread fabrications (in the old tales) and accepted views that do not tally with experience. This tension between the discourse of self and others over the representation of female destiny in general, and the heroine's life in particular, is mediated by the narration, which at once speaks *with* and speaks *of* the heroine. The heroine articulates her feelings, gives shape to her memories, and justifies her thoughts and actions as she invokes (as the counterpoint) the discourses of others — the sense of difference from others turns the gaze back onto the self. This self-reflexivity, however, is captured by a frame that is neither self nor others — an estranged voice that has no fixed place in the story-world. We must avoid understanding this process through a causal relation that installs self as the origin, that the estranged voice is produced by the preexisting heroine who tells her life-story. In fact, the temporality of the text works in reverse. We may recall that the text opens with a voice that speaks *of* the heroine from a remove. Seen through the overall structure of the text, the estranged voice is that which precedes and enables the construction of the heroine as a discursive agent. I return to this issue in the epilogue. Here I end the chapter by noting that I do not claim novelty in the observation that *Kagerō* presents a rejoinder to existing expectations about female destiny. The issue addressed here, which has not received much attention, is *how* the text inscribes this tension and what kind of subject it constitutes in this process. I continue this analysis in the epilogue, reframing my discussion in relation to ongoing debates over feminist subject and agency.

Heian Texts and Feminist Subjects

In this book, I have argued that the gender ideology embedded in kokubungaku has to be examined in relation to the concept of national subject, which has underwritten the discipline's project of modernizing premodern literature. I tried to develop an alternative strategy for analyzing Heian literary texts through a critique of the national subject, not only in the disciplinary orthodoxy but in revisionist movements that have sought to overcome modernist and nationalist tendencies of kokubungaku. In particular, I cautioned against the textual and formal approach to Heian literature that ends up postulating the subject of narration as an abstract structural principle shaping the text. I extended this critique by showing how the reading of *Kagerō nikki* against the assumptions pertaining to the modern subject (engrained in the concept of the first-person narration) helps us understand not only the specificity of its narrative economy but the ways in which the text constitutes the heroine as a socially situated *self.* Through these discussions, I tried to suggest some new approaches to the question of gender in the study of Heian narrative.

The attempt to insert feminist perspectives in Heian literary studies, therefore, cannot avoid engaging with the problem of modern subject. Otherwise, the critique of normative gender identity and gender relations in Heian kana texts, for instance, will most likely end up invoking the paradigm of the modernist feminist subject, who resists external social regulations. Such an analysis would inadvertently reproduce kokubungaku's appropriation of Heian literature, albeit from a feminist point of view. Thus in chapter 4, I suggested that in order to challenge the romanticized image of Heian kana narratives it is not enough to merely locate the tension between the gendered difference of interests in the texts. We need to simultaneously question the conceptualization of politics that presupposes the modern notions of individual subject. And in chapter 6 I examined the rejoinder against existing expectations about women and women's lives found in *Kagerō nikki* in relation to narratological and characterological discourses that refract the modern subject form.

The Feminist Critique of the Modern Subject

The methodological approach of this study was deeply informed by contemporary feminist theory, which sheds light on the centrality of the question of subject in understanding and challenging modern gender constructions. Simone de Beauvoir's *Second Sex*, for instance, helped lay the groundwork for the feminist critique of the modern subject by arguing that the feminine has been defined through its status as the alterity, the negative Other, to the sovereign subject articulated in masculine terms.[1] Thus, Beauvoir argued that misogyny cannot be truly overcome by the assertion of human equality alone.[2] Rather, we need to question the asymmetrical and nonreciprocal ways in which women have been construed as objects rather than subjects, marked by the particularity of sexed identity against which the abstract and disembodied universality of the subject proper has been posited.

Beauvoir appears to have believed in the possibility of recuperating a genuinely universal subject that avoids reifying (as the feminine Other) the negation integral to its dialectical becoming.[3] The creation of an authentic "brotherhood" of humanity that includes both sexes, then, would liberate not only women but men from a false transcendence won at the expense of women. Feminist theory, particularly

since the 1970s, however, has increasingly identified the source of sexist epistemology in the dualism foundational to the modern subject —
subject versus object, mind versus body, universal versus particular, to
name a few. Two of the most influential strains of feminist theory that
have emerged in the last several decades — radical feminism and gender constructionism — can be seen as divergent responses to the problem of how to break the deadlock of this logic, which posits "woman"
as the inferior and negative pole of binary values. Roughly put, radical
feminism asserted the feminine subject, which cannot be represented
by a phallogocentric economy that produces a masculinist epistemological subject and its object, while gender constructionism sought to
undercut the substantiality of the male-female dichotomy by arguing
that gender categories refer to mutable and contingent constructs of
social and historical forces.

So-called postmodern feminism, often associated with the influential work of Judith Butler in the early 1990s, may be seen as a critical extension of both of these positions. Butler offered a sophisticated theorization on the ways in which gender and sexuality work together as a
central matrix of the modern order of power, which operates through
the constitution of individuals as subjects. The forces governing the
normativity of sex and gender, in other words, are not only juridical
and prohibitive but generative, creating the very subjects that they appear to merely represent and place under their injunctions.[4] Like radical feminism, postmodern feminism insisted not on restoring truly
universal subject but on exposing the masculinist and hetrosexist ideology at the core of modern subject formation. It drew attention to
the exclusionary mechanism through which the idealized subject of
modernity has been construed — the process through which the universality of the humanistic subject has been naturalized by the civilizational hierarchy of the world, which incessantly produces inferior
others (marked, for instance, by gender, sexual, racial, ethnic, class,
and cultural particularities). At the same time, however, postmodern feminism was reluctant to accept the alternative feminine subject
called forth by radical feminism. For one thing, it was perceived that
such a proposition reproduces the essentializing model of identity that
occludes the irreducible diversity of the way women are constituted —
through the complex intersection of gender and other axes of identity,
including race, class, ethnicity, sexuality, and culture. Furthermore,

the identification of the feminine in the exteriority of a phallogocentric economy was thought to risk hypostatizing the very process that produces gendered subjects. Butler, drawing on Foucault, rejected the emancipatory strategy that relies on positing the outside of the modern order of power, locating instead the subversive possibilities immanent to its operation.[5]

Calling into question the mechanism of the modern subject formation, which posits the preexisting metaphysical basis of identity, postmodern feminism spurred the radicalization of gender constructionism as well. Butler and others challenged the givenness of sexed/gender identity in general, interrogating the residual substantiality of biological and anatomical sex retained in many versions of gender constructionism. Rejecting the duality of gender versus sex, or the understanding of gender as the cultural and historical interpretation of the sexed body and its biological functions, they argued that sexed bodies themselves are made intelligible through the signifying structure that produces the gendered subject.[6]

By removing some of the last vestiges of the substantive identity of "woman," the postmodern version of gender constructionism posed a number of highly fraught problems for feminism. Given that feminism and feminist politics have been generally defined by their projects of representing women against existing systems of gender inequality and misogyny, the question of how to reformulate feminism and feminist praxis in the face of the deconstruction of the category "woman" became a source of heated controversy. Just as important, radically constructionist understandings of gendered subject brought into sharper focus the question of how we may conceptualize the agency of the feminist subject. If the gendered subject is thoroughly constructed in the juncture of regulatory forces, how can such a subject contest and transform this process? The field of feminist studies in the last decade has tirelessly debated, and perhaps even stagnated, over the seemingly irreconcilable dilemma between social determinism and individual voluntarism (and the related impasse between constructionism and essentialism). There has been much accusation directed against postmodern feminism for reducing the materiality of the sexed body and social institutions such as the economic gender division of labor to all-encompassing forces of discursive production and consequently eradicating the possibility of theorizing feminist political agency. Seyla Benhabib, for instance, wrote that "the subject that is but another position in language can no longer master and create that distance between itself and the chain of significations in which it is immersed such that it can reflect upon them and creatively alter them."[7] Benhabib set up a neat dichotomy between the subject constituted in the discursive field and the subject capable of reflecting on and actively transforming the existing order of signification by virtue of being separate (and autonomous) from it, and she delimited the status of the properly political subject to the latter. Thereby she sounded alarmed that feminist politics cannot afford to give up the autonomous, individual, and rational notion of subject.

Butler objected to this defense of the self-constituting subject in feminist criticism by pointing out that the constructedness of the gendered subject does not translate into absolute determinism.[8] Normative forces of gender and sexual regulations are not to be reified as an infallible Law pronounced once and for all, for they are themselves in flux, never self-identical. They are shaped and sustained by the repeated, collective articulation of norms, which always violate the putative purity, autonomy, and completeness of the original to which they refer (e.g., the intent of the paternal law, the phallic ideal, compulsive heterosexuality, the naturalized essence of gender identity). This is what Butler referred to as gender performativity—citational practices that are always already the modification and betrayal of the normative gender and sexuality that they invoke. Butler argued that, paradoxically, one can envision the possibility of subverting the regulatory/productive order of gender and sexuality only if we understand the gendered subject to be constructed through this reiterative process.[9]

While I do not dispute the theoretical coherence of Bulter's argument against the resuscitation of the liberal subject and the valuable contributions she has made to feminist theory, there are aspects of her analysis of gendered subject that raise serious questions. One of the obvious problems in Butler's notion of gender performativity may be summed up as follows: if gendered subject formation always simultaneously configures and refigures the existing codes of articulating gender and sexuality, then both the observation and the subversion of norms seem to appear everywhere and thus nowhere. On what basis do we evaluate a particular instance of observation/subversion of the law? The issue at stake is not simply how to secure the ethical standard of differentiation or even a strategic standard for feminist politics. More fundamentally, it is unclear whether it is possible to apprehend a certain gender performance and its effects in their specificity on the basis of Butler's account — for instance, distinguishing between the repetition that sustains the norm (even when it fails to replicate it exactly) and that which disrupts it (even when it reinvokes the norm in order to do so).[10] Butler attributes a privileged critical potential to what she calls an abject subject, disavowed by the exclusionary matrix of subject formation and made to serve as its constitutional (i.e., structural rather than ontological) outside. If abject subjects are *internal* limits of gender/sexual intelligibility, however, we are once again without the means to distinguish the observation and subversion, the preservation and disruption, of norms.

Further implications of this problem in Butler's conceptualization of gender performativity may be teased out by examining its basis in her particular deployment of the poststructuralist theory of signification. According to Butler, gender performativity as a signifying practice does not constitute an airtight, closed structure in the vein of a linguistic system associated with orthodox structuralism. Rather, it remains open by means of its citational reproduction, which forecloses self-coincidence; and she insists on its historicity and discontinuity on the basis of this nonclosure. Nevertheless, one cannot help but detect the static quality of her analytic schema. The totalization of the structure is avoided by positing the perfect dispersion of effectivity and the failure of its logic, which, in turn, suggests the fixed complementarity between them. Citational dynamics of the signifying chain, as described by Butler, sustained by the compulsion to repeat, are strictly speaking atemporal and ahistoric despite the appearance of incessant movement. The reiterative operation may disable conventional historicist causality (and the metaphysical origin and teleological closure it invokes), but we are left without an effective means of historicization. The conceptualization of history that is not historicist (the succession of empty homogeneous time stretched along a linear axis) must be able to articulate more definitive forms of break as well as consistency than what can be mapped out by the even diffusion of difference generated by citational practice. To the extent that it cannot speak in temporally inflected terms such as production, generation, transformation, and degeneration, it also curtails the discussion of the social as an aggregate of irreducibly *multiple* (rather than simply differential) relationality.[11]

The structural and synchronic tendencies of Butler's theoretical framework explain why her analysis often appears to recoil from addressing the subject's experience in the social space of history or its acts therein.[12] The specificity of these events appears to be epiphenomenal to the juridical/productive inscription of the gendered subject that is both effective and incomplete, constituting always already impossible, divided identity. Surely, however, the conditions under which we find ourselves gendered, or our negotiations with them, involve not only the nonclosure of the signifying operation (the ground of intelligibility) but our relations to discreet, multiple, and unevenly distributed forces organized through social institutions and practices. They refer not only to our self-division vis-à-vis the symbolic mediation of identity but to our antagonistic as well as associative interactions with others. We may rephrase these questions from a slightly different angle: if the regime of gender and sexuality is located in the signifying operation itself, how does it induce (or inhibit) one to take one form of gendered identity over another or desire a particular object over another? To say that the discursive field shapes our epistemological access to gendered subjectivity suggests that it should support both the normative and the perverse object of desire or the identities that are despised as well as valorized. While Butler explains the structural impossibility of self-same gender identity, her discussion does not get us very far in understanding specific ways in which we find ourselves marked for gender with some degree of consistency and how we act through or against them in a given social context.[13] It seems to me that the weakness of Butler's theoretical approach lies in its conflation, on one hand, of the signifying process as the fundamental condition of sociality and social being with, on the other, concrete articulations of individual and collective identities through which the relation of power materializes (and thus sets in motion the dialectic of domination and resistance, prohibition and sanction, etc.). Thus, the constitutive contingency of the linguistic field (the sphere of adeterminacy) is made to stand in and account for *overdetermined* social and historical processes (constituted via multiple and dynamic force fields of power).

The Question of I and the Narrative of Self

It may have been noticed that there are some echoes between my objections to Butler's analysis of the gendered subject and my critique of Tokieda's and his followers' conceptualizations of the discursive subject. Despite the obvious and substantial differences between these two sets of discussions, they do share common interests in critiquing the modern (nominalized) subject, proposing instead to examine the subject performatively through its signifying practices. Moreover, I believe that they both exhibit the shortcomings of analytic approaches that seek to counter the normative and deterministic notion of subjective identity without recognizing that such a project calls for an alternative (nonhistoricist) approach to historicization. In the following, I attempt to link my critique of shutai and Butler's analysis of the gendered subject by extending my study of the narrative form of *Kagerō nikki*. I suggest that a study of Heian narrative may help us rethink the postmodernist discussions of feminist agency, particularly their references to the contingency of the signifying operation in their critique of the modern, humanist model of the subject.

I have argued that in *Kagerō nikki* the heroine as a self is articulated through the tension established between her perspective and the existing discourses on women and female destiny. In this sense, the specific locus that the self occupies are marked by antagonistic and oppositional relations to the discourses of others. At the same time, the articulation of self is enabled by the discursive frame that I have referred to as the estranged voice, which has no determinate identity vis-à-vis the story-world. Neither that of the heroine nor of others, this voice sounds irregular to our modern ears, leading many to assume that the text oscillates between the first- and third-person points of view. I have argued against such a view by discussing the text's narrative economy in terms of three interrelated yet discrete discursive levels: that of the heroine in the story-world, that of the estranged voice, and that of others (in the story-world) who are mediated largely by the heroine. While the narrating voice in much of the text may appear indistinguishable from that of the heroine, there are clear instances in which the distinction between them is marked (hence, the designation "estranged voice")—especially in transitional sections of the text and in moments of the heroine's self-reflection. The understanding of the discourse of self therefore hinges largely on elucidating its distinction from the estranged voice.

Despite my insistence on the fundamental inapplicability of modern narratological concepts to a Heian text such as *Kagerō*, the narrative apparatus of the text that I have laid out may appear suspiciously resonant with the discourse of the self-divided subject articulated in modern narratives. The unity of the modern subject (e.g., the coincidence between the subject of utterance and the subject of statement or of the empirical self and the transcendent "I") of course is a fraught ideal, an antinomy that has animated the theory and practice of modern narrative. One of the fundamental perspectives that catalyzed contemporary narratology is precisely the identification of the difference (and complex relationality) between the context of the narration and the context of narrated or the distinction between the narrating subject and the subject narrated. As I discussed in chapter 5, this insight has helped displace the centrality and unproblematic unity of the realist subject. So what is the difference between the discourse of the self-divided subject of modern narratives and the noncoincidence between the discourse of the self and the estranged voice in the narrative economy of *Kagerō nikki*?

An influential theory on the modern novel offered by Georg Lukács identifies the classic structure of the novel as composed of two layers: the outer form being the biography of a problematic individual (problematic, above all, in his or her relation to the society) and the inner form being the individual's search for self-recognition.[14] That is to say, in the modern novel the individual seeks to resolve troubles arising from relations with others or one's place in the world by discovering his or her authentic self-identity as "I"—the first-person subjectivity as an originary and absolute point of reference from which one makes sense of the self and the world. It is worth noting that in the analysis offered by Lukács the unity of the narrating subject and the subject narrated ("I" and self) is not a given. Instead, it shapes the modern novelistic form as its central problem. In other words, it is the *question* of subject ("Who am I?") that supplies consistency to the modern narrative, which anticipates and tends toward the union of transcendent and empirical subjects as its ultimate telos (even if achievement of such a goal is impossible). The ideological force of the question resides in its status as a project, announcing the awakening of Man from the slumber of static unity between the self and the world. The antinomy generated by the self-reflexivity of the modern subject (looking at myself looking) is cast as the inevitable price of its freedom, independence, and self-awareness. Thus, discussions of the modern subjectivity represented in literature and other mediums have often vacillated between mourning for the lost oneness ascribed to premodern man and his world, on one hand, and valorization of the Promethean struggle of modern consciousness on the other. The question of subject is indissociable from the ethics of humanism, which celebrate the civilizational quest through which modern Man seeks to challenge and move beyond the externalized form of the absolute. The disenchantment of the world (bleaching the world of its mystery) thus turns into the enchantment of the subject and its heroic battle to transcend the prohibition and sanction of the Other (e.g., the residual force of divine and cosmological order, externalized social regulations embodied in the state and so on). In this process, the supposed plenitude of the abstract "I" becomes the basis of human morality—the guarantor of its rationality, freedom, and accountability. It is important to underscore the fact that the structuring force of the question of subject does not depend on whether it is possible to reach complete union between "I" and the self.

The perception that the search for self-recognition that is central to the modern narrative convention is an open-ended, liberating, and ethical process functions as an important ideological apparatus in modernity. The great frontier of the adventure of interiority is also a fertile ground for the modern disciplinary regime.[15] The question of subject translates the dilemma of identity into a problem to be solved in the realm of abstraction where the subject itself figures as the principal enigma. The reification of first-person "I" via the question of subject provides a powerful excuse for humanism to disavow or render secondary socially immanent bases for affirming human freedom and agency. It gives the appearance of inevitability to the either/or choice between the self-constituting, individuated, and socially abstracted sovereign subject, on one hand, and the externally determined, subjected self on the other. This dichotomy has had a profound effect on the conceptualization of modern social and political orders, including the organization of gender identities. For instance, it supports the logic that excludes women and the feminine from disembodied universal subjectivity (and its status as the only legitimate model of a free, ethical, and socially transformative agent), as feminist critics have pointed out.

The modern narrative form suggests, therefore, that subject formation in modernity is not sustained by the injunction to assume an identity with which one can never fully coincide. Rather, what characterizes the modern subject is the internalization of the equivocal and ultimately nonsensical question "Who am I?" Understanding the modern subject in terms of the *question* of "I" helps us avoid the linguistic determinism that reduces the modern formation of identity to the first-person singular reference and its grammatical properties. Furthermore, it suggests that what is forced on the subject via this question is not so much the dilemma of identity itself but the way this dilemma is articulated (narrativized) in relation to the perpetually deferred identification with the empty "I." The structurally delayed self-identification of "I" underwrites the quasitemporality of abstract futurity, giving shape and meaning to the forward march of time in a modern narrative.

From this perspective, we may gain a clearer understanding of the difference between *Kagerō nikki*'s construction of self and the modern narrative of the subject. The discourse of self in the text does not negotiate with the teleological aspirations of the modern narrative, which seeks its closure (resolution of its antinomy) in the subsumption of the narrated subject (self) by the narrating subject (I). This is another way to say that it is not structured around the question of subject. Thus, the analysis in chapter 6 bracketed the question of "I"—that is, who is the subject outside the story-world to whom this estranged voice belongs? By contrast, even Mitani's notion of washa, which postulates the incessant dispersion of the subject in Heian kana narrative, presumes the inevitability of this question—that is, that the narrating voice necessarily implicates not so much the unified identity of the subject as the *question* of "I." Despite the avowed intent of critiquing the paradigmatic status of modern novels, Mitani read into Heian texts the enigma that anchors the narrative of the modern subject.

If *Kagerō nikki* does not assume the question of subject, the issue of identity in the text has to be approached at the level of self and its situatedness in the social/diegetic world. It is important to emphasize, however, that the constitution of the heroine as a self is not reducible to her discursive agency inscribed within the diegetic horizon—as if her will to tell her story in itself generates the self. The establishment of self as the node of reflexivity and a locus of distinct perspective from which others are perceived is enabled by the estranged voice that is neither self nor other. The voice that frames the self implies not a hidden speaking subject but the enunciatory context from which the self emerges and into which it recurrently disappears, most notably at the moment of self-reflection. What I am referring to, however, should not be confused with an intersubjective sphere of communication—a seamless space where the speaker and the spoken, addresser and addressee, coexist. The spatiality invoked by the term *context* obscures the peculiar temporal relation that obtains between the discourse of self and its frame. As I have argued, the overall structure of the text, beginning with the prologue that introduces the heroine as an "other," suggests that the estranged voice must be activated prior to that of the heroine. Yet the (narrative) temporality begins only with the installment of the self in the world, where it is set in relation to the others. The priority of the estranged voice to the discursive agency of self, therefore, cannot be temporalized vis-à-vis narrative time. The discourse of self and its frame, then, are discontinuous in the sense that they are not locatable on the single spatio-temporal horizon. The discursive frame serves as the context of individual or collective enunciation precisely because it cannot be identified with and unified from any specific position internal to it—again, it is neither self nor the Other. This difficulty of temporalizing/spatializing the relationship between the estranged voice and the self also means that we cannot assume the conventional notion of a causal link between them.

The way the discourse of self and the estranged voice are interwoven in *Kagerō* suggests not the abstract and transcendental quest for the self-identity of the subject itself but the project of narrating the social self and its relation to others. Self is etched by its differentiation from others—for example, the heroine articulates herself against the grain of the received notion of female roles and normative gendered values through which others judge and define her. It is by both invoking these conventional pieces of wisdom and placing herself against them that the specificity of the heroine's identity is marked. And the self as a discursive agent that relates oneself with and against others reconstitutes the world from its own perspective, both reproducing and altering the existing social formations. The associations that the heroine forges outside the social relations she is supposed to align herself with are integral to her attempt to question the received notions of female destiny.

Although the agency of self in the text is not inscribed in terms of "I," this does not mean that it is not reflexive, contested, or oppositional. That the self does not constitute the abstract autonomy attributed to the first-person subject does not translate into immersion in a collective identity or its inability to critique social norms. The creative force of the text gathers around the effort to establish and draw meaning from the antagonistic relationship between self and others — the self's discontent with the prescribed social position it is to occupy and its inability (refusal) to offer affective responses that relate her to others in expected ways. Furthermore, it is by inscribing this lack of fit between the self and the conventions that the possibility of new social relations is suggested — the heroine's self-initiated associations with others and the text's invitation to readers to view her life from her point of view. The heroine's refiguration of established views and accepted social codes becomes effective and concrete through such sociality and the discursive acts of sharing her feelings and insights. In other words, the discourse of self activates the force directed not in self-positing — the impulse attributed to "I" that seeks to wrest its freedom and agency from extrinsic forces of determination. Rather, the self's agency tends toward suasion — contesting, affecting, and influencing. Furthermore, the identity of self is constituted in these dialogues with existing discourses and through the creation of specific social relations. What is absent in *Kagerō*, compared to the modern narrative of subject, is not the differentiation but the binary structure between self and others or the individual and the collective. The strict binary between these terms is not possible without positing the "I" outside the diegetic horizon as the essence of the individual self. In *Kagerō*, the estranged voice frames the division between self and others while preventing that difference from ossifying into the structure of mutually exclusive opposition. The self constituted in the text refracts the modernist notion of subject both through its enframement by the no-self of the estranged voice and through its constitutive relation to others.

Historicizing the Negativity of Subject

An individual, by virtue of being inserted into the social network, relates to himself or herself in terms that are extrinsic. Any category of identity that one may invoke in this process is marked by the contingency of the differential relation through which the signifying operation works. At this level, the negativity of identity is not so much the *effect* of social codes and regulations as the very prerequisite for a human to be a social being whose sense of self is mediated by language and other symbolic practices. The paradigmatic tendency of the modern narrative is to disavow this condition, seeking instead to contain the discontinuity between the formal enunciatory frame (the field of language) and the enframed subject via the question of "I," which insinuates the possibility of a unified subject. Thereby, the founding negativity of identity is rearticulated as the source of the ultimate solution to the enigma of "I." Butler's poststructuralist critique of this process foregrounds the *impossibility* of a unified, selfsame subject or the coincidence between the formal, empty signifier "I" and the specificity of the self. The teleology of the narrative of subject is disabled, and its evolutionary trajectory is revealed to be a perpetual remarking of the failure of full identification. Furthermore, she suggests that once we properly understand "I" as an empty signifier, we may proceed with the critical operation of denaturalizing the specific terms of identification that cultural norms force onto it, potentially exposing any prescribed form of identity to contestation.[16] Understood as such, it no longer obscures the impasse of identification but opens it up to critical and political possibilities. The function played by the question of subject is radically inverted—it does not repress the symbolic mediation of identity but exposes it as a source of struggle for emancipation.

That the discourse of self in *Kagerō* is framed by the discourse of the no-self (the estranged voice) indicates that it also inscribes the fundamental misfire of identification. This point is clearly overlooked by modern commentators, who read the text as a narcissistic monologue of the heroine. The text, in other words, suggests that the dilemma of identity need not be a prerogative of the modern narrative of subject. At the same time, however, the text articulates the negativity of identity formation in a manner different from that found in the modern narrative of subject. In the absence of the circular, hyperreflexive movement structured by the question of "I," the division between the enuciatory frame and the self is not turned into a problem to be resolved, a lack to be compensated for, or a limitation to be overcome. It does not coalesce into an absolute confrontation between the "I" and the Other, whose prohibition and sanction the subject must overcome. Rather, the dilemma of identity catalyzes the discursive force that engages the self with and against others in creative and nondeterminate ways. The discourse of self invokes the world not as the site of a solution to the primordial failure of identification but as a site where the impasse becomes socially productive. The self's agency is inscribed in its act of relating to others, which in turn participates in the formation of sociality as a collective, dialogic process.

■　　■　　■

I would like to end by addressing somewhat more specifically the ways in which my analysis of *Kagerō* speaks to the debates over feminist agency. It goes without saying that the narrative of self in *Kagerō nikki*, in terms of both its content and its form, does not automatically translate into contemporary feminist discourses and strategies. I certainly do not wish to suggest that the enabling discursive mode for feminism was more readily available in the Heian period. In this study, I have emphatically rejected the possibility of treating a text from the past as offering a shortcut to resolving the problems of the present. Seeking ready-made, immediately available knowledge in Heian texts risks repeating some of the fallacies of kokubungaku I have critiqued. Previous chapters argued against the viability of reading Heian texts through the project of modernization or a reactive critique of modernization. In order to break from these two stances, we need to envision a different kind of relation to the past as well as the present. We cannot hope to engage with Heian texts—texts that were not written for us—in the same ways we read more historically approximate texts. I am the first to admit that my analysis of the formal economy of Heian kana narrative, for instance, merely gropes at what ultimately eludes us—how individual identities and social relations were lived in a time vastly different from our own. Yet these texts continue to be meaningful to us because they compel us to question the implicit frame of reference that we invoke in order to relate to our selves and our world historically. They energize not the relativization of the present but the critical reflection of the way we approach the present as a problem.

I have tried to suggest in my analysis of *Kagerō* that Heian narratives offer us an opportunity to consider the contingency not so much of the putative positivity of the gendered subject as of its negativity. It urges us to consider whether the question of the gendered subject as an empty signifier is the unsurpassable horizon for rethinking the feminist subject and agency today. Without such an investigation, the problematization of the metaphysical grounding of the gendered subject may risk becoming a totalizing horizon that determines in advance the terms of negativity that it is to explore. What I call for is not that the question of subject be simply dismantled but that it be historicized and that we deliberate on its adequacy for diverse facets of the feminist project accordingly.

If, as I have argued, the "question of I" is historically constituted, it would be insufficient to merely locate its internal antinomy—the points at which it undermines itself. We will need to investigate its foreclosure of other questions, other modes of articulating the negativity of subject. Such a reflection needs to be worked out, at least in part, through attention to the specific and multiple contours of gendered social practices, institutions, and identity formations that are rendered opaque or indistinct via the question of subject. Our concern here, however, does not lie in the discovery of yet another form of exclusionary mechanisms, which would merely reaffirm the question of subject as the frame within which the internal difference is to be recognized. At stake is, above all, the question of method. I suggested through my critique of Butler's work that we need to find ways to simultaneously address both the symbolic mediation of subject, which has no history of its own, and the historicity and sociality of the subject. We need to resist the sterile division of disciplinary or methodological labor—for instance, between modes of investigation that prioritize cultural over economic and vice versa. The interrogation of the question of "I" suggests a point of departure for unblocking the divide between inquiries into the formal impossibility of a selfsame gendered subject and engagements with the concrete social constitution and negotiation of gendered identities. It seems to me that feminism must take on the question of the gendered subject as a whole — as a genuinely complex assemblage of heterogeneous conditions that demands diverse and creative forms of inquiry. And I believe that the study of sources as historically remote as Heian texts, too, can participate in such methodological explorations.

NOTES

The place of publication of all Japanese sources is Tokyo unless otherwise noted.

Introduction

1 Rey Chow, *Writing Diaspora: Tactics of Intervention in Contemporary Cultural Studies* (Bloomington: Indiana University Press, 1993), 110.

2 For helpful studies on the interrelated formation of national literary studies, modern university, and modern national identity in Great Britain and the United States, see Franklin E. Court, *Institutionalizing English Literature: The Culture and Politics of Literary Study, 1750–1900* (Stanford: Stanford University Press, 1992); Terry Eagleton, *The Idea of Culture* (Oxford: Blackwell, 2000); Terry Eagleton, *Literary Theory: An Introduction* (Minneapolis: University of Minnesota Press, 1982); Gerald Graff, *Professing Literature: An Institutional History* (Chicago: University of Chicago Press, 1987); and Bill Reading, *The University in Ruins* (Cambridge: Harvard University Press, 1996).

3 In particular, this study is indebted to the study of the nationalization/modernization of Heian literature in Thomas LaMarre, *Uncovering Heian Japan: An Archeology of Sensation and Inscription* (Durham: Duke University Press, 2000). Haruo Shirane and Tomi Suzuki, eds., *Inventing the Classics: Modernity, National Identity, and Japanese Literature* (Stanford: Stanford University Press, 2001), is a highly in-

formative collection of essays on the modern invention of Japanese classical canon. Although it is not focused on literary tradition per se, another relevant collection is Stephen Vlastos, ed., *Mirror of Modernity: Invented Traditions of Modern Japan* (Berkeley: University of California Press, 1998).

4 On Orikuchi's critique of kokubungaku's modernizing project, see Harry Harootunian, *Overcome by Modernity: History, Culture, and Community in Interwar Japan* (Princeton: Princeton University Press, 2000), 328–57.

5 Mitani Kuniaki, "Monogatari to kakukoto: Monogatari bungaku no imisayō arui wa fuzai no bungaku," *Nihonbungaku* 25 (October 1976): 3.

Chapter 1: The Feminization of Heian

1 I use the term, *eighteenth-century poetics* loosely to refer to discourses on poetry that developed roughly between the early eighteenth and early nineteenth centuries.

2 Sakai Naoki reminds us that, although kokugaku discourses expressed yearning for the transparency of language, it should not be assumed that this was simply a response to the *existing* opacity of language. Rather, the notion of the opacity of language was itself constituted through the desire for transparency. Thus, we need to focus our attention on the conditions under which this desire came to be. See Sakai Naoki, *Voices of the Past: The Status of Language in Eighteenth-Century Japanese Discourse* (Ithaca: Cornell University Press, 1991), 213.

3 Takahashi Masa'aki, "Jōshikiteki kizokuzō, bushizō no sōshutsu katei," in *Nihonshi ni okeru ōyake to watakushi*, ed. Rekishi to hōhō henshū iinkai (Aoki shoten, 1996).

4 Mabuchi was the scholar and poet who established the highly influential school of kokugaku. He produced a massive study on *Man'yōshū*, (*Man'yōkō* 1768).

5 Kamo no Mabuchi, "Nihimanabi," in *Kinsei shintōron, zenki kokugaku*, ed. Taira Shigemichi and Abe Akio, NST 39 (Iwanami shoten, 1972), 368.

6 This is the oldest anthology of Japanese poetry in existence, dating from about the late eighth century, but some of the poems are believed to have been composed in much earlier periods.

7 *Waka*, which translates as "Japanese [as opposed to Chinese] poem," often refers more specifically to the thirty-one-syllable poems that became the dominant form of vernacular poetry after the Heian period.

8 Kamo no Mabuchi, "Kokuikō," NST 39, 381.

9 See Kanno Kakumyō, *Motoori Norinaga: Kotoba to miyabi* (Perikansha, 1991), 83–85.

10 Kada Arimaro (1706–51) wrote the tract at the request of his patron, Tayasu Munetake, the second son of the Shogun Yoshimune. The content of *Kokka hachiron* enraged Munetake, who believed in the political power of waka and its ability to foster self-cultivation.

11 Kada Arimaro, "Kokka hachiron," in *Karonshū*, ed. Hashimoto Fumio, Ariyoshi Tamotsu, and Fujihira Harua, NKBZ 50 (Shōgakkan, 1975), 541.

12 I also need to note that, although Mabuchi did associate genuine poetry with the prosperity of imperial rule and a harmonious society, he did not subordinate poetry to sociopolitical effects. He wrote: "Since poetry is that which expresses human feelings, it may not always follow general moral principles. Yet when it is seen through the perspective of the poet it can be quite compelling and draw our empathy" ("Futatabi kingo no kimi ni kotahematsuru fumi," in *Nihon kagaku taikei*, ed. Sasaki Nobutsuna, NKT 7 [Kazama shobō, 1965], 153).

13 Kamo no Mabuchi, "Kokka hachiron yogen shūi," NKT 7, 123.

14 Kamo no Mabuchi, "Kokkaron okusetsu," NKT 7, 128. On the relationship between the poetic and the political in Mabuchi's stance in the *Kokka hachiron* debate, see Watanabe Osamu, *Kinsei waka shisō kenkyū* (Jichōsha, 1991), 44–45; and Peter Nosco, "Nature, Invention, and National Learning: The *Kokka hachiron* Controversy, 1742–46," *Harvard Journal of Asiatic Studies* 41:1 (1981): 88.

15 Kagawa Kageki (1768–1843) was an influential poet and a critic who founded the school of poetry that dominated the late Tokugawa and early Meiji waka scene. The school was known for a clear and elegant style of poetry that incorporated some elements of contemporary language and themes.

16 Kagawa Kageki, "Nihimanabi iken," in NKBZ 50, 589.

17 Ibid., 590.

18 Ibid., 596–97.

19 It may be worth noting that in the Meiji period, the descendents of Kageki's poetic lineage, which was regarded as the most powerful faction of waka poets at the time, were harshly criticized by promoters of poetic modernization (such as Masaoka Shiki) in a campaign to free Japanese poetry from the bonds of tradition.

20 Kagawa, "Nihimanabi iken," 597–98.

21 Motoori Norinaga (1730–1801), a highly prolific scholar and a poet, was arguably the most influential theorist of kokugaku thought in the eighteenth century.

22 Motoori Norinaga, *Isonokami sasamegoto*, in *Motoori Norinaga Zenshū*, ed. Ōno Susumu, MNZ 2 (Chikuma shobō, 1968), 151.

23 Ibid.

24 Motoori Norinaga, *Shibun yōryō*, MNZ 4, 95.

25 Motoori Norinaga, "Ashiwake obune," MNZ 2, 40–41.

26 Ibid., 62. In "Uhiyamabumi," Norinaga repeats the notion that *Kokinshū* represents the apogee of waka history, but some aspects are more fully developed in the twelfth-century imperial anthology *Shinkokinshū* ("Uhiyamabumi," MNZ 1, 25–26).

27 Motoori, *Shibun yōryō*, 94.

28 While Norinaga located the source of exemplary native spirit in the discourses of the past, we need to note that the contrast between the corrupt present and the pristine past is complicated by the distinction between cultural interiority (native) and exteriority (foreign). For the discussion of the eighteenth-century poetics and its formation of socio-cultural interiority, see Sakai, *Voices of the Past*. Sakai's study focuses on the kokugaku construction of language, a topic that is not addressed in detail in this chapter but is highly relevant to the issues I discuss.

29 Motoori Norinaga, *Genji monogatari tama no ogushi*, MNZ 4, 199.

30 Norinaga insists on describing affect as that which is constantly in motion (*Isono-kami sasamegoto*, 99–100).

31 Motoori, "Uhiyamabumi," 22.

32 Motoori, *Isonokami sasamegoto*, 112.

33 Ibid.

34 Norinaga never wavered from this position, from his earliest poetic treatise to what he wrote toward the end of his career ("Uhihyamabumi," 53; "Ashiwake obune," 70).

35 Harry D. Harootunian, *Things Seen and Unseen: Discourse and Ideology in Tokugawa Nativism* (Chicago: University of Chicago Press, 1988), 29.

36 Norinaga's contention against neo-Confucian ethical doctrines, for instance, may be better described as the rejection of rationalization rather than of rationality. Rationalization is driven by the impetus to regulate human behavior and thoughts on the basis of the reified distinction between the rational and nonrational, promoting the former while censoring the latter. To the extent that Norinaga was staunchly against positing such a division as a regulatory principle, his critique was directed not so much against rationality itself as against rationalization.

37 On the relationship between past and present in Norinaga's thought, see Watanabe Hiroshi, "Michi to miyabi [pt. 1]," *Kokkagaku gakkai zasshi* 87:9–10 (1974): 65–70.

Chapter 2: Gender and Nationalization

1 Tokyo University (Tokyo Diagaku) became Imperial University (Teikoku Daigaku) in 1886; with the opening of Kyoto Imperial University in 1890, it was renamed Tokyo Imperial University. On the history of imperial universities in Japan and their role in the nation's modernization process, see James R. Bartholomew, "Japanese Modernization and the Imperial Universities, 1876–1920," *Journal of Asian Studies* 37:2 (February 1978).

2 A seminar for the study of classical literature, *koten kōshūka*, was organized in 1882 by a kokugaku scholar, Konakamura Kiyonori, with the support of Katō Hiroyuki, the president of Imperial University. Although the seminar was closed when wabungakuka was established, within the short span of its operation, it trained students who went on to become prominent figures of kokubungaku such as Ueda Kazutoshi, Haga Yaichi, Mikami Sanji, and Watanabe (Konakamura) Yoshikata.

3 For a discussion in English of the transition from kokugaku to kokubungaku and the formation of a new literary canon, see Michael C. Brownstein, "From *Kokugaku* to *Kokubungaku*: Canon Formation in the Meiji Period," *Harvard Journal of Asiatic Studies* 47:2 (1987).

4 Ueda Kazutoshi proclaimed in his *Kokubungaku* that "Like *wagakusha* [kokugaku scholars], I value Nara and Heian literature, but at the same time I also value war narratives, essays, No, puppet dramas, novels, nonstandard poems, and comic poems from other periods.... I would not blindly adhere to the opinions of today's

wagakusha" ("Kokubungaku shogen," in *Ochiai Naobumi, Ueda Kazutoshi, Haga Yaichi, Fujioka Sakutarō shū*, ed. Hisamatsu Sen'ichi, MBZ 44 [Chikuma shobō, 1968], 107).

5   Mikami Sanji and Takatsu Kuwasaburō, *Nihon bungakushi* (Kinkōdō, 1890), 1:1.

6   For a summary of Taine's notion of literary history, see the introduction to his *History of English Literature*, trans. H. Van Laun, vol. 1 (New York: Holt, 1891).

7   Haga Yaichi and Tachibana Sensaburō, eds., *Kokubungaku tokuhon*, in *Haga Yaichi senshū*, ed. Haga Yaichi senshū henshūiinkai, HYS 2 (Kokugakuin, 1983), 28.

8   Ibid., 14.

9   Mikami and Takatsu, *Nihon bungakushi*, 1:200–201.

10   For an analysis of eighteenth-century phoneticism, see Naoki Sakai, *Voies of the Past: The Status of Language in Eighteenth-Century Discourse* (Ithaca: Cornell University Press, 1991), esp. 250–66. Sakai himself notes the ambivalent attitude toward writing in eighteenth-century discourse: "Writing puts both spatial and temporal distance between voice and reader in an effect similar to the distancing and separating effect of representational language which Ogyu sensed. On the other hand, the voice would have been lost irredeemably had its trace not been secured and fixed in writing" (259).

11   "Although Japanese literature emerged through the introduction of a writing system from abroad, through the invention of kana script we gained what was uniquely Japanese, something of which we can be proud" (Mikami and Takatsu, *Nihon bungakushi*, 1:106).

12   Ibid., 32.

13   Ibid., 216.

14   Ibid., 34.

15   Karatani Kōjin, *Origins of Japanese Literature*, ed. and trans. Brett de Bary (Durham: Duke University Press, 1993), 45–75.

16   Mikami and Takutsu, *Nihon bungakushi*, 1:4.

17   Haga Yaichi, "Kokugaku to wa nanzo ya?" HYS 1, 159.

18   His vision of kokubungaku as the modern avatar of kokugaku was reinforced by his study of philology during his stay in Germany. Haga was influenced by the discipline, which posited language as the most crucial foundation of human culture and thus the basic material for the study of civilization. He saw the commonality between romantic philology and kokugaku not only in their interest in language and written texts but in their focus on the national as a critical frame of reference. Thus, he found in the field of philology a model for kokubungaku, restoring the original purpose of kokugaku while also incorporating the scientific and empirical rigor of Western knowledge.

19   Haga Yaichi, *Kokubungaku jukkō*, HYS 2, 188.

20   Haga and Tachibana, *Kokubungaku tokuhon*, 192–93.

21   "Since the origin of our nation in the antiquity, for thousands of years, our nation has never been invaded by a foreign country. We have upheld the single lineage of imperial rule and eternally unchanging national language" (Haga, *Kokubungaku jukkō*, 189, 317).

Notes to Chapter 2   235

22 Ibid., 222–23.

23 Ibid., 193.

24 Tomi Suzuki discusses this ambivalence regarding the feminization of national language and literature by male Japanese intellectuals and academics in her study on the construction of so-called Heian women's diary literature ("Gender and Genre: Modern Literary Histories and Women's Diary Literature," in *Inventing the Classics: Modernity, National Identity, and Japanese Literature*, ed. Haruo Shirane and Tomi Suzuki [Stanford: Stanford University Press, 2001]).

25 Haga Yaichi, "Nihonjin," *HYS* 6, 106.

26 "When we speak of miyabi, we mean 'courtly,' that is, the way of the imperial court" (Haga Yaichi, "Nihon bungaku to waka," *HYS* 3, 36).

27 Ibid., 37.

28 The understanding of Fujiwara rule as the affirmation rather than the negation of imperial rule is an idea with an old pedigree. For instance, in *Jinnō shōtōki*, one of the best-known chronicles of the imperial dynasty from the fourteenth century, the era of Fujiwara regency is represented in an extremely favorable light. Paul Varley explains this aspect of *Jinnō shōtōki* in terms of the partisan interest of the author, Kitabatake Chikafusa, who wished to promote the legitimacy of the aristocratic clans that traditionally held the ministerial posts at the court, including the house of Murakami Genji, of which he was a descendent. See H. Paul Varley, trans., *A Chronicle of Gods and Sovereigns: Jinnō Shōtōki of Kitabatake Chikafusa* (New York: Columbia University Press, 1980), 24.

29 Anne McClintock, *Imperial Leather: Race, Gender and Sexuality in the Colonial Contest* (London: Routledge, 1995), 354.

30 George L. Mosse, *Nationalism and Sexuality* (Madison: University of Wisconsin Press, 1985), 90–113.

31 Takashi Fujitani, *Splendid Monarchy* (Berkeley: University of California Press, 1996), 161.

32 Here I am trying to draw some distinctions between the femininity of the emperor as the passive center of national unity and, for instance, the maternalization of the emperor that Kanō Mikiyo identified in the popular construction of the emperor during the Fifteen-Year War. See Kanō Mikiyo, "'Ōmigokoro' to 'hahagokoro': 'Yasukuni no haha' o umidasu mono," in *Josei to tennōsei*, ed. Kanō Mikiyo (Shisō no Kagakusha, 1979), 64–81 (cited in Fujitani, *Splendid Monarchy*, 273).

33 Fujioka Sakutarō, *Kokubungaku zenshi: Heianchōhen* (Heibonsha, 1971), 1:350–51.

34 Ibid., 4.

35 Ibid., 6.

36 Ibid., 24.

37 Ibid., 25.

38 Fujioka's attention to the historical agency of Heian women and women writers was no doubt influenced by the changing perception of women in the Meiji period. By late 1880s, there were debates on women's political rights and participation, and by the 1890s there were broad discussions on social reforms centered on the

advancement of women's education and the modernization of domestic life. Especially among liberals, the improvement of women's social status and the promotion of their contributions to society were deemed critical to the national modernization project.

39 Fujioka, *Kokubungaku zenshi*, 2:154.

40 For instance, *Genji monogatari ipponkyō* (1168) by Chōken criticized the *Genji* for encouraging men and women to harbor lustful desires and claimed that the author, Murasaki Shikibu, had been condemned to hell for writing such a harmful text. On the history of the early didactic criticism of the *Genji*, see Shigematsu Nobuhiro, *Shinkō Genji Monogatari kenkyūshi* (Kazama shobō, 1980), 92–115.

41 Leading scholars in the field such as Haga were directly involved in designing the state's policies on education. Haga's *Kokubungakushi jukkō* was based on a lecture to schoolteachers, and it explicitly exhorts educators to study literary history in order to design school curricula.

42 For a discussion of the Meiji state's regulation of sexual practices, see Gregory M. Pflugfelder, *Cartographies of Desire* (Berkeley: University of California Press, 1999), chap. 3.

43 Haga writes, "It is deplorable that we have to treat the *Genji*, which depicts a corrupt society, as if it were the foremost work of our national literature. At the very least, it is not suitable material to be included in a textbook. Yet it is a massive work that sheds light on life in the Heian period, it is an important source for those who study the history or language of the time. From a purely literary point of view, moreover, the text displays a truly impressive ability to depict varied characters with distinct personalities, bringing them all into life. Nor can we dismiss the power of its writing and its influence on subsequent literary history" (*Kokubungaku jukkō*, 244).

44 Ibid., 240.

45 Although Tsubouchi himself conflated the authenticity of feelings and desires with the faithful representation of social and historical reality, he gave priority to the former: "The main point of the novel is human sentiment. Social conditions and practices rank second. By 'human sentiment' I mean man's desire and passion" (Tsubouchi Shōyō, *Shōsetsu shinzui*, in *Tsubouchi Shōyōshū*, ed. Inagaki Tetsurō, MBZ 16 [Chikuma shobō, 1969], 16).

46 Haga, *Kokubungaku jukkō*, 240.

47 Fujioka, *Kokubungaku zenshi*, 2:133–34.

48 Prior to Fujioka's *Kokubungaku zenshi* Mikami and Takatsu in *Nihon bungakushi* presented a similar argument. They praised Norinaga's refutation of the didactic interpretation of the text, but they also objected that Norinaga's critique of Confucian bias did not go far enough. While, like Haga, they equated mono no aware with realism—noting that it advocated the realistic representation of society—they deemed this view insufficient as an analytic perspective for studying the *Genji*. Instead, they suggested that precisely because amorous adventures were accepted

practices of the day the text sought to explore the ideal in the context of such pursuits, even to the extent of portraying the scandalous liaison between Genji and Fujitsubo. They faulted Norinaga for evading the question of locating a specific ideal in the text and thereby failing to read the "meaning" conveyed by literary texts (1:268).

49 Fujioka Sakutarō, *Kokubungakushi kōwa* (Iwanami shoten, 1993), 4.

50 Ibid., 9.

51 Ibid., 10. While Haga explained this "weakness and monotony" as a general characteristic of Japanese literature resulting from the nature of its language, Fujioka attributed these characteristics specifically to Heian literature due to the stagnant social organization of the Heian aristocracy.

52 Ibid., 13.

53 Ibid., 21–24.

54 Ibid., 25.

55 Ibid., 26.

56 Ibid., 138.

57 Ibid., 141.

58 Fujioka, *Kokubungaku zenshi* 1:8.

59 Fujioka, *Kokubungakushi kōwa*, 94.

60 Ibid., 220.

61 Ibid., 224.

62 Fujioka, *Kokubungaku zenshi*, 1:46.

63 Harry D. Harootunian, "Between Politics and Culture: Authority and the Ambiguities of Intellectual Choice in Imperial Japan," in *Japan in Crisis: Essays on Taishō Democracy*, ed. Bernard S. Silberman and H. D. Harootunian (Princeton: Princeton University Press, 1974), 140.

64 Watsuji Tetsurō, *Nihon seishinshi kenkyū* (Iwanami shoten, 1992), 221–35.

65 Ibid., 232.

66 Ibid., 234.

67 Ibid., 235.

68 Ibid.

69 See, for instance, Nomura Seiichi, *Nihon bungaku kenkyūshiron* (Kasama shoin, 1983), 33–35.

70 We need to caution against reducing Haga's model of national unity to a retrogressive nativism, a holdover from pre-Meiji thought. As I have tried to suggest, the ideological function served by the emperor (and classical aesthetics associated with the imperial court) in Haga's schema can be fathomed by its isomorphic relation to the deployment of feminine symbols found in diverse brands of modern nationalism.

71 Lloyd and Thomas argue that the concept of "representation" in modern cultural theories ultimately affirms a political structure that presupposes the modern state. See David Lloyd and Paul Thomas, *Culture and the State* (London: Routledge, 1998), esp. 59–81.

Chapter 3: Women and Heian Kana Writing

1 For a discussion of the complicity of kokubungaku scholars in the war effort and their postwar denial of that past, see Murai Osamu, "Kokubungakusha no jūgonen sensō," pts. 1–2. *Hihyō kūkan* 2:17; 2:18 (1998).

2 Étienne Balibar, "The Nation Form: History and Ideology," in *Race, Nation, Class: Ambiguous Identities*, ed. Étienne Balibar and Immanuel Wallerstein (London: Verso, 1991), 94.

3 A leading postwar scholar of Heian literature, Tamagami Takuya, for instance, characterized *The Tale of Genji* as a tale about women, by a woman, and for women, "the world within the text is represented from the point of view of women: the author is a woman, and the readers were also women." He thus emphasized Heian women's literary agency and the autonomy of their literary community ("Genji monogatari no dokusha: Monogatari ondokuron [1955]," in *Genji monogatari kenkyu* [Kadokawa shoten, 1965], 249).

4 Surviving material evidence of early kana texts in general is very rare. Although there is a body of Japanese poems by female poets from the late ninth to the mid-tenth centuries, there are very few kana prose texts prior to the late tenth century attributed to women. One example is the narrative section of *Ise shū*, an anthology of poems attributed to the female poet Ise, who was highly regarded when *Kokinshū* was compiled in the early tenth century. The authorship and the date of *Ise shū* and other kana texts from the period, however, are highly problematic.

5 Kimura Masanori reviews some of the major hypotheses on Tsurayuki's female impersonation in *Tosa nikki*. He concludes that the most widespread contemporary view on the question explains Tsurayuki's adoption of a female persona as a way to liberate himself from his bureaucratic identity, enabling the free, honest, and concrete expression of human emotions. See Kimura Masanori, "Nikki bungaku no honshitsu to sōsaku shinri," in *Kōza nihon bungaku no sōten*, ed. Abe Akio (Meiji shoin, 1968), 2:108–13. An identical view on *Tosa nikki* can also be found in more recent publications as well. See, for instance, Itō Hiroshi, "Nikki bungaku no kaika," in *Nihon bungaku shinshi, kodai II*, ed. Suzuki Kazuo (Shibundō, 1990), 117. A summary of various hypotheses on the female narrator of the text in English can be found in Lynne K. Miyake, "*The Tosa Diary*: In the Interstices of Gender and Criticism," in *The Woman's Hand: Gender and Theory in Japanese Women's Writing*, ed. Paul Gordon Schalow and Janet A. Walker (Stanford: Stanford University Press, 1996), 44–47.

   The argument that links the gender of the narrator with the emotional and personal content of the text, however, has lost some of its force in recent years. This may be due, in part, to the compelling critique against the autobiographical reading of *Tosa nikki* presented in Hasegawa Haruo, *Ki no Tsurayukiron* (Yūseidō shoten, 1984), 24–27.

6 There is a fragment of an earlier kana diary, the *Taikō gyoki* of Fujiwara Onshi (885–954), the principal consort of the emperor Daigo, cited in *Kakaishō* (ca. 1362–68), a medieval commentary on *The Tale of Genji* by Yotsutsuji Yoshinari. Whether

such a text truly existed and was originally written in kana is open to debate. One of the most prominent proponents of the view that *Tosa nikki* was based on existing kana diaries by women is Ishihara Shōhei. See Ishihara Shōhei, "Kana bungaku to Kana moji: *Tosa nikki* ni itaru made," *Bungei to hihyō* 1 (1971): 49–57.

7 Fujii Sadakazu, "Hyōgen to shite no nihongo: Bunpōteki jikan no chōhatsu," *Hihyō kūkan* 2:2 (1994): 204–5.

8 Fujii is not alone in associating the rise of kana literature in the mid-Heian period and the *genbun itchi* movement in the nineteenth and twentieth centuries. As I discuss later, such a view ignores highly specific ideological and historical bases for the rise of modern vernacularization movements in Japan and elsewhere.

9 Kojima Naoko, "Utagatari to tsukuri monogatari," in *Iwanami kōza nihon bungakushi*, ed. Kubota Jun, et. al. (Iwanami shoten, 1996), 2:8.

10 Miyake, "*The Tosa Diary*," 65.

11 The text refers to Chinese poems composed on the continent or in Japan as *kara uta* (*T'ang song*) after the T'ang dynasty in China: Japanese poems are called *yamato uta* (yamato song) after the archaic site of the imperial court.

    Citations of *Tosa nikki* are based on Hagitani Boku, ed., *Tosa nikki zen chushaku* (Kadokawa shoten, 1967). I consulted the English translation of *Tosa nikki* in Helen McCullough, *Kokin Wakashu: The First Imperial Anthology of Japanese Poetry* (Stanford: Stanford University Press, 1985). At the end of citation, I note the day the passage is from; this is followed by the page number in McCullough's translation. Translations are mine unless otherwise noted.

12 Hagitani, *Tosa nikki zen chūshaku*, 491.

13 Aside from the Kana Preface, *Kokinwakashū* has a preface written in Chinese, the so-called Mana Preface (*mana jo*) attributed to Ki no Yoshimochi. While there is much overlap in the content of the two texts, there are some important and revealing differences. Significantly for our present discussion, the Mana Preface attributes the decline of Japanese poetry to the incursion of Chinese poetry and the Chinese writing system. See Ozawa Masao, ed., *Kokinwakashū*, NKBZ 7 (Shōgakkan, 1975), 415.

14 Ibid., 54–55.

15 Suzuki Hideo argues that the image of the emperor and his subjects bonding through poetry presented in the Kana Preface has no relevant historical precedent in the tradition of Japanese poetry but is reminiscent of the ideal upheld by the sinophile emperor Saga and his members of his literary circle, who were active in composing Chinese poetry. See Suzuki Hideo, *Kodai wakashiron* (Tokyo daigaku shuppankai, 1993), 324.

16 Takeoka Masao argues that sama is a poetic principle developed by Tsurayuki that refers to the figuration of affect by perceptual objects (Kokin wakashū zenhyōshaku [Yūbun shoin, 1983], 87–119). According to Takeoka, this is the process invoked in the famous opening passage of the Kana Preface of *Kokinwakashū*, "Since people's deeds and experiences in the world are varied, they put their feelings into words through things they have seen and heard." (*Kokinwakashū*, NKBZ 7, 47.)

17 The only time the text mentions kara uta being composed is when the narrator de-

scribes Chinese poems being dedicated to Abe no Nakamaro at his farewell party (First Month, Twentieth Day, 277).

18 One of the seminal expressions of this view is in Hagitani Boku, "Tosa nikki wa karonsho ka," in *Heianchō nikki I*, ed. Nihon bungaku kenkyū shiryō kankōkai, (Yūseidō, 1971).

19 For an example, see Higuchi Hiroshi, "Tosa nikki ni okeru tsurayuki no tachiba," in *Heianchō nikki I*, 36–52.

20 Fujioka Tadami, Nakano Kō'ichi, Inukai Ken, and Ishii Fumio, eds., *Izumi shikibu nikki, Murasaki shikibu nikki, Sarashina nikki, Sanuki no suke nikki*, NKBZ 18 (Shōgakkan, 1971), 240; Richard Bowring, *Murasaki Shikibu, Her Diary and Poetic Memoir: A Translation and Study* (Princeton: Princeton University Press, 1982), 133.

21 Abe Akio, Akiyama Ken, and Imai Gen'e, eds., *Genji monogatari 1*, NKBZ 12 (Shōgakkan, 1970), 165; Edward Seidensticker, trans., *The Tale of Genji* (New York: Knopf, 1987), 36.

22 Endō argues that, being less constrained by the knowledge of proper calligraphic techniques developed in China, women may have taken more liberties in their cursive simplification of characters, creating the distinct shapes of the feminine hand. See Endō Yoshimoto, "Chūko," in *Kokugo no rekishi*, ed. Kokugogakkai (Osaka: Akitaya, 1948), 58.

23 Marshal Unger, "The Etymology of the Japanese Word *Kana*," *Papers in Japanese Linguistics* 7 (1980): 173–77. For an analysis and critique of Unger's argument, see Thomas LaMarre, *Uncovering Heian Japan: An Archaeology of Sensation and Inscription* (Durham: Duke University Press, 2000), 26–27.

24 Unger, "Etymology," 177.

25 Kōno Tama, ed., *Utsuho monogatari III*, NKBT 12 (Iwanami shoten, 1963), 101. Komatsu Shigemi points out that this is the first extant reference to the term *kana*. See also Komatsu Shigemi, *Kana* (Iwanami shoten, 1972), 64–65.

26 Matsuo Sō and Nagai Kazuko, eds., *Makura no sōshi*, NKBZ 11 (Shōgakkan, 1974), 232.

27 One of the earliest expressions of this view is found in Ban Nobutomo, *Kana no motosue* (1850). Even Nobutomo, however, maintains that Kūkai created the basic forty-seven kana graphs. See *Kana no motosue I* (Benseisha, 1979), 19.

28 Thomas LaMarre, "Writing Doubled over, Broken: Provisional Names, Acrostic Poems, and the Perpetual Contest of Doubles in Heian Japan," *positions* 2:2 (fall 1994): 253. For further elaboration of LaMarre's argument, see his *Uncovering of Heian Japan*.

29 Ibid.

30 LaMarre, *Uncovering Heian Japan*, 192, n. 24.

31 Benedict Anderson, *Imagined Communities: Reflections on the Origin and Spread of Nationalism* (London: Verso, 1991); Eric Hobsbawn, *Nations and Nationalism since 1780* (Cambridge: Cambridge University Press, 1990), 14–79.

32 Naoki Sakai discusses the unity of Japanese language as an idea that emerged out of a broad range of discourse on language, society, history, and culture in the eighteenth century. He also notes, however, the critical difference between this

eighteenth-century conception of "Japanese" and that of the post-Meiji period. In the eighteenth century, the wholeness of Japanese language was perceived as an ideal that existed in the archaic past but was lost to the contemporary society. In modernity, in contrast, this unity was posited in the very present, sutured to the totalizing project of the nation-state. See Naoki Sakai, *Voices of the Past: The Status of Language in Eighteenth-Century Japanese Discourse* (Ithaca: Cornell University Press, 1991), 335–36.

33   The philosophical significance of phonocentrism in modernity was, of course, brought to a wide attention by Jacques Derrida. Derrida sheds light on the ideological stakes involved in the privileging of speech over writing or phonetic scripts over other systems of writing. The hierarchy of speech and writing (speech being closer to the internal essence of linguistic unity and systematicity) serves to reify the interiority of language, the self-present voice, and ultimately an identity and presence primordial to representation. See his *Of Grammatology*, trans. and ed. Gayatri Spivak (Baltimore: Johns Hopkins University Press, 1976).

34   Karatani Kōjin argues that the call to eliminate the use of kanji was a critical component of the vernacularization movement in Japan, signaling the introduction of the modern concept of interiority (Brett de Bary, ed. and trans., *Origins of Japanese Literature* [Durham, Duke University Press], 45–75).

35   *Kokinwakashū*, NKBZ 7, 50.

36   This is mentioned in the Mana Preface of the anthology (NKBZ 7, 415).

37   Most notable was princess Uchiko (?–847), the daughter of the sinophile emperor Saga, whose poems appear in an imperial anthology of Chinese poems.

38   The process may have been facilitated by the rising prominence of the *kōkyū* (rear court), the private quarters of the emperor organized around imperial consorts and their circles, as opposed to the *zenden* (front court), where official state business was conducted. The period is well known for the so-called marriage politics of powerful aristocratic clans such as the northern branch of the Fujiwara family, which exerted great political influence by successfully installing its daughters as high-ranking imperial consorts and placing its offspring on the throne. Kana and literary productions employing this style of writing flourished as relations of power at the court were increasingly brokered not only in the official sites of bureaucratic administration but in the supposedly more personal space of the emperor and his consorts, where court women had considerable cultural and political leverage.

39   *Genji monogatari III*, NKBZ 14, 407. See also Seidensticker, *The Tale of Genji*, 517.

40   *Genji monogatari III*, 408. See also Seidensticker, *The Tale of Genji*, 517.

41   Shimura Midori points out that even female courtiers had to have some knowledge of reading and an understanding of official documents ("Heian jidai josei no mana kanseki no gakushū," *Nihon rekishi* 457 [June 1986]: 35).

42   *Murasaki shikibu nikki*, NKBZ 18, 244; Bowring, *Murasaki Shikibu*, 137. The text also recounts how as a child the author learned to read Chinese texts faster than her brother just by listening to him read and study them, causing her father to lament that she was not born a male (NKBZ 18, 244; Bowring, *Murasaki Shikibu*, 139).

Later, in her adulthood, she gave lessons on Chinese poetry to her mistress and an imperial consort, Shōshi, with approval from both the emperor and Shōshi's father, Fujiwara Michinaga, the most powerful politician at the court (NKBZ 18, 245; Bowring, *Murasaki Shikibu*, 139).

43 *Makura no soshi*, NKBZ 11, 169–75. Ivan Morris, *The Pillow Book of Sei Shōnagon* (New York: Columbia University Press, 1991), 88–93.

44 *The Diary of Murasaki Shikibu* notes that men, too, could ruin their chances of success if they flaunted their training in Chinese letters (NKBZ 18, 244; Bowring, *Murasaki Shikibu*, 139).

45 Shimura, "Heian jidai josei no mana kanseki no gakushū," 22–38.

46 Roy Miller, for instance, comments that Heian society by and large began to treat both Chinese and Japanese as if they were the same language (*The Japanese Language* [Chicago: University of Chicago Press, 1967], 131) In the light of the argument made in this chapter, however, the perception that the proper distinction between Chinese and Japanese languages became lost in Heian society is a retroactive formation that presupposes the modern conception of national language.

47 Anne McClintock, *Imperial Leather: Race, Gender, and Sexuality in the Colonial Contest* (London: Routledge, 1995), 354. On the issue of woman as symbolic bearers of national culture, see chapter 3, "Cultural Reproduction and Gender Relations," in Nira Yuval-Davis, *Gender and Nation* (London: Sage, 1997), 39–67.

48 For example, writings in Heian literary studies by leading female scholars such as Mitamura Masako, Kawazoe Fusae, and Kojima Naoko frequently treat these issues. There are also works by a growing number of younger researchers in the field informed by feminist and gender studies. A series of edited volumes on Heian literature that focus on the issues of gender and sexuality published in the last decade include Monogatari Kenkyūkai, ed., *Monogatari: Otoko to onna* (Yūseidō shuppan, 1995); Kojima Naoko, ed., *Ōchō no sei to shintai: Itsudatsusuru monogatari* (Shinwasha, 1996); Gotō Shōko, ed., *Heian bungaku no shikaku: Josei* (Benseisha, 1995); and a special issue on sexuality and the body "Ōchō no bunka to sei," in the journal *Genji kenkyū* (1 [1996]), edited by Mitamura Masako, Kawazoe Fusae, and Matsui Kenji.

There are also a number of studies on Heian literature that engage feminist problematics produced by scholars in the United States. These include Norma Field's *The Splendor of Longing in "The Tale of Genji"* (Princeton: Princeton University Press, 1987), which reexamines the construction of female characters in *The Tale of Genji*, highlighting their discursive and social agencies. Edith Sarra analyzes Heian women writers' construction of the feminine through the study of Heian kana diaries in her *Fictions of Femininity: Literary Interventions of Gender in Japanese Court Women's Memoirs* (Stanford: Stanford University Press, 1999). Carole Cavanaugh studies the sociopolitical and economic agency of female subjects as depicted in Heian texts by focusing on women's role as producers of textile art in her "Text and Textile: Unweaving the Female Subject in Heian Writing," *positions* 4:3 (winter 1996).

49 The association among kana, native language, and feminine writing in Heian lit-

erature has been powerfully reinforced by the sense of an overarching binary between the Chinese and Japanese modalities (and attendant gendered associations) that allegedly organized Heian aristocratic culture—extending from language, calligraphy, and literary genres to paintings. Even scholars such as Chino Kaori, a leading Heian art historian, who seek to introduce contemporary feminist theory into Heian studies, subscribe to this view. For instance, see Chino's "Nihon bijutsu no jendā," *Nihon bijutsu* 136 (1994). I have tried to suggest in this chapter that we need to exercise great caution in projecting the modern notion of national cultural identity onto the Heian context. For the critique of Chino's discussion of gender and cultural identity in Heian society, see my "*Seisa, moji, kokka:* Feminizumu hihyō to heian bungaku kenkyū," in *Tekisuto no seiaijutsu: Monogatari bunseki no riron to jissen*, ed. Takagi Makoto and Andō Tōru (Shinwasha, 1999).

50 Suzuki Tomi's thoughtful analysis of the modern origin of the term *joryū nikki bungaku* (female diary literature) is one of the few studies that offers a sustained critique of the gender and national ideologies that inform modern Heian literary scholarship and the role it has carved out for Heian literature within the broader horizon of Japanese literary history. See her "Gender and Genre: Modern Literary Histories and Women's Diary Literature," in *Inventing the Classics: Modernity, National Identity, and Japanese Literature*, ed. Harao Shirane and Tomi Suzuki (Stanford: Stanford University Press, 2001). Yoshino Mizue has also studied the modern construction of the "female diary literature" in Heian literary studies; see "Onna e no toraware: Joryū nikki bungaku to iu seido," in *Heian bungaku to iu ideorogī*, ed. Kawazoe Fusae (Benseisha, 1999).

Chapter 4: Politics and Poetics in *Genji*

1 It was the father and son leaders of Kamakura poetry, Fujiwara Shunzei (1114–1204) and Teika (1162–1241), who designated the text as the repository of aesthetic sensibility. In his often quoted comment in a poetry contest, "Roppyakuban utaawase," Shunzei intoned that the poets who do not read the *Genji* are regrettable (*Utaawaseshū*, ed. Hatitani Boku and Taniyama Sigeru, NKBT 74 [Iwanami shoten, 1965], 442). His son, Teika, commended the text for its broader literary values. In "Kyōgoku chūnagon sōgo," he speaks derisively of those who fret over the author's lineage or the exact references to the text's poetic allusions. He draws attention instead to the profundity of Shikibu's writing, stating that in reading the text one's mind becomes clearer and one's poems improve in their words and style (*Chūsei no bungaku, Karonshū* I, ed. Hisamatsu Sen'ichi [Kyoto: Miyai shoten, 1971], 335).

2 Each citation of Motoori Norinaga's writing in this chapter is followed by the title of the piece and the volume and the page number in Ōno Susumu, ed., *Motoori Norinaga zenshū* (Chikuma shobō, 1968–77). See, for example, the citation in note 3.

3 A similar argument is made in Motoori, *Shibun yōryō*, 4:107. See also Motoori, *Isonokami sasamegoto*, 2:112.

4   Naoki Sakai, *Voices of the Past: The Status of Language in Eighteenth-Century Japanese Discourse* (Ithaca: Cornell University Press, 1991), 307.

5   As I suggested in chapter 1, although Norinaga was highly critical of the esoteric teachings of courtier poetics—for example, their traditionalism and the quasi-spiritual mystification of waka—the poetic composition he practiced and preached did not stray far from a highly conservative style. On Motoori Norinaga and Nijō school poetry, see Kanno Kakumyō, *Motoori Norinaga kotoba to miyabi* (Perikansha, 1991), 67–106.

6   The Kana Preface of *Kokinwakashū* states that poetry emerges from the organic link between *kokoro* and *kotoba*.

7   Harry Harootunian writes of kokugaku's problematization of the fissure between form and content and the resignification of "form" not as a mere vehicle of meaning but as an integral element of signification: "They charged that contemporary forms of representation were not adequately referring to 'reality' and that form had been separated from content, language from authentic experience. . . . In their valorization of poetry, they made 'visible as ideological what otherwise was disregarded as merely means' or instrument of representation" (*Things Seen and Unseen: Discourse and Ideology in Tokugawa Nativism* [Chicago: University of Chicago Press, 1988], 41–42).

8   The English translations of chapter titles of the *Genji* are based on Seidensticker's translation of the text.

9   Norinaga writes: "Poems in the *Genji* are all composed by the author, but there is hardly an inferior verse; they are generally well made, and some are quite exquisite" (*Genji monogatari Tama no ogushi*, 4:235). An example of a more representative view can be found in Fujiwara Shunzei's comment in the "Roppyakuban Utaawase," quoted earlier, in which he praises Murasaki Shikibu's talent as a writer but not as a poet (NKBT 74, 442).

10   Masuda Katsumi, "Genji monogatari no sengo: Watashi no baai," *Nihon bungaku* 10:6 (1961): 291–93.

11   On the postwar democratization debates and the participation of literary scholars in them, see J. V. Koschmann, *Revolution and Subjectivity in Postwar Japan* (Chicago: University of Chicago Press, 1996), especially 41–87.

12   Saigō Nobutsuna, "Bungakushi to hihyō, bungaku janru o megutte," *Bungaku* 19 (December 1951): 4.

13   The article was renamed "Kyūtei joryū bungaku no kaika" when it was later collected in *Nihon bungaku no hōhō* (Miraisha, 1955).

14   "Creating a prose narrative requires construction of a particular fictional world mediated by materials taken from reality and experience. The author thereby must express his or her own position through this world with some degree of objectivity and intention of persuading the audience one way or another. To be a writer of such fictional tales, it seems to me, entailed a background not in Japanese poetry but in Chinese letters" (Saigō, "Kyūtei joryū bungaku no kaika," 165).

15   Ibid., 167.

16   Masuda drew directly on Saigō's study in his "Genji monogatari no ninaite," in

Genji monogatari 1, ed. Nihon bungaku kenkyū shiryō kankōkai (Yūseidō shuppan, 1974).

17   Masuda Katsumi, "Waka to Seikatsu: Genji monogatari no naibu kara," in *Genji monogatari 4*, ed. Nihon bungaku kenkyū shiryō kankōkai (Yūseidō shuppan, 1974).

18   Ibid., 235.

19   Ibid., 233.

20   Ibid.

21   Ibid., 238.

22   Ibid., 234.

23   Roman Jakobson, "Linguistics and Poetics," in *Language in Literature*, ed. Krystyna Pomorska and Stephen Rudyed (Cambridge: Belknap, 1987), 66–71.

24   Ibid., 66.

25   Roland Barthes, "Is There Any Poetic Writing?" In *Writing Degree Zero*, trans. Annette Lavers and Colin Smith (New York: Hill and Wang, 1968), 41.

26   For an example, see the exchanges between Kaguyahime and Prince Ishitsukuri in Katagiri Yōichi, ed., *Taketori monogatari, Ise monogatari, Yamato Monogatari, Heichū monogatari*, NKBZ 8 (Shōgakkan, 1972), 59–60.

27   It should be noted that Chinese poems are paraphrased by the narrator on a few occasions—for instance, the kanshi composed by a Korean physiognomist in the "The Paulownia Court" (Kiritsubo) chapter, which predicts events in Genji's future. Chinese poems must be "told" rather than "shown" in a kana text narrated in the female voice, although, as famously recorded in her diary, the text's author, Murasaki Shikibu, was apparently fully versed in kanshi.

28   At a banquet described in the "The Maiden" (Otome) chapter, the narrator, after recording four poems recited by principal guests and hosts, states: "These are the only poems I have from the banquet. Was it the case that, the occasion being an informal one, the cup did not completely make the rounds? Or were there more, but they were never written down?" (Abe Akio, Akiyama Ken, Imai gen'e, eds., *Genji Monogatari 3*, NKBZ 13 [Shōgakkan, 1972], 67; see also Edward Seidensticker, trans., *The Tale of Genji* [New York: Knopf, 1987], 381). The text thus explains the scarcity of poems cited in relation to the expected number of guests, who should have recited a verse as they received the cup of wine being passed around.

29   In translating passages from the *Genji*, I consulted Edward Seidensticker's translation, *The Tale of Genji*; and Royall Tyler, trans., *The Tale of Genji 1* (New York: Viking, 2001). Each citation is followed by the volume number of the six-volume *Genji monogatari* published in *Nihon koten bungaku zenshū* and the page number in the volume; this is followed by the page number in the Seidensticker translation, marked with an S.

30   In fact, at night the imperial guard is assigned to the division in which Genji is a captain. A reference to this detail is found in Tamagami Takuya, *Genji monogatari hyōshaku* (Kadokawa shoten, 1965), 2:542–43.

31   The term *ku* refers to either five or seven syllabic units by which 5-7-5-7-7 syllabic waka is constituted.

32 Koyasu Nobukuni comments that Norinaga's concept of mono no aware represents an understanding of monogatari from the position of a reader ("Motoori Norinaga: Waka no zokuryūka to bi no jiritsu," *Shisō* 879 (1997): 13–15).

33 Harootunian writes, "Archaism for Motoori meant returning to the tangible; it demanded closing the gap between word and thing in order to reach the origin of discourse itself" (*Things Seen and Unseen*, 81).

34 Gerald Genette, *Figures of Literary Discourse*, trans. Alan Sheridan (New York: Columbia University Press, 1982), 97.

35 This is, of course, not an issue exclusive to discussing poetry in Japanese literary history. As Barbara Johnson writes, "What, indeed, is the problem in any modern theory of poetic language, if not the problem of articulating authenticity with conventionality, originality and continuity, freshness with what is recognizably 'fit' to be called poetic?" (*A World of Difference* [Baltimore: Johns Hopkins University Press, 1987], 95).

36 Suggestively, the female characters who repeatedly send poetic addresses to Genji are comic figures such as the lecherous old woman Gen no Naishi or the unworldly princess with the ruddy nose, Suetsumuhana.

37 Not only plot development but the description of performative elements of poetic exchanges—tone of voice if a poem is delivered orally or in written exchanges the calligraphic style and epistolary format (the choice of paper, ornamentation, and various modes of delivery)—function as contexts that inflect a poetic communication.

38 Again, formal specificity assures a certain level of autonomy in the signification of poetry. For instance, the convention of *hikiuta* (traditional allusion) may invoke a series of other poetic discourses and their contexts of composition, regardless of their relevance to the narrative context.

39 Quite aptly, it is Fujitsubo, rather than Genji, who shortly after this meeting suddenly becomes a nun and forecloses any possibility of further overtures from the hero.

40 As if to echo the very manner in which the text portrays Genji's life at Suma, Genji himself records his experience of exile in a lyrical picture-diary with waka interspersed with prose. The diary is later presented at a court event, captivating the audience with its affective power.

41 Of the scholarship in English, an article by Esperanza Ramirez-Christensen presents an insightful analysis of how what she calls the "lyrical mode" dominates certain scenes in the *Genji*, digressing from the linear flow of narrative progression. See her "The Operation of the Lyrical Mode in the *Genji monogatari*," in *Ukifune: Love in The Tale of Genji*, ed. Andrew Pekarik (New York: Columbia University Press, 1982), 21–61.

42 A note in NKBZ states that some commentators have understood the narratorial intrusion—about the difficulty of composing poems under such circumstances—to refer specifically to Rokujō, attributing, for that reason, not only the first but also the second waka to Genji. Modern editions of the text, however, generally treat the second waka as Rokujō's response to Genji.

The translation of this exchange has been transcribed from Seidensticker's text with some minor modifications.

43 According to Ramirez-Christensen, such fusion between the elements of the external setting and the character's emotion expressed by the poem that he or she composes at the moment functions as the central motif of the text's lyrical mode, a structure that anchors a scene dominated by poetic function ("Operation of the Lyrical Mode," 38–39).

44 In *Shibun yōryō*, Norinaga refers to Ukifune, the heroine in the final section of the *Genji* who suffers from the romantic triangle and tries to commit suicide, as "losing her very self and sensing the mono no aware of two men completely." This association with death is another facet of the negativity of mono no aware (*Shibun yōryō* 4: 74–75).

45 Buddhist doctrines locate the root of human suffering in desire and greed, which stem from the deluded attachment to the self. Any earthly passion, therefore, poses a serious impediment to spiritual salvation. Indeed, the text is populated by a number of "ghosts" who after their deaths are trapped between their past lives and their next incarnations due to their attachment to the world.

46 Masuda, "Waka to seikatsu," 232.

47 What Masuda fails to recognize is that his investment of transcendent value in transgressive romance presupposes a whole complex of notions associated with individuated subject and the sociality based on this modern conceptualization of human existence. His definition of genuine poetry as the expression of individual interiority and its transcendence of prosaic sociality is also inextricably linked to the modern, humanistic notion of subject.

48 Matsumoto Sannosuke's classic study of kokugaku views the concept of mono no aware as a new theory of governance in which the political status quo is maintained by a specific construction not of the rulership but of the ruled — aestheticizing passive subjection to regulations that are beyond one's control. See Matsumoto Sannosuke, *Kokugaku seiji shisō no kenkyū* (Miraisha, 1972), 51–55. This is not to say, however, that the vision of culture and society suggested by Norinaga's corpus of work may be reduced to its reactionary potential. As Harootunian reminds us, Norinaga's projects, in relation to the dominant ideology at the time, offered a theoretical basis for empowering the townspeople as newly emerging political subjects, affirming the political relevance of their daily experience, which lay outside the conventional definition of public institutions and practices (*Things Seen and Unseen*, 114–17).

49 Motoori, *Tama no ogushi*, 4:209–21.

50 Although LaMarre's research does not discuss poetic exchanges in monogatari, his caution against the hasty politicization of Heian poetic practice is highly relevant to the issue I am trying to raise here: "In literary studies, it is not uncommon for scholars to treat poetics as a site of political contestation and to analyze poetic exchanges in which poets air their grievances in a competitive arena. Such competition is often construed by contemporary scholars as a form of resistance — usually to the ruling elite — and is interpreted in terms of the individual versus the

group; in effect, they presume a modern apparatus of resistance. In this study, I do not treat such exchanges primarily as a form of resistance but rather as a mode of participation in a poetic order of things" (*Uncovering Heian Japan: An Archeology of Sensation and Inscription* [Durham: Duke University Press, 2000], 7).

Chapter 5: Tokieda's Imperial Subject

1   Mitani Kuniaki, *Monogatari bungaku no hōhō 1* (Yūseidō, 1989), 3. Mitani and Takahashi both used the nonperspectival representational mode of the *Genji*'s hand scroll paintings as a model with which to explicate its distinct (from modern and Western) narratological principles and structure. See also Takahashi Tōru, *Monogatari to e no enkin hō* (Perikansha, 1991).

2   Monogatari kenkyūkai (Monoken), a study group founded in 1971 by scholars including Mitani and Takahashi provided an important forum for this new generation of researchers and students in Heian literary studies, challenging both the hierarchical organization of the academic institutions and their methodological orthodoxy. Abe Yoshiomi, in his reflection of the twenty-five years of the Monoken's activities, emphasized the relationship between the group's formation and the political/intellectual climate of the early 1970s. See his "Monoken nijūgonen no seika to kongo no tenbō," *Monogatari kenkyu kaihō* 27 (August 1998): 2.

3   Mitani began his seminal 1976 article by raising the question, "What is monogatari?" pointing out how existing scholarship in the field had largely ignored this basic inquiry. He went on to argue that in the few instances when the question was addressed scholars had merely explained monogatari in light of the original causes they had posited, falling short of analyzing the monogatari texts themselves. He proposed instead a phenomenological approach that begins with the effect, considering, for instance, how *katari* (speech, narration, communication) constituted monogatari. See his "Monogatari to kakukoto," *Nihon bungaku* 25 (October 1976): 3–4. The question, "What is *monogatari*?" not only was the central problematic for Mitani but a theme that brought together the members of Monoken (Abe, "Monoken no seika to kongo no tenbō," 2).

4   Between 1976 to 1980, four out of the five annual themes of Monoken were related to the issue of katari, testifying to the centrality of the issue for the group during this period.

5   It should be mentioned that even prior to the early 1970s there was an existing body of scholarship in Heian literary studies that focused on formal issues such as the structural organization of the text and linguistic and stylistic analysis. Members of the new generation of formalist scholars, however, differed from them in their emphasis on the disjunction between the modern and premodern narratives, seeking the logic of Heian tales that is distinct from that of modern novels. They brought to the foreground of their intellectual agenda, therefore, the critique of the normative status of realism, which was hardly ever questioned by the earlier generation of scholars.

6   Fujii Sadakazu, another leading scholar of the new trend in Heian studies, pointed

out that in the 1960s and 1970s the global critique of the academic establishment stimulated an effort to overcome the hierarchical dissemination of knowledge (including that between the West and the rest). Thus, in the context of the study of Heian tales as well the issue of confronting the global study of narrative emerged as a major problematic (*Kokubungaku no tanjō* [Sangensha, 2000], 160).

7   Lee Yeounsuk argued that the conflict between gengogaku and kokugogaku must be understood not simply in terms of methodological differences but in relation to the tension between modernity and tradition found at the very core of the nation's modern history. We will see later, however, that the association of kokugogaku with traditionalism does not adequately capture the project of Tokieda Motoki. See Lee Yeounsuk, *Kokugo to iu shisō: Kindai nihon no gengo ninshiki* (Iwanami shoten, 1996), 178.

8   Miura Tsutomu, *Nihongo wa dōyū gengo ka* (Kōdansha, 1956); Yoshimoto Taka'aki, *Gengo ni totte bi to wa nanika*, vol. 1 (Keisō shobō, 1965). For Tokieda's own critique of Stalin's *Marxism and Linguistics*, see his "Stālin 'gengogaku ni okeru marukusushugi' ni kanshite," *Chūō kōron* 65: 740 (October 1950): 97–103.

9   In the preface to his book, Tokieda wrote that language is one type of subjective process of expression (*shutaiteki na hyōgen katei*) (Tokieda, *Kokugogaku genron* [Iwanami shoten, 1947], v).

10   An informative discussion of Tokieda's theory and the intellectual scene in Japan in the 1960s is found in Kamei Hideo's preface to the English translation of his book. See Kamei Hideo, *Transformations of Sensibility*, trans. and ed. Michael Bourdaghs (Ann Arbor: Center for Japanese Studies, University of Michigan, 2002).

11   For a discussion of this current in the study of modern Japanese literature, see James Fujii, *Complicit Fictions: The Subject in the Modern Japanese Prose Narrative* (Berkeley: University of California Press, 1993).

12   The exact date of the text is unknown, but it is generally thought to be from the late ninth or early tenth century. The earliest surviving manuscript of the text is from the late sixteenth century. Sakakura Atsuyoshi contended in his study on the narration of *Taketori monogatari* that, although the surviving manuscripts of the text most certainly contain later revisions, the widespread notion that the text retains a vestige of earliest kana narrative may be justified by its distinct stylistic features, which mix elements of *kanbun kundoku* style as well as those of kana prose ("*Taketori monogatari* ni okeru 'buntai' no mondai," *Kokugo Kokubun* 25 [November, 1956]).

13   Mitani Kuniaki, "Genji monogatari ni okeru katari no kōzō," *Monogatari bungaku no hōhō* 1, 170.

14   What is called jodōshi by modern Japanese grammarians is postpositional and inflecting morphemes that attach to verbals and adjectivals. Various types of jodōshi express negation, speculation, hearsay, desire, and so on.

15   In pre-Heian narrative texts written in kanbun or hybrid kanbun, there are very few jodōshi used, even in a text with a relatively strong vernacular flavor such as *Kojiki* (the oldest Japanese chronicle dating from the early eighth century). Although *Kojiki* used *man'yōgana* to inscribe the phonetic values of proper names

and some distinctly native grammatical elements, *keri* was rarely written out explicitly. We find it in a few instances of speech or poetry but never in prose narration. On the absence of jodōshi in *Kojiki*, see Sugiyama Yasuhiko, "Kodai sanbun no jikan," *Nihon bungaku* 26 (November 1977): 2.

16   Takeoka Masao, "Jodōshi 'keri' no hongi to kinō," *Kokubungaku Gengo to bungei* 5 (November 1963): 4.

17   Ibid., 9–8. Here is the opening passage of *Taketori*.

Ima ha mukashi, Taketori no wokina to ifu mono ari*keri*. Noyama ni majirite take wo toritsutsu, yorozu no koto ni tsukahi*keri*. Na wo ba, sanuki no miyatsuko to namu ihi*keru*. Sono take no naka ni, moto hikaru take namu hitosuzi ari*keru*. Ayashigarite, yorite miru ni, tsutsu no naka hikari*tari*. Sore wo mireba, sansun bakarinaru hito, ito utsukushiūte wi*tari*.

Now is the time past. There was a man known as the old bamboo cutter. He roamed around the mountains cutting bamboo trees and crafting many kinds of things out of them. His name was Sanuki no Miyatsuko. One day, among the bamboo trees that he was about to cut down, he noticed a shining trunk. The old man found this strange and went to take a closer look. He saw that the tree was shining from within, and inside it he found a beautiful tiny girl (Katagiri Yōichi, ed., *Taketori monogatari*, Ise monogatari, Yamato monogatari, NKBZ 8 [Shōgakkan, 1972], 51).

After the first three uses of *keri*, the narration switches to the jodōshi *tari* (signifying the continuation of a state or action), followed by the phrase ending with verbal stems without jodōshi. The switching of sentence endings from *keri* to *tari*, and to verbal stems without jodōshi, seems to conform to Takeoka's argument, indicating the movement of the narratorial perspective from the context of narration into the story-world (speaking from a position placed within it). We should also note that the temporal location of the narrator is ambiguous. Furthermore, in the passage "the [old man] found this strange and went to take a closer look. [He] saw that the tree was shining from within" (ayashigarite yoritemiruni, tsutsu no naka hikaritari), the grammatical subject placed in brackets in the translation is absent in the original. The phrase itself, if we disregard the context, can be translated into English as a first- or third-person discourse.

18   Of course, in modern novels, too, the tense system is not always strictly observed. Novels in English commonly use the historical present and tense switching. Yet the deployment of such techniques is more marked and limited than in the case of Heian kana texts.

19   The "instance of discourse" is a term coined by Emile Benveniste, a French structuralist linguist whose work provided some of the theoretical foundations to contemporary narratology. (*Problems in General Linguistics*, trans. Mary Elizabeth Meek [Coral Gables: University of Miami Press, 1971], 217).

20   It has been pointed out that Tokieda's understanding of Saussure was largely based on a widespread misconception of the latter's theory in Japan. Saussure, in fact,

was squarely opposed to what he perceived as a positivistic approach to language in evolutionary linguistics and historical philology. He sought to examine language intrinsically, without resorting to external causes. Far from analyzing language as an inert object, he insisted on approaching it in terms of the lived linguistic experience of native speakers, rejecting the evolutionary notion that endows language with continuity and substance that transcend any particular context of linguistic practice. Saussure's notion of the synchronic, therefore, posited the inseparability of language from its pragmatic frame. It was only on the assumption of this fundamental contextuality of language that he spoke of its systematicity in terms of *langue* and its individual enactment in terms of *parole*. On the misrepresentation of Saussure in Japan, see Maruyama Keizaburō, *Soshūru no shisō* (Iwanami shoten, 1993), 46–49.

21   In this chapter, I frequently refer to the discursive subject discussed in Tokieda using the Japanese term *shutai*, as this is a central concept in his thought and the focal point of my analysis.

22   As the practice of waka composition became increasingly bound by strict rules of precedent and prohibitions concerning diction, theme, and rhetorical technique, the subtle modification and modulations of verses by means of te-ni-wo-ha became major technical and aesthetic concerns. The esoteric and pedantic tendencies of the influential Nijō school further emphasized and mystified te-ni-wo-ha, the mastery of which was equated with the ultimate skill in waka composition. Because these morphemes are frequently found at the end of a phrase, marking a completion or conjunction with the next phrase, te-ni-wo-ha was carefully studied in the theory of *renga* (linked verse) in which the links as well as the cuts between verses are of vital importance.

23   Norinaga approached te-ni-wo-ha primarily through the issue of *kakari musubi*. *Kakari musubi* today is defined as a grammatical phenomenon in which a word in the sentence-final position takes an irregular inflection in the presence of a class of particles called *kakarijoshi* or *keijoshi*. Norinaga, however, understood the relations between particles and the inflection of the final morpheme as a grammatical rule in general (not limited to the irregular cases). He thereby established te-ni-wo-ha as a grammatical principle.

24   Widely considered to be the first treatise on te-ni-wo-ha from the fourteenth century, and apocryphally attributed to Fujiwara Teika, the text has a famous commentary by the renga master Sōgi.

25   Kanno Kakumyō, *Motoori norinaga: kotoba to miyabi* (Perikansha, 1991), 269.

26   Sakai, Naoki, *Voices of the Past: The Status of Language in Eighteenth-Century Japanese Discourse* (Ithaca: Cornell University Press, 1991), 269–70.

27   Tokieda, *Kokugogaku genron*, 235.

28   Ibid., 247.

29   Ji, in this sense, may be likened to the notion of copula as applied to Indo-European languages. A copula may not be found in every sentence, but it suggests that the basic unifying principle of an utterance is to be localized in its middle. Ji, in contrast, indicates that the Japanese syntax has its anchor at the end of a phrase.

30 Tokieda, *Kokugogaku genron*, 347.

31 Karatani Kōjin, "Nihon seishin bunseki 4," *Hihyō kūkan* 8 (1993): 242.

32 Ibid., 242.

33 Tokieda, *Kokugogaku genron*, 8–9. These issues raised by Tokieda are far from obsolete, as attested by the ongoing debate in the academy over the configuration of area studies and its relation to "theory."

34 Kamei, *Transformations of Sensibility*, xxxvii–xxxviii.

35 Tokieda, *Kokugogaku genron*, ii.

36 Tokieda Motoki, "Chōsen ni okeru kokugo seisaku oyobi kokugo kyōiku no shō-rai," *Nihongo* 2:2 (August 1942): 61–63.

37 This means that the explicit grammatical subject in Japanese discourse is distinguished not only from the phenomenological agent of utterance, shutai, but from the subject of statement that is always already implied in the predicate.

38 My discussion on the application Tokieda's theory in the formalist study of Heian narrative focuses on Japanese scholarship, especially the influential work of Mitani Kuniaki. I should mention, however, Amanda Stinchecum's fine study of narrative voice in the *Genji*, which skillfully deploys elements of Tokieda's theory, "Who Tells the Tale? 'Ukifune': A Study in Narrative Voice," *Monumenta Nipponica*, 35:4 (April, 1980).

   Although Richard Okada's *Figures of Resistance: Language, Poetry, and Narrating in "The Tale of Genji" and Other Mid-Heian Texts* (Durham: Duke University Press, 1991) does not directly refer to Tokieda, its approaches bear some striking resonance with the linguist's insights, providing us with an example of innovative and sophisticated extension of Tokieda's theory in the study of Heian kana narrative. Just as Tokieda argued that Japanese discourse cannot help but exteriorize shutai, Okada contends that in Heian narrative the narrating register never truly disappears from the narration, privileging the discourse over the story, so that "the narrative discourse itself, the performative event, becomes an important, perhaps *the* important, story" (170; also see 180). Okada points to jodōshi as the signifiers that "mark the continual emphasis placed on an implied speaker or enunciative position and on the (modal) attitude that speaker or position adopts toward the discourse" (18).

39 Fujii Sadakazu, "Katarite ninshō wa doko ni aruka," in *Ronshū heian bungaku* (Benseisha 1994), 46.

40 Takahashi, *Monogatari to e no enkin hō*, 25–26.

41 Mitani Kuniaki, *Monogatari bungaku no gensetsu* (Yūseidō, 1992), 324.

42 Ibid., 105–6.

43 Although Mitani's attention to the issue of writing serves as a means of questioning some of the existing assumptions in the field, it should be pointed out that there are some serious theoretical problems in the manner in which he uses the term. He reifies the distinction between orality and literacy and largely ignores the historicity of this concept as it is deployed by poststructuralist critics such as Derrida, that is, bound up with the technology of inscription, communication, and distribution and their social effects in modernity.

44 Mitani, *Monogatari bungaku no hōhō 2*, 463.

45 Mitani, *Monogatari bungaku no gensetsu*, 194.

46 Ibid., 323.

47 Mitani, *Monogatari bungaku no hōhō 2*, 463.

48 This view is similar to Takahashi's attribution of greater critical insights to narrators because of their marginality vis-à-vis the story-world.

49 According to Tokieda, utterance is produced when someone (the discursive agent: shutai) speaks about something (the theme: sozai) to someone (the context: bamen). All three elements in this triad are conditions of existence for language, but at the same time none inheres in words and sentences.

50 As Sakai Naoki points out in his analysis of Tokieda, it takes a perspective other than that of the present shutai to posit shutai as the origin of utterance. To apprehend shutai's externalization of its intention, one needs a perspective other than that of the shutai intending. Tokieda "neglects to mention that a viewpoint away from the position marked as the shutai is essential to comprehend the original situation of the shutai; the representation of the shutai as such requires a viewpoint other than the *shutai*" (*Voices of the Past*, 328).

51 See V. N. Volsinov [M. M. Bakhtin], *Marxism and Theory of Language*, trans. L. Matejka and I. R. Titunik (New York: Seminar Press, 1973), esp. pts. 1–2.

52 "The boundaries of each concrete utterance as a unit of speech communication are determined by a *change of speaking subjects*, that is, a change of speakers" (M. M. Bakhtin, *Speech Genres and Other Late Essays*, trans. Vern W. McGee, ed. Caryl Emerson and Michael Holquist [Austin: University of Texas Press, 1986], 71).

53 Elsewhere Bakhtin associates the consciousness of the inconclusivity of any given moment with the historicization of time and the world. See *The Dialogic Imagination*, trans. Caryl Emerson and Michael Holquist (Austin: University of Texas Press, 1981), 30.

54 Bakhtin himself was cognizant of this problem, as is clear in his analysis of "quasi-indirect discourse," a form of literary discourse in which a given utterance is stratified dialogically between the registers of characterological and authorial voices.

55 Jacques Lacan, *Écrits*, trans. Alan Sheridan (New York: Norton, 1977), 306.

56 Ludwig Wittgenstein, *Philosophical Investigations*, trans., G. E. Anscombe (New York: Macmillan, 1968), 404.

57 "I pointed, but I robbed the pointing of its sense by inseparably connecting that which points and that to which it points" (Ludwig Wittgenstein, *Preliminary Studies for the "Philosophical Investigations," Generally Known as the Blue and Brown Books* [New York: Harper and Row, 1958], 71).

58 "This cut in the signifying chain alone verifies the structure of the subject as discontinuity in the real. If linguistics enables us to see the signifier as the determinant of the signified, analysis reveals the truth of this relation by making 'holes' in the meaning of the determinants of its discourse" (Lacan, *Écrits*, 299).

59 "What this structure of the signifying chain discloses is the possibility I have, precisely in so far as I have this language in common with other subjects, that is to

say, in so far as it exists as a language, to use it in order to signify *something quite other* than what it says" (ibid., 155).

60   Slavoj Žižek's critique of historical relativism offers a valuable caution in this regard: "The fascinating 'diversity' of the Other functions as a fetish by means of which we are able to preserve the unproblematic *identity* of our subjective position: although we pretend to 'historically relativize' our position, we actually conceal its split; we deceive ourselves as to how this position is already 'decentered from within' " (*For They Know Not What They Do: Enjoyment as a Political Factor* [London: Verso, 1991], 102).

61   "The philosophy of disengagement and objectification has helped to create a picture of the human being, at its most extreme in certain forms of materialism, from which the last vestiges of subjectivity seem to have been expelled. It is a picture of the human being from a completely third-person perspective. The paradox is that this severe outlook is connected with, indeed, based on, according a central place to the first-person stance. Radical objectivity is only intelligible and accessible through radical subjectivity" (Charles Taylor, *Sources of the Self: The Making of the Modern Identity* [Cambridge: Harvard University Press, 1989], 175–76).

62   Takagi Makoto, "Tekisuto riron no kishikata, yukusue: Nihontekina, amari ni nihontekina," in *Tekisuto no seiaijutsu: Monogatari bunseki no riron to jissen*, ed. Takagi Makoto and Endō Tōru (Shinwasha, 1999).

63   Yasuda Toshiaki, *Shokuminchi no naka no kokugogaku* (Sangensha, 1977), 162.

64   Tokieda Motoki, "Chōsen ni okeru kokugo: Jissen oyobi kenkyū no shosō," *Kokuminbungaku* 3:1 (1943): 12, quoted in Yasuda, *Shokuminchi no naka no kokugogaku*, 133–34.

65   Accordingly, the exemplary figure of feminine negativity called forth in the process of subject construction takes on a much more biological cast (although, of course, a mother's educative function is essential in Tokieda's program of linguistic hygiene).

66   Tokieda, *Kokugogaku genron*, 7; 136–39.

Chapter 6: Gender and Heian Narrative Form

1   Ikeda Kikan, *Kyūtei joryū nikki bungaku* (Shibundō, 1967), 36.

2   Watanabe Minoru, *Heian Bunshōshi* (Tokyo Daigaku Shuppankai, 1981), 102–3.

3   Edward Seidensticker, trans., *The Gossamer Years* (Tokyo: Charles E. Tuttle, 1990), 33.

4   *Hito* generally means "person," but in certain contexts it could specifically mean "other(s)."

5   Matsumura Seiichi, Kimura Masanori, and Imuta Tsunehisa, eds., *Tosa nikki, Kagerō nikki*, NKBZ 9 (Shōgakkan, 1973), 125.

6   Linguists disagree, however, over whether there is a grammatical *person* in Japanese discourse. Aside from the "ellipsis" of the grammatical subject, we should note that both modern and classical Japanese makes no distinction between the

subject pronoun ("I"/*ware*) and object pronoun ("me"/*ware*). Also, in classical Japanese there are no specific third-person pronouns such as "he," "she," or "it." The closest approximations are demonstrative pronouns such as "this" (*kore*) and "that" (*are*) used as an oblique reference to a third party. In *Kagerō nikki*, a common noun, *hito* is one of the words most frequently used to represent the Other. In both classical and modern Japanese, furthermore, common nouns expressing a person's profession, rank, kinship relations, and so on are frequently used in first-, and second-, and third-person references.

7   The widely held assumption that *Kagerō nikki* was written in the first person is supported in part, by the text's generic identity as a *nikki*, which is understood to mean "journal" or "diary." Modern commentaries on the text seem to adopt not only the Western grammatical category of person but the Western generic category of diary as the model for analyzing Heian kana texts. In the Heian period, however, narratives that had *nikki* in their titles were closer to biography than autobiography.

8   The citations of *Kagerō nikki* are based on NKBZ 9. I consulted English translations of *Kagerō* by Edward Seidensticker, and Sonja Arntzen (*The Kagerō Diary* [Ann Arbor: Center for Japanese Studies, 1997]). At the end of the citation, I note the date the passage is from followed by the page number from NKBZ. This is followed by the page number in the Seidensticker translation, marked with an S. Translations are mine unless otherwise noted.

9   That is, these are passages in which ware is used in narration (i.e., excluding the usage in waka and in utterances presumably voiced within the diegesis) that explicitly refer to the heroine. I have not counted ware when it is used in cliché expressions. Saeki Umetomo and Imuta Tsunehisa, eds., *Kagerō nikki sōsakuin* (Kazama shobō, 1981).

10 Out of thirty-eight examples, all but two uses of ware do not neatly fit this model. In the two exceptions, ware is used rhetorically. For instance, on the way back from a pilgrimage, the heroine spends an evening watching night fishing on the Uji River: "Whenever I dozed off, I would start up at a rapping at the prow of a boat, which sounded as if it were meant to awaken *me*" (Seventh Month of Tenroku 2:295; S:117).

In the other example, when a suitor of the heroine's daughter appears to be agitated, the text comments, "I thought his pestering [me] was due to the fact that he had only *me* to count on [to help arrange his marriage to her daughter]" (Seventh Month of Ten'en 2:381; S:161). The heroine soon finds out that he has other reasons to be jittery. He has apparently stolen another man's wife—a scandal that soon reaches her ears. In both cases, ware is used rhetorically: "I thought it had something to do with *me*—but it didn't" and "I thought he was counting on *me*—but he wasn't." Ware again carries the contrastive nuance of specifying self as opposed to Other.

11 Fukazawa Tōru, "*Kagerō nikki no tasha ishiki*," in *Issatsu no kōza: Kagerō nikki*, ed. Issatsu no kōza henshūbu (Yūseidō, 1971), 190.

12 Tokieda Motoki, *Nihon bunpō kōgohen* (Iwanami shoten, 1978), 72.

13   Fukazawa, "Kagerō nikki no tasha ishiki," 192.

14   Scholars have pointed out that in literary texts this grammatical norm can be transgressed, especially in the third-person narration that effaces the presence of the speaker. Discussing the opening line of Hemingway's short story "The Short Happy Life of Francis Macomber," Wallace Martin writes, "By eliminating all self-reference, a narrator cuts deictics loose from their normal connection to an identifiable speaker; thus they are free to gravitate toward the here-and-now of the characters" (*Recent Theories of Narrative* [Ithaca: Cornell University Press, 1986], 137). This is one way in which writers have tried to circumvent the problem identified as a major dilemma in the history of modern narration: how to reconcile the retrospectivity of the event (from the point of view of the narrator) and the prospectivity of narrative unfolding.

15   *Waga* is generally understood as a compound of *wa* etymologically related to *ware* and the possessive particle *ga.* The word *wa* in the Heian period was used almost exclusively in combination with *ga* and is usually translated as the first-person possessive "my."

16   The English and modern Japanese translations of the text change the word *today* to *that day*, making the utterance consistent with the narrator's point of view.

17   Fujioka Tadami, Nakano Kō'ichi, Inukai Ken and Ishii Fumio, eds., *Izumi shikibu nikki, Murasaki shikibu nikki, Sarashina nikki, Sanuki no suke nikki*, NKBZ 18 (Shō-gakkan, 1971), 327. See also Ivan Morris, trans., *As I Crossed a Bridge of Dreams: Recollections of a Woman in Eleventh-Century Japan* (London: Penguin, 1971), 75.

18   We may also note a phenomenon in modern Japanese in which English phrases such as "my home" or "my car" undergo a transformation when they become "Japanized." These phrases used in Japanese contexts become divorced from the diectic ties to the speaker and come to mean "someone's *own* house" or "someone's *own* car" as opposed to rental properties or company-owned vehicles. Hence, one may ask "May I drive your *my car*?" or "Have you visited her *my home*?" Again the reflexivity is relative to the context of the spoken topic and not necessarily to the context of the speaker. Thus, even in contemporary Japanese the distinction between *self* and "I" are not as clearly demarcated as in English.

19   Erwin Panofsky, *Perspective as Symbolic Form*, trans. Christopher S. Wood (New York: Zone, 1997), 67–68.

20   It is precisely because the third-person voice is never simply "objective," always implying the subject that mediates the representation, that it can often adopt the narratorial perspectives and voices of central characters. Unlike Heian narrative discourse, however, modern third-person narrative sets up the "neutral" narratological discourse as the default mode. In other words, the voices and perspectives of the characters are structurally subordinate to those of the narration, which serves as the primary principle of unity that binds the text together.

21   Fukazawa, "Kagerō nikki no tasha ishiki," 191.

22   John Locke, *Second Treatise of Government*, ed. C. B. Macpherson (Indianapolis: Hacket, 1980), 19.

23   "There are so-called *monogatari*, which have such an effect upon ladies' hearts.

They flourish in numbers greater than the grasses of Ōaraki Forest, more count-
less than the sands on Arisomi beaches. They attribute speech to trees and plants,
mountains and rivers, birds and beasts, fish and insects that cannot speak; they
invest unfeeling objects with human feelings and ramble on and on with meaningless phrases like so much flotsam in the sea, with not two words together that
have any more solid basis than does swamp grass growing by a river bank. *The
Sorceress of Iga, The Tosa Lord, The Fashionable Captain, The Nagai Chamberlain,*
and all the rest depict relations between men and women just as if they were so
many flowers or butterflies, but do not let your heart get caught up even briefly in
these tangled roots of evil, these forests of words." The translation is from Edward
Kamens, *The Three Jewels* (Ann Arbor: Center for Japanese Studies, University of
Michigan, 1988), 93. I have consulted Yamada Yoshio, ed., *Sanbōe ryakuchū* (Hō-
bunkan, 1971), 6–7.

24   The heroine discovers an estranged daughter of her husband and one of his mistresses and adopts her as her own daughter. She sets up a dramatic meeting between her husband and the girl he has not seen for years (Second Month of Tenroku 3:318; S:129).

25   The term *watakushi* is thought to have originated as a *kundokugo* (translation
word), that entered the lexicon of the Yamato language through the translation
of Chinese texts. The explicit use of the term as a first-person pronoun (or a reflexive pronoun comparable to ware in Heian texts) begins around the late medieval period. See Mizubayashi Takeshi, "Waga kuni ni okeru 'kōshi' kannen no
rekishiteki tenkai," in *Nihonshi ni okeru oyake to watakushi*, ed. Rekishi to hōhō
henshūi'inkai (Aoki shoten, 1996), 96.

26   The heroine's general weariness with Kanei's fast-track career and her dismay over
the Anna Disturbance may also be understood through their association with the
historical trend that contradicted traditional aristocratic values. Ishimoda Shō
has argued that the Anna Disturbance punctuated the final stage of the process
through which the internal contradiction of Heian aristocratic society led to the
undermining of the very principles that underwrote its order. See Ishimoda Shō,
"Utsuho monogatari ni tsuite no oboegaki," *Ishimoda shō chosakushū* (Iwanami
shoten, 1990), 11:23. In other words, the contest for power within the insular world
of court politics led to the downfall of a large number of principal aristocratic
clans, culminating in the unrivaled supremacy of the northern branch of Fujiwaras. This process marked the final disintegration not only of the ritsuryō system
but of the social order of an aristocracy based on blood (i.e., the equivalence of
status with birth vis-à-vis the established hierarchy of clans and families). While
I do not mean to suggest that the heroine perceived the Anna Disturbance from
a perspective proposed by Ishimoda, his analysis is suggestive. It suggests a reason why the banishment of Taka'akira would strike a chord of terror and anxiety
in Heian aristocratic society in general, even among those who were not closely
related to the clan. It also suggests a way to understand the ambivalent attitude
toward realpolitik and the kind of career that Kaneie exemplifies expressed in
a number of Heian kana texts, including *Kagerō*. Whether we adopt Ishimoda's

thesis or not, it is worth considering the sociopolitical implications of *Kagerō*'s repeated expressions of sympathy for those who are deemed the "losers" from the point of view of Heian aristocratic order.

Epilogue

1   Simone de Beauvoir, *Second Sex*, trans., H. M. Parshley (New York: Vintage, 1989), xxi–xxii.

2   Ibid., xxxi.

3   Ibid., 728–32.

4   Judith Butler, *Gender Trouble* (New York: Routledge, 1990), 2.

5   Ibid., 29.

6   Judith Butler, *Bodies That Matter* (New York: Routledge, 1993), 1–4.

7   Seyla Benhabib, "Feminism and Postmodernism," in *Feminist Contentions: A Philosophical Exchange*, ed. Seyla Benhabib, Judith Butler, Druciall Cornell, and Nancy Fraser (London: Routledge, 1995), 21.

8   Judith Butler, "Contingent Foundations," in *Feminist Contentions: A Philosophical Exchange*, ed. Seyla Benhabib, Judith Butler, Druciall Cornell, and Nancy Fraser (London: Routledge, 1995), 46.

9   "Paradoxically, it may be that only through releasing the category of women from a fixed referent that something like 'agency' becomes possible. For if the term permits of a resignification, if its referent is not fixed, then possibilities for new configurations of the term become possible" (ibid., 50).

10 For a thoughtful discussion on this problem in Butler's work and its ramifications for queer theory, see Brett Levinson, "Sex without Sex, Queering the Market, the Collapse of the Political, the Death of Difference, and AIDS: Hailing Judith Butler," *Diacritics* 29:3 (1999).

11 We may also note that while Butler's discussion frequently refers to works by Michel Foucault her notion of gender performativity and her analyses of power that organizes gender and sexual identities clearly depart from some of the basic features of Foucault's perspective. In *The History of Sexuality* Foucault argues that the relation of power should *not* be understood juridically, not simply because its effects are always undermined by the resistance that it produces but more importantly because he understands it in tactical terms — as a complex configuration of multiple strategems arising out of local relations of forces, including, but not reducible to, those that may be categorized in terms of domination and resistance. This suggests that the Foucauldian relation of power refracts the linear structure (even those interspersed by gaps) that the notion of the reiterative "chain" seems to invoke. Rather, it takes shape as a network that is extralinear and even rhizomic. See Michel Foucault, *The History of Sexuality* vol. 1, trans. Robert Hurley (New York: Pantheon, 1978), 102. Deleuze's study of Foucault is particularly helpful in highlighting this aspect of the latter's thought. See Gilles Deleuze, *Foucault*, trans. and ed. Séan Hand (Minneapolis: University of Minnesota Press, 1988).

12 For instance, let me point to the way Butler responded to bell hooks's comment

that the film *Paris Is Burning* tacitly confines the subjects it represents to the world of a drag ball, failing to inquire into their connections to the world beyond it — for example, their relations to their families and communities. In response, Butler argued that the drag ball constitutes an *alternative* kinship structure that subversively configures/refigures the terms of domination in society. The social space inside and outside the drag ball are thus vitally interlinked even though the film does not refer to the exterior world. What deserves our attention here is the reduction that occurs in Butler's rhetorical move, which conflates subjects' "connections to a world of family and community" with the "kinship system." Butler's argument seems to imply that we know in advance what would be revealed by the subjects' articulation of their relations to family and community. The assumption that the kinship system adequately stands in for the specificity of individual men's social relations outside the drag ball (which the film passes over in silence), in turn, authorizes Butler's assertion that the sociality of the drag ball is constituted through and against the existing law of kinship in mainstream society. The relations between the world of the drag ball and the world outside it are established at the cost of reducing them both to the highly schematic structure of a kinship organization (Butler, *Bodies That Matter*, 136–137; see also bell hooks, "Is Paris Burning?" in *Black Looks: Race and Representation* [Boston: South End, 1992]).

13 Kathi Weeks points out that Butler's insistence on the "absolute contingency" or a strict opposition between contingency and necessity suggests that the contingency of subject is secured by its underdeterminacy — that is, the refraction of historical baggage (*Constituting Feminist Subjects* [Ithaca: Cornell University Press, 1999], 132–33).

14 Georg Lukács, *The Theory of the Novel*, trans. Anna Bostock (Cambridge: MIT Press, 1971), 77–81.

15 As Louis Althusser puts it, "the individual is interpellated as a (free) subject in order that he shall submit freely to the commandments of the Subject" (*Lenin and Philosophy*, trans. Ben Brewster [New York: Monthly Review Press, 1971], 182).

16 The question of subject, in other words, becomes a site for the "hegemonic struggle" in the sense that Ernesto Laclau discusses this concept. See his *Emancipation(s)* (London: Verso, 1996); and, with Chantal Mouffe, his *Hegemony and Socialist Strategy: Towards a Politics* (London: Verso, 1985). Butler refers to the compatibility between her theory of performativity and the theory of hegemony; see "Restaging the Universal," in *Contingency, Hegemony, Universality: Contemporary Dialogues on the Left*, ed. Judith Butler, Ernesto Laclau, and Slavoj Žižek (London: Verso, 2000), 14.

BIBLIOGRAPHY

The place of publication of all Japanese sources is Tokyo unless otherwise noted.

Abe Akio, Akiyama Ken, and Imai Gen'e, eds. *Genji monogatari*. 6 vols. NKBZ 12–17.

Abe Yoshiomi. "Monoken nijūgonen no seika to kongo no tenbō." *Monogatari kenkyū kaihō* 27 (August 1998).

Althusser, Louis. *Lenin and Philosophy*. Trans. Ben Brewster. New York: Monthly Review Press, 1971.

Anderson, Benedict. *Imagined Communities: Reflections on the Origin and Spread of Nationalism*. London: Verso, 1991.

Arntzen, Sonja, trans. *The Kagerō Diary*. Ann Arbor: Center for Japanese Studies, 1997.

Bakhtin, M. M. *The Dialogic Imagination*. Trans. Caryl Emerson and Michael Holquist. Austin: University of Texas Press, 1981.

———. *Speech Genres and Other Late Essays*. Trans. Vern W. McGee, ed. Caryl Emerson and Michael Holquist. Austin: University of Texas Press, 1986.

Balibar, Étienne. "The Nation Form: History and Ideology." In *Race, Nation, Class: Ambiguous Identities*, ed. Étienne Balibar and Immanuel Wallerstein. London: Verso, 1991.

Ban Nobutomo. *Kana no motosue* I. Benseisha, 1979.

Barthes, Roland. *Empire of Signs*. Trans. Richard Howard. New York: Hill and Wang, 1982.

———. "Is There Any Poetic Writing?" In *Writing Degree Zero*. Trans. Annette Lavers and Colin Smith. New York: Hill and Wang, 1968.

Bartholomew, James R. "Japanese Modernization and the Imperial Universities, 1876–1920." *Journal of Asian Studies* 37:2 (February 1978).

Beauvoir, Simone de. *Second Sex*. Trans. H. M. Parshley. New York: Vintage, 1989.

Benhabib, Seyla. "Feminism and Postmodernism." In *Feminist Contentions: A Philosophical Exchange*, ed. Seyla Benhabib, Judith Butler, Druciall Cornell, and Nancy Fraser. London: Routledge, 1995.

Benveniste, Emile. *Problems in General Linguistics*. Trans. Mary Elizabeth Meek. Coral Gables: University of Miami Press, 1971.

Bowring, Richard, trans. *Murasaki Shikibu, Her Diary and Poetic Memoir: A Translation and Study*. Princeton: Princeton University Press, 1982.

Brownstein, Michael C. "From *Kokugaku* to *Kokubungaku*: Canon-Formation in the Meiji Period." *Harvard Journal of Asiatic Studies* 47:2 (1987).

Butler, Judith. *Bodies That Matter*. (New York: Routledge, 1993).

———. "Contingent Foundations." In *Feminist Contentions: A Philosophical Exchange*, ed. Seyla Benhabib, Judith Butler, Druciall Cornell, and Nancy Fraser. London: Routledge, 1995.

———. *Gender Trouble*. New York: Routledge, 1990.

———. "Restaging the Universal." In *Contingency, Hegemony, Universality: Contemporary Dialogues on the Left*, ed. Judith Butler, Ernesto Laclau, and Slavoj Žižek. London: Verso, 2000.

Cavanaugh, Carole. "Text and Textile: Unweaving the Female Subject in Heian Writing." *positions* 4:3 (winter 1996).

Chino Kaori. "Nihon bijutsu no jendā." *Nihon bijutsu* 136 (1994).

Chow, Rey. *Writing Diaspora: Tactics of Intervention in Contemporary Cultural Studies*. Bloomington: Indiana University Press, 1993.

Court, Franklin E. *Institutionalizing English Literature: The Culture and Politics of Literary Study, 1750–1900*. Stanford: Stanford University Press, 1992.

Deleuze, Gilles. *Foucault*. Trans. and ed. Séan Hand. Minneapolis: University of Minnesota Press, 1988.

Derrida, Jacques. *Of Grammatology*. Trans. and ed. Gayatri Spivak. Baltimore: Johns Hopkins University Press, 1976.

Eagleton, Terry. *The Idea of Culture*. Oxford: Blackwell, 2000.

———. *Literary Theory: An Introduction*. Minneapolis: University of Minnesota Press, 1983.

Endō Yoshimoto. "Chūko." In *Kokugo no rekishi*. Ed. Kokugogakkai. Osaka: Akitaya, 1948.

Field, Norma. *The Splendor of Longing in "The Tale of Genji."* Princeton: Princeton University Press, 1987.

Foucault, Michel. *The History of Sexuality*. Trans. Robert Hurley. Vol. 1. New York: Pantheon, 1978.

Fujii, James. *Complicit Fictions: The Subject in the Modern Japanese Prose Narrative*. Berkeley: University of California Press, 1993.

Fujii Sadakazu. "Hyōgen to shite no nihongo: Bunpōteki jikan no chōhatsu." *Hihyō kūkan* 2:2 (1994).

———. "Katarite ninshō wa doko ni aruka." In *Ronshū heian bungaku*. Benseisha, 1994.

———. *Kokubungaku no tanjō*. Sangensha, 2000.

Fujioka Sakutarō. *Kokubungaku zenshi: Heianchōhen*. 2 vols. Heibonsha, 1971.

———. *Kokubungakushi kōwa*. Iwanami shoten, 1993.

Fujioka Tadami, Nakano Kō'ichi, Inukai Ken, and Ishii Fumio, eds. *Izumi shikibu nikki, Murasaki shikibu nikki, Sarashina nikki, Sanuki no suke nikki*. NKBZ 18.

Fujitani, Takashi. *Splendid Monarchy*. Berkeley: University of California Press, 1996.

Fujiwara Teika. "Kyōgoku chūnagon sōgo." In *Chūsei no bungaku*. Ed. Hisamatsu Sen'ichi. *Karonshū* 1. Kyoto: Miyai shoten, 1971.

Fukazawa Tōru. "Kagerō nikki no tasha ishiki." In *Issatsu no kōza: Kagerō nikki*. Ed. Issatsu no kōza henshūbu. Yūseidō, 1971.

Genette, Gerard. *Figures of Literary Discourse*. Trans. Alan Sheridan. New York: Columbia University Press, 1982.

Gotō Shōko, ed. *Heian bungaku no shikaku: Josei*. Benseisha, 1995.

Graff, Gerald. *Professing Literature: An Institutional History*. Chicago: University of Chicago Press, 1987.

Haga Yaichi. *Kokubungaku jukkō*. HYS 2.

———. "Kokugaku to wa nanzoya?" HYS 1.

———. "Nihon bungaku to waka." HYS 3.

———. "Nihonjin." In HYS 6.

Hagitani Boku. "Tosa nikki wa karonsho ka." In *Heianchō nikki I*. Ed. Nihon bungaku kenkyū shiryō kankōkai. Yūseidō, 1971.

———. ed. *Tosa nikki zenchūshaku*. Kadokawa shoten, 1967.

Hagitani Boku and Taniyama Shigeru, eds. *Utaawaseshū*. NKBT 74.

Harootunian, Harry D. "Between Politics and Culture: Authority and the Ambiguities of Intellectual Choice in Imperial Japan." In *Japan in Crisis: Essays on Taishō Democracy*, ed. Bernard S. Silberman and H. D. Harootunian. Princeton: Princeton University Press, 1974.

———. *Overcome by Modernity: History, Culture, and Community in Interwar Japan*. Princeton: Princeton University Press, 2000.

———. *Things Seen and Unseen: Discourse and Ideology in Tokugawa Nativism*. Chicago: University of Chicago Press, 1988.

Hasegawa Haruo. *Ki no Tsurayuki ron*. Yūseidō shoten, 1984.

Higuchi Hiroshi. "Tosa nikki ni okeru tsurayuki no tachiba." In *Heianchō nikki I*. Ed. Nihon bungaku kenkyū shiryō kankōkai. Yūseidō, 1971.

Hobsbawn, Eric. *Nations and Nationalism since 1780*. Cambridge: Cambridge University Press, 1990.

bell hooks. "Is Paris Burning?" In *Black Looks: Race and Representation*. Boston: South End, 1992.

Ikeda Kikan. *Kyūtei joryū nikki bungaku*. Shibundō, 1967.

Imuta Tsunehisa, Kimura Masanori, and Matsumura Sei'ichi, eds. *Tosa nikki, Kagerō nikki*. NKBZ 9.

Ishihara Shōhei. "Kana bungaku to kana moji: Tosa nikki ni itaru made." *Bungei to hihyō* 1 (1971).

Ishimoda Shō. "Utsuho monogatari ni tsuite no oboegaki." In *Ishimoda shō chosakushū*. Ed. Aoki Kazuo et al. Vol. 11. Iwanami shoten, 1990.

Itō Hiroshi. "Nikki bungaku no kaika." In *Nihon bungaku shinshi, kodai 2*. Ed. Suzuki Kazuo. Shibundō, 1990.

Jakobson, Roman. "Linguistics and Poetics." In *Language in Literature*, ed. Krystyna Pomorska and Stephen Rudy. Cambridge, Mass.: Belknap, 1987.

Johnson, Barbara. *A World of Difference*. Baltimore: Johns Hopkins University Press, 1987.

Kada Arimaro. "Kokka hachiron." In *Karonshū*. Ed. Hashimoto Fumio, Ariyoshi Tamotsu, and Fujihira Haruo. NKBZ 50.

Kagawa Kageki. "Nihimanabi iken." In *Karonshū*. Ed. Hashimoto Fumio, Ariyoshi Tamotsu, and Fujihira Haruo. NKBZ 50.

Kamei Hideo. *Transformations of Sensibility*. Trans. and ed. Michael Bourdaghs. Ann Arbor: Center for Japanese Studies, University of Michigan, 2002.

Kamens, Edward. *The Three Jewels*. Ann Arbor: Center for Japanese Studies, University of Michigan, 1988.

Kamo no Mabuchi. "Futatabi kingo no kimi ni kotahematsuru fumi." Ed. Sasaki Nobutsun. NKT 7.

———. "Kokka hachiron yogen shūi." NKT 7.

———. "Kokkaron okusetsu." NKT 7.

———. "Kokuikō." In *Kinsei shintōron, zenki kokugaku*. Ed. Taira Shigemichi and Abe Akio. NST 39.

———. "Nihimanabi." In *Kinsei shintōron, zenki kokugaku*, NST 39.

Kanno Kakumyō. *Motoori norinaga: Kotoba to miyabi*. Perikansha, 1991.

Kanō Mikiyo, ed. *Josei to tennōsei*. Shisō no Kagakusha, 1979.

Karatani Kōjin. "Nihon seishin bunseki." *Hihyō kūkan* 8 (1993).

———. *Origins of Japanese Literature*. Trans. and ed. Brett de Bary. Durham: Duke University Press, 1993.

Katagiri Yōichi, ed. *Taketori monogatari, Ise monogatari, Yamato Monogatari, Heichū monogatari*. NKBZ 8.

Kimura Masanori. "Nikki bungaku no honshitsu to sōsaku shinri." In *Kōza nihon bungaku no sōten*. Ed. Abe Akio. Vol. 2. Meiji shoin, 1968.

Kitabatake Chikafusa. *A Chronicle of Gods and Sovereigns: Jinnō Shōtōki of Kitabatake Chikafusa*. Trans. H. Paul Varley. New York: Columbia University Press, 1980.

Kojima Naoko. "Utagatari to tsukuri monogatari." In *Iwanami kōza nihon bungakushi*. Ed. Kubota Jun, et al. Vol. 2. Iwanami shoten, 1996.

Komatsu Shigemi. *Kana*. Iwanami shoten, 1972.

Kōno Tama. *Utsuho monogatari*. 3 vols. NKBT 10–12.

Koschmann, J. V. *Revolution and Subjectivity in Postwar Japan*. Chicago: University of Chicago Press, 1996.

Koyasu Nobukuni. "Motoori norinaga: Waka no zokuryūka to bi no jiritsu." *Shisō*
879 (1997).

Lacan, Jacques. *Écrits*. Trans. Alan Sheridan. New York: Norton, 1977.

Laclau, Ernesto. *Emancipation(s)*. London: Verso, 1996.

Laclau, Ernesto, and Chantal Mouffe. *Hegemony and Socialist Strategy: Towards a
Politics*. London: Verso, 1985.

LaMarre, Thomas. *Uncovering Heian Japan: An Archeology of Sensation and
Inscription*. Durham: Duke University Press, 2000.

————. "Writing Doubled over, Broken: Provisional Names, Acrostic Poems, and the
Perpetual Contest of Doubles in Heian Japan." *positions* 2:2 (fall 1994).

Lee Yeounsuk. *Kokugo to iu shisō: Kindai nihon no gengo ninshiki*. Iwanami shoten,
1996.

Levinson, Brett. "Sex without Sex, Queering the Market, the Collapse of the Political,
the Death of Difference, and AIDS: Hailing Judith Butler." *Diacritics* 29:3 (1999).

Lloyd, David, and Paul Thomas, *Culture and the State*. London: Routledge, 1998.

Locke, John. *Second Treatise of Government*. Ed. C. B. Macpherson. Indianapolis:
Hacket, 1980.

Lukács, Georg. *The Theory of the Novel*. Trans. Anna Bostock. Cambridge: MIT Press,
1971.

Martin, Wallace. *Recent Theories of Narrative*. Ithaca: Cornell University Press, 1986.

Maruyama Keizaburō. *Soshūru no shisō*. Iwanami shoten, 1993.

Masuda Katsumi. "Genji monogatari no ninaite. In *Genji monogatari 1*. Ed. Nihon
bungaku kenkyū shiryō kankō kai. Yūseidō shuppan, 1974.

————. "Genji monogatari no sengo: Watashi no baai." *Nihon bungaku* 10:6 (1961).

————. "Waka to Seikatsu: Genji monogatari no haibu kara." In *Genji monogatari 4*.
Ed. Nihon bungaku kenkū shiryō kankōkai. Yūseidō shuppan, 1974.

Matsumoto Sannosuke. *Kokugaku seiji shisō no kenkyū*. Miraisha, 1972.

Matsuo Sō and Nagai Kazuko, eds. *Makura no sōshi*. NKBZ 11.

McClintock, Anne. *Imperial Leather: Race, Gender and Sexuality in the Colonial
Contest*. London: Routledge, 1995.

McCullough, Helen. *Kokin Wakashū: The First Imperial Anthology of Japanese Poetry*.
Stanford: Stanford University Press, 1985.

Mikami Sanji and Takatsu Kuwasaburō. *Nihon bungakushi*. Vol. 1. Kinkōdō, 1890.

Miller, Roy. *The Japanese Language*. Chicago: University of Chicago Press, 1967.

Mitani Kuniaki. *Monogatari bungaku no gensetsu*. Yūseidō, 1992.

————. *Monogatari bungaku no hōhō*. 2 vols. Yūseidō, 1989.

————. "Monogatari to kakukoto: Monogatari bungaku no imisayō arui wa fuzai no
bungaku." *Nihonbungaku* 25 (October 1976).

Miura Tsutomu. *Nihongo wa dōyū gengo ka*. Kōdansha, 1956.

Miyake, Lynne K. "*The Tosa Diary*: In the Interstices of Gender and Criticism." In
The Woman's Hand: Gender and Theory in Japanese Women's Writing, ed. Paul
Gordon Schalow and Janet A. Walker. Stanford: Stanford University Press, 1996.

Monogatari Kenkyūkai, ed. *Monogatari: Otoko to onna*. Yūseidō shuppan, 1995.

Morris, Ivan, trans. *As I Crossed a Bridge of Dreams: Recollections of a Woman in Eleventh-Century Japan*. London: Penguin, 1971.

———, trans. *The Pillow Book of Sei Shōnagon*. New York: Columbia University Press, 1991.

Mosse, George L. *Nationalism and Sexuality*. Madison: University of Wisconsin Press, 1985.

Motoori Norinaga. "Ashiwake obune." MNZ 2.

———. *Genji monogatari tama no ogushi*. MNZ 4.

———. *Isonokami sasamegoto*. MNZ 2.

———. *Shibun yōryō*. MNZ 4.

———. "Uhiyamabumi." MNZ 1.

Murai Osamu. "Kokubungakusha no jūgonen sensō." Pts. 1–2. *Hihyō kūkan* 2:17; 2:18 (1998).

Nomura Seiichi. *Nihon bungaku kenkyūshiron*. Kasama shoin, 1983.

Nosco, Peter. "Nature, Invention, and National Learning: The *Kokka hachiron* Controversy, 1742–46." *Harvard Journal of Asiatic Studies*, 41:1 (1981).

Okada, Richard. *Figures of Resistance: Language, Poetry, and Narrating in "The Tale of Genji" and other Mid-Heian Texts*. Durham: Duke University Press, 1991.

Panofsky, Erwin. *Perspective as Symbolic Form*. Trans. Christopher S. Wood, New York: Zone, 1997.

Pflugfelder, Gregory M. *Cartographies of Desire*. Berkeley: University of California Press, 1999.

Ramirez-Christensen, Eperanza. "The Operation of the Lyrical Mode in the *Genji monogatari*." In *Ukifune: Love in "The Tale of Genji*," ed. Andrew Pekarik. New York: Columbia University Press, 1982.

Readings, Bill. *The University in Ruins*. Cambridge: Harvard University Press, 1996.

Saeki Umetomo and Imuta Tsunehisa, eds. *Kagerō nikki sōsakuin*. Kasama shobō, 1981.

Saigō Nobutsuna. "Bungakushi to hihyō: Bungaku janru o megutte." *Bungaku* 19 (December 1951).

———. "Kyūtei joryū bungaku no kaika." In *Nihon bungaku no hōhō*. Miraisha, 1955.

Sakai, Naoki. *Voices of the Past: The Status of Language in Eighteenth-Century Japanese Discourse*. Ithaca: Cornell University Press, 1991.

Sakakura Atsuyoshi. "*Taketori monogatari* ni okeru 'buntai' no mondai." *Kokugo Kokubun* 25 (November 1956).

Sarrah, Edith. *Fictions of Femininity: Literary Interventions of Gender in Japanese Court Women's Memoirs*. Stanford: Stanford University Press, 1999.

Seidensticker, Edward, trans. *The Gossamer Years*. Tokyo: Tuttle, 1990.

———. *The Tale of Genji*. New York: Knopf, 1987.

Shigematsu Nobuhiro. *Shinkō Genji Monogatari kenkyūshi*. Kazama shobō, 1980.

Shimura Midori. "Heian jidai josei no mana kanseki no gakushū." *Nihon rekishi* 457 (June 1986).

Shirane, Haruo, and Tomi Suzuki, eds. *Inventing the Classics: Modernity, National Identity, and Japanese Literature*. Stanford: Stanford University Press, 2001.

Stinchecum, Amanda. "Who Tells the Tale? 'Ukifune': A Study of Narrative Voice." *Monumenta Nipponica* 35:4 (April 1980).

Sugiyama Yasuhiko. "Kodai sanbun no jikan." *Nihon bungaku* 26 (November 1977): 2.

Suzuki Hideo. *Kodai wakashiron.* Tokyo daigaku shuppankai, 1993.

Suzuki, Tomi. "Gender and Genre: Modern Literary Histories and Women's Diary Literature." In *Inventing the Classics: Modernity, National Identity, and Japanese Literature,* ed. Haruo Shirane and Tomi Suzuki. Stanford: Stanford University Press, 2001.

Taine, Hyppolite. *History of English Literature.* Trans. H. Van Laun. Vol. 1. New York: Holt, 1891.

Takagi Mokoto. "Tekisuto riron no kishikata, yukusue: Nihontekina, amari ni nihontekina." In *Tekisuto no seiaijutsu: Monogatari bunseki no riron to jissen.* Ed. Takagi Makoto and Andō Tōru. Shinwasha, 1999.

Takahashi Masaaki. "Jōshikiteki kizokuzō, bushizō no sōshutsu katei." In *Nihonshi ni okeru ōyake to watakushi.* Ed. Rekishi to hōhō henshū iinkai. Aoki shoten, 1996.

Takahashi Tōru. *Monogatari to e no enkinhō.* Perikansha, 1991.

Takeoka Masao. "Jodōshi 'keri' no hongi to kinō." *Kokubungaku gengo to bungei* (November 1963).

———. *Kokinwakashū zenhyōshaku.* Yūbun shoin, 1983.

Takeshi, Mizubayashi. "Waga kuni ni okeru 'kōshi' kannen no rekishiteki tenkai." In *Nihonshi ni okeru ōyake to watakushi.* Ed. Rekishi to hōhō henshūi'inkai, Aoki shoten, 1996.

Tamagami Takuya. "Genji monogatari no dokusha: Monogatari ondokuron." In *Genji monogatari kenkyū.* Genji monogatari bekkan 1. Kadokawa shoten, 1965.

———. *Genji monogatari hyōshaku.* Vol. 2. Kadokawa shoten, 1965.

Taylor, Charles. *Sources of the Self: The Making of the Modern Identity.* Cambridge: Harvard University Press, 1989.

Tokieda Motoki. "Chōsen ni okeru kokugo seisaku oyobi kokugo kyōiku no shōrai." *Nihongo* 2:2 (August 1942).

———. "Chōsen ni okeru kokugo: Jissen oyobi kenkyū no shosō." *Kokuminbungaku* 3:1 (1943).

———. *Kokugogaku genron.* Iwanami shoten, 1947.

———. *Kokugogakushi.* Iwanami shoten, 1940.

———. *Nihon bunpō kōgohen.* Iwanami shoten, 1978.

———. "Stālin 'gengogaku ni okeru marukusushugi' ni kanshite." *Chū'ō kōron* 65:740 (October 1950).

Tsubouchi Shōyō. *Shōsetsu shinzui.* In *Tsubouchi shōyōshū.* Ed. Inagaki Tetsurō, MBZ 16.

Tyler, Royall, trans. *The Tale of Genji.* 2 vols. New York: Viking, 2001.

Ueda Kazutoshi. "Kokubungaku shogen." In *Ochiai Naobumi, Ueda Kazutoshi, Haga Yaichi, Fujioka Sakutarō shū.* Ed. Hisamatsu Sen'ichi. MBZ 44.

Unger, Marshal. "The Etymology of the Japanese Word *Kana.*" *Papers in Japanese Linguistics* 7 (1980).

Vlastos, Stephen, ed. *Mirror of Modernity: Invented Traditions of Modern Japan.* Berkeley: University of California Press, 1998.

Volsinov, V. N. [M. M. Bakhtin]. *Marxism and Theory of Language.* Trans. L. Matejka and I. R. Titunik. New York: Seminar, 1973.

Watanabe Hiroshi. "Michi to miyabi, part 1." *Kokkagaku gakkai zasshi* 87:9–10 (1974).

Watanabe Minoru. *Heian bunshōshi.* Tokyo Daigaku Shuppankai, 1981.

Watanabe Osamu. *Kinsei waka shisō kenkyū.* Jichōsha, 1991.

Watsuji Tetsurō. *Nihon seishinshi kenkyū.* Iwanami shoten, 1992.

Weeks, Kathi. *Constituting Feminist Subjects.* Ithaca: Cornell University Press, 1999.

Wittgenstein, Ludwig. *Philosophical Investigations.* Trans. G. E. Anscombe. New York: Macmillan, 1968.

———. *Preliminary Studies for the "Philosophical Investigations" Generally Known as the Blue and Brown Books.* New York: Harper and Row, 1958.

Yasuda Toshiaki. *Shokuminchi no naka no kokugogaku.* Sangensha, 1977.

Yoshimoto Taka'aki. *Gengo ni totte bi to wa nanika.* Vol. 1. Keisō shobō, 1965.

Yoda, Tomiko. "*Seisa, moji, kokka*: Feminizuma hihyō to heian bungaku kenkyū." In *Tekisuto no seiaijutsu: Monogatari bunseki no riron to jissen.* Ed. Takagi Makoto and Andō Tōru. Shinwasha, 1999.

Yuval-Davis, Nira. *Gender and Nation.* London: Sage, 1997.

Žižek, Slavoj. *For They Know Not What They Do: Enjoyment as a Political Factor.* London: Verso, 1991.

INDEX

Deixis: in *Kagerô nikki*, 189, 191–192

Dialectics, gendered, 67–72

Dialogue, poetic, 131, 133–136; in *The Tale of Genji*, 137, 142, 144–145

Diary *(nikki)*, 206, 208, 211–213; literary *(nikki bungaku)*, 22, 85–88

Diary of Murasaki Shikibu, The, 95, 106

Discursive subject. See *Shutai*

Edo period, 66–67; associated with masculinity, 68–70. *See also* Tokugawa period

Eighteenth century: conditions in Japan during, 37; nativism in, 19, 21; poetics in, 19, 25–40, 63

Emotion, definitions of, 35–36

Emperor, image of, 53–55

Eurocentrism, critique of, 160, 176

European linguistics, influence of, 149

European literary theory, 151, 159

Feelings, authentic: in poetry, 37–38

Female narrators, 94

Female point of view, 205

Females, literacy of, 88–95

Feminine: aestheticism, 71; Heian literature as, 6, 13, 19, 25, 27, 40–42, 71–72; Heian period as, 68, 73–74, 76; voice, 109

Femininity: and the emperor, 53–55; and *kana*, 103; and negativity, 8, 26, 33–37, 39, 179; in poetry, 28, 39–40; understanding of the term, 4, 35; of writing, 84

Feminism: and Heian studies, 13–16, 214–215; postmodern, 216–217; radical, 216; on subject, 214–230

Feminist agency, 228

Feminization: and Heian literature, 2, 19, 25–40, 78; of the national, 52–55

First-person narration, 194–197, 203

Formalist methodologies: on Heian literature, 177

Fûdo, 66

Fujioka Sakutarô, 41–42, 181; background of, 55; on Bushidô, 56, 68; on Edo period, 68–69; on Heian, 56–57, 75; on Japanese culture and nation, 50, 56, 64–66, 70; on *kokubungaku*, 56, 64; on literature, 62–64, 72, 76; methodology of, 62–64; on *mono no aware*, 61; on national subject, 79, 179; on native identity, 67; on *The Tale of Genji*, 58; on Tokugawa scholarship, 56; use of gender metaphor, 70; on warrior class, 68

Fujii Sadakazu, 87, 165

Fujitsubo, 125, 127–129, 135–136, 143

Fukazawa Tôru, 189, 197

Furu monogatari (old tales), 207

Gender: of author, 3, 6; construction of, 22, 216–217; differences in literature, 7, 14, 142; and Heian narrative form, 3, 182–213; and historical eras, 31–32; and *Kagerô nikki*, 22–23, 205; in *kokubungaku*, 41, 72; modern conception of, 15; and nationalization of literature, 41–80; and poetics, 37–40; and *Tosa Nikki*, 86–89; understanding of the term, 15–16

Gender categories: and poetics, 26, 75

Gendered dialectics, 67–72

Gendered periodization, Kageki's critique of, 31–33

Gendered subject, 217–218, 221, 229–230. *See also* Subject

Gendered terms: in eighteenth-century poetics, 19

Gender ideology, 4, 14–15, 76–77, 214

Gender metaphor, 6, 26–29, 32–33, 39–40, 70, 78

Gender performativity, 218–219

Gengogaku (modern linguistics), 149

Genji, 127; and Fujitsubo, 143; and *mono no aware*, 129; poems of, 134–138; and Rokujô Lady, 138–140; *waka* recited by, 124–125, 127

Genji, Shika shichiron, 60

Ghostly spirits: in *The Tale of Genji*, 165

Ghostly subject: in Heian narratives, 164–169

Grammatical subject *(shugo)*, 156, 163

Gu Dao, 94

Haga Yaichi, 41–43; background of, 50–51; on the emperor, 53–55; on Heian, 46, 52; on *kokubungaku*, 50–52; on language, 51; on literature, 51–52, 55, 64; on *mono no aware*, 60; on nation, 50, 77; on *The Tale of Genji*, 60; on *waka*, 53

Hagitani Boku, 89

Hartootunian, Harry, 26, 37, 71

Heianchôhen, 55–56, 64

Heian female diary literature *(heian joryû nikki bungaku)*, 22, 86–88, 182. *See also* Heian literature; *and under titles of specific works*

Heian literature: calligraphy in, 98; female agency in, 72–73, 77; as feminine, 13, 19, 25, 27, 41–42, 76; and feminization, 2, 19, 26, 78; Fujioka on, 56, 64, 75; and gender topics, 4, 15–16, 40; and *kokubungaku*, 45–50, 78–80. *See also* History: of Heian literature; *Kana*; *and under titles of specific works*

Heian period, 66–67; Chinese in, 90–91, 106–107; conditions of, 57; as feminine, 68, 71–74; feminization of, 25–40; Fujioka on, 70–71; function of *keri* in, 151–152; Haga on, 52; *kokugaku* on, 46; old tales from, 207; poetry of, 27–31, 69, 101; society, 46, 56–57; women's writing in, 1–2, 83. *See also* Aristocracy, Heian; *Kana*

Hero: in *The Tale of Genji*, 142–143

Heroine: in *Kagerô nikki*, 183–193, 197–198, 201–214, 221–222, 225–226, 228; in *The Tale of Genji*, 142–144

Hideo, Kamei, 161

History: of Heian literature, 55–58, 120;

feminine hand in, 83–88; *kana* in, 110; modern renditions of, 107; Saigo's account of, 119; scholarship on, 17–18

Hito (other), 183–190, 207, 210, 213

"I," question of, 223, 227–229; in *Kagerô nikki*, 199, 205; and "self," 196–204, 221–227

Ikeda Kikan,182

Imperial subject, 146–181

Individual subject: in modern literary discourse, 7

Irekogata kôzô (box-in-box structure), 155, 156

Ise monogatari, 109, 119

Ishimoda Shô, 119

Jakobson, Roman, 122

Japan: Chinese influences on, 47; compared with the West, 66; conditions in, 37

Japanese history: intellectual, 39; literary, 41, 67, 72. *See also* Heian literature

Japanese identity: and masculinity, 189

Japanese language, 48; and colonialism, 161–162, 177–181; post-1970s scholarship on, 11; in tenth century, 84; Tokieda on, 11, 21, 146, 150, 161. See also *Kana*

Japanese literature: classical, 42–43; Haga on, 51–52; influences on, 49–50; post-1970s study of, 8–9, 11; in postwar period, 81–82; scholarship on, 43, 72; tradition of, 51

Japanese national character, 51, 64–65

Japanese nationhood, 50

Japanese poems *(yamato uta)*, 89–90

Japanese poetry, 84; in "Kana Preface," 91; and lover's exchanges, 134; in tenth century, 90–91; in *Tosa Nikki*, 91–92, 94

Ji: Tokieda on, 153–156, 158–159, 163–164, 170, 173–174

Haga on, 51; in Heian period, 110; literature as expressing, 4–5; national (kokugo), 43, 99–100, 106–110; and nationalism, 99; poetic, 133; sociality of, 169–175; understanding of the term, 99–100. *See also* Chinese language; Japanese language; *Kana*; Language process theory

Language process theory, 10, 153–160, 169–170, 177

Linear perspectivism, 192–196

Linguistic empire, Tokieda's logic of, 176–181

Linguistics, 10–11, 149

Literacy, female, 88–95

Literary aesthetics: feminine, 8; and gender metaphors, 6; Haga on, 51; and national subject, 79; in past historical periods, 45; Takayama on, 70–71; Watsuji on, 74–75

Literary criticism, 43

Literary discourses, 7, 26

Literary history, Heian, 83–88

Literary scholarship, postwar, 150

Literary theories, from abroad, 149

Literature: as expressing language, 4–5; Heian (*see* Heian literature); Japanese classical, 42–43; national, 41, 44, 48–49, 55, 64–65, 76; study of (see *Kokubungaku*); on women's everyday activities, 84

Lovers' poetic exchanges: in Japanese poetry, 134; in *The Tale of Genji*, 112, 121–122, 127–130, 133, 137–142, 144

Lukács, George, 222

Mabuchi. *See* Kamo no Mabuchi

Male script *(wotokomoji)*, 92

Man, understanding of the term, 16

Mana (Chinese characters): as calligraphic term, 102; and *kana*, 20, 84, 95–102, 98; understanding of the term, 96–98; and women, 95, 102–106

Man'yôgana, 84, 97

Man'yôshû: language in, 84, 98; as masculine, 69–70; poetry of, 30–32, 66; and *waka*, 28

Masculine: discursive subject, 109; Edo period as, 68; and Japanese identity, 189; literature as, 6; *Man'yôshû* as, 69–70; Norinaga on, 34; in poetry, 39–40; writing, 84; Yamato region as, 31–32

Masuda Katsumi, 116; on Heian literature, 118; on poetic dialogue, 131; on poetry and prose, 137; on *The Tale of Genji*, 120–123, 126, 132, 134, 140, 142; on *waka*, 131, 132

Meiji kokubungaku: and gender, 41–42; and Heian literature, 45, 78–80; and *kana* writing, 48–49; and *kokugaku*, 44; and nationalism, 50, 81; poetics of, 63; and *The Tale of Genji*, 59. See also *Kokubungaku*

Meiji period, 48, 50, 59–60, 66

Metaphors, gender. *See* Gender metaphor

Mikami Sanji, 44, 46–47, 49

Minamoto no Shitago'o, 118

Minamoto no Taka'akira, 211–212

Mi no uhe, 211

Minzokugakusha (folklorist), 8–9

Mitani Kuniaki, 9, 147, 165–169, 224

Mitchitsuna, Mother of, 182, 189, 197

Miura Tsutomu, 150

Miyabi, concept of, 34, 40, 53

Miyake, Lynn K., 87

Modernity, critique of, 10, 160

Modern period: commentaries from, on *Kagerô nikki*, 184–186; gender in, 15; and Heian literature, 18; linguistics of, 10–11; literature studies in, 17–18; and narration, 200, 223–224, 226–228; novels in, 147, 222; subject in, 7–8, 214–217, 221–222, 224

Monogatari, 113, 135, 208

Mono no aware: Fujioka on, 61; Haga on, 60; and Heian literature, 111–112; influence of, 116–117; and *kokubungaku*, 116–117; Norinaga on, 34, 111, 113–115;

Tomiko Yoda is an associate professor in Asian and
African Languages and Literature, Women's Studies,
and the Program in Literature at Duke University.

Library of Congress Cataloging-in-Publication Data

Yoda, Tomiko.

Gender of national literature : Heian texts in the emergence

of Japanese modernity / Tomiko Yoda.

p. cm. Includes bibliographical references and index.

ISBN 0-8223-3187-X (cloth : alk. paper)

ISBN 0-8223-3237-X (pbk. : alk. paper)

1. Japanese literature—Heian period, 794–1185—Women

authors—History and criticism. 2. Feminism and literature—

Japan. 3. Feminist literary criticism—Japan. I. Title.

PL726.26.W64Y63 2003   895.6'099287'0902—dc21

2003014178